THE WAR IN THE NORTH

0 20 40 60 80 100 120 140
Statute Miles

BROADSIDES

And

BAYONETS

BROADSIDES
And
BAYONETS
The Propaganda War of the American Revolution

★★★

by

CARL BERGER

Philadelphia

University of Pennsylvania Press

Published in Great Britain, India, and Pakistan
by the Oxford University Press
London, Bombay, and Karachi

Library of Congress Catalog Card Number: 61–5358

To Rae Berger's Memory

Preface

★★

In this book I have attempted to encompass the story of propaganda and subversion in the American Revolutionary War. The archives and literature of the Revolution contain many intriguing references to "secret arts and machinations," some relating to incidents familiar to us, others touching on events long forgotten. This book for the first time brings them together in a single narrative, examining their role and importance.

During its eight-year progression the war gave birth to many divisive operations, well planned in some instances and often involving minority groups on the scene as well as Englishmen and Americans. Drawn into the colonial struggle were French Canadians and German mercenaries, Indian tribes and Negro slaves, Irishmen, and other peoples. From the beginning it was a war of words as well as gunpowder, with each major protagonist seeking to subvert and weaken the enemy camp with carefully prepared arguments. It was a provocative war in which the atrocity story, kidnappings, false rumors, and bribery stirred the people. It was a conflict which inevitably spread to Europe and there engaged the talents of Benjamin Franklin and John Adams, in America's first organized overseas propaganda campaign.

In reconstructing this tale, I have been much less concerned with the important military operations of the war than with what was said and done in support of them, and also less concerned with the political issues than with the techniques of propaganda and subversion employed by each side. The reader will note that the word "propaganda" is used in this volume without evil connotations, that is, in accordance with the dictionary definition of: "Any organized or concerted group effort or movement to spread particular doctrines, information, etc." The American Revolution was such an organized movement, which spread doctrines of liberty and independence throughout the world.

CARL BERGER

Santa Maria, Calif.
October 27, 1959

Contents

★★★

Illustrations

★★★

Acknowledgments

★★

There are two general English-language studies dealing with what might be called the domestic side of the propaganda struggle, Arthur M. Schlesinger's *Prelude to Independence: The Newspaper War on Britain, 1764–1776,* New York, 1958, and Philip Davidson's *Propaganda and the American Revolution, 1763–1783,* Chapel Hill, 1941. The emphasis in both is on the prewar pamphlet and newspaper competition between the Revolutionary leaders on one side and the pro-English Tories and the British government on the other, for the hearts and minds of the American people. The present work, which concentrates on the war period, takes its lead from Dr. Lyman H. Butterfield's article on "Psychological Warfare in 1776: The Jefferson-Franklin Plan to Cause Hessian Desertions," *Proceedings of the American Philosophical Society,* 194 (June 1950). Dr. Butterfield's report provided the main inspiration which led to this volume. The bulk of research for the book was conducted at the Library of Congress and the National Archives, Washington, D.C.

BROADSIDES
And
BAYONETS

1

★★★

American Propaganda and the
Struggle for Canada

Boston's martyrdom had already aroused the countryside when
fifty-six predominantly middle-aged Americans gathered in the
first Continental Congress in Philadelphia to consult "on the
present state of the Colonies." For seven weeks, beginning on
September 5, 1774, the delegates argued and debated "the un-
wise, unjust, and ruinous policy" of Great Britain. In late
October, after adopting various anti-Parliamentary resolves
and issuing several important political papers, they adjourned
peaceably. One of those state papers was an appeal to the King
for redress of grievances; another was a lengthy and indignant
Address to the People of Great Britain, and a third was an *Address to the Inhabitants of the Province of Quebec.*[1]

It is this latter document that particularly concerns us,
because it was the beginning of an American propaganda
campaign to bring Canada over to the side of the colonies. This
campaign was highly successful in subverting the new and
tenuous allegiance of the French Canadians to the British
government, especially after the entrance of France into the
war in 1778. The combined Franco-American verbal assault on
the Canadian mind was so effective that the British authorities
in Canada were placed almost entirely on the defensive. Indeed,

so worried was the British government over the impact of the ideas emanating from the south that British commanders in Canada undertook to seal off the province from the colonies. With English bayonets a futile attempt was made to create an eighteenth-century "Iron Curtain" to halt the movement of American agitators and propaganda into that uneasy territory.

I

To understand why American propaganda to the north was so successful, we must review briefly Canada's population complexion. Most of the white inhabitants of Canada at the time of the Revolution were of French descent, adherents of the Roman Catholic faith, and tenant-farmers by occupation. They had fallen under British rule as a result of England's victory over France in the French and Indian War (Seven Years' War). By 1763 the prolific French Canadian population had reached an estimated 70,000 persons, while the English residents totalled scarcely 400 people, these being mostly traders from the southern colonies or discharged British soldiers.[2]

During the decade after 1763 the British military government—overseeing a large and formerly hostile Canadian population with but a small force of regular troops—was troubled by fears of a popular uprising. Rumors of Canadian plots were reported periodically to London by members of the British minority. In 1768 the military governor, Sir Guy Carleton, although unable to discover any of the supposed subversive plots, wrote to the London government that "there was no doubt of their secret and natural affection for France," an affection which he said would continue so long as they were excluded from all appointments in the British service.[3] Carleton was referring specifically to the French Canadian seigneurs and clergy, the privileged minority which had dominated the peasant class under French rule but which had lost much of its power under Britain.

It was clear London would have to "conciliate the affections of the conquered" in order to insure its rule. There was subsequently initiated a governmental study which led, in 1774, to the passage by Parliament of the famed Quebec Act. This act, which has become known as "the Magna Carta of the French Canadians," guaranteed to the inhabitants the free exercise of their religion and French judicial procedure. It also provided for an advisory council to the British governor, to be composed of seventeen to twenty-six members, chosen from among the French Canadian nobility and clergy. In addition, the act extended the boundaries of Quebec south to the Ohio, and west to the Mississippi.

The Quebec Act did not go down well with the Americans, especially its boundary provisions which would have the effect of blocking American expansion into the western territories. This was the situation when the colonists learned to their surprise that many of the Canadian peasants also were not pleased with the act. On the contrary, wrote a "Gentleman in Montreal" to a New York friend: "The Canadians, in general, are greatly alarmed at being put under their former laws, of which they had long severely felt the bad effects; though the French noblesse and gentry, indeed, are very well pleased with the new act, which restores the old, and they expect to lord it over the industrious farmer and trader, and live upon their spoils, as they did before the conquest."[4]

It was in these circumstances that the first propaganda address of the Continental Congress was published. In what was to be its procedure in producing propaganda documents throughout the war, Congress appointed a committee—composed of Thomas Cushing of Massachusetts, Richard Henry Lee of Virginia, and John Dickinson of Pennsylvania—to write the first appeal to the people of Quebec for support against Parliament. It was Dickinson's famous pen which produced the address, dated October 26, 1774, in which Congress suggested to the Canadians "whether it may not be expedient for you to meet together, in your several towns and districts, and elect deputies who, after meeting in a Provincial Congress, may choose delegates to represent your province in the Continental Congress."[5]

As to their differences in religion, Congress argued smoothly: "We are too well acquainted with the liberality of sentiment distinguishing your nation, to imagine the difference in religion will prejudice you against a hearty amity with us. You know that the transcendent nature of freedom elevates those who unite in her cause, above all such low-minded infirmities. The Swiss Cantons furnish a memorable proof of this truth. Their union is composed of Roman Catholic and Protestant states, living in the utmost concord and peace with one another."[6] Responsibility for translating this American address into French was given to the delegates from Pennsylvania, who were also directed to have it printed and disseminated in Canada with the help of agents of New Hampshire, New York, and Massachusetts.

There were, however, a number of flaws in this initial propaganda to Canada. Among them were the undeveloped political consciousness of the Canadians, resulting largely from their feudal background, and the fact that many of the peasants could not read. A pro-American writer in Montreal, after receiving English-language copies of Congress' address, predicted the Canadians would "avoid taking any part in the matter" because "they have been so little accustomed to speak or think on subjects of that kind," and were also afraid "of giving the smallest offence to government."[7]

There was still another important flaw in this address, connected with Congress' simultaneous appeal to the people of Great Britain. In this latter appeal, which was written largely by John Jay, Congress had attacked the Quebec Act on religious grounds, professing astonishment "that a British Parliament should ever consent to establish in that country a *Religion* that has deluged your island in blood, and dispersed impiety, bigotry, persecution, murder, and rebellion, through every part of the world."[8]

Congress' faux pas soon came home to roost. A letter from Montreal* described what happened:

> The Address from the Continental Congress attracted the notice of some of the principal Canadians; it was soon translated into very tolerable French. The decent manner in which the religious matters were touched; the encomiums on the French nation, flattered a people fond of compliments. They begged the translator, as he had succeeded so well, to try his hand on that Address to the People of Great Britain. He had equal success in this, and read his performance to a numerous audience. But when he came to that part which treats of the new modelling of the province; draws a picture of the Catholic religion . . . they could not contain their resentment, nor express it but in broken curses. "Oh! the perfidious double-faced Congress. . . ."[9]

Because they had failed to co-ordinate their propaganda, the Americans created ill-feeling instead of good will for their cause. However, they continued to address the Canadians. Prior to Congress' adjournment on October 26, 1774, the task of corresponding with the northern province was turned over to that important agency of American propaganda, the Boston Committee of Correspondence. Several months later, in February 1775, this committee received and accepted a proposal from one John Brown that he and other agents be sent to Canada to obtain intelligence and to spread American viewpoints.

To help him on his mission, the Boston Committee supplied him with a stock of American patriotic propaganda pamphlets, as well as a number of letters to English friends in Montreal, including a letter to the Canadians from that master agitator,

* For a note on the style adopted in this study for the various passages and documents cited (spelling, capitalization, and punctuation), see the Introduction to Bibliography, p. 238.

Samuel Adams. Adams' letter, dated February 21, 1775, was a lengthy review of colonial grievances which contained the hopeful sentence: "The enemies of American liberty will surely be chagrined when they find that the people of Quebec have in common with other Americans the true sentiments of liberty."[10]

Brown headed north accompanied by several frontiersmen, and they distributed American literature in the hamlets on the way. In searching out the sentiments of the Canadians, Brown found that, while they were not unfriendly to the colonies, they preferred "to stand neuter." Reaching Montreal in March, 1775, Brown immediately contacted the pro-American faction in the town. He also had the brashness to apply to Governor Carleton for a public printing of the address of Congress—which was refused. On March 29 Brown sat down to write a report to Sam Adams on the political conditions he had found in Canada; and, in his letter, he revealed "a profound secret." Wrote Brown: "The fort at Ticonderoga must be seized as soon as possible should hostilities be committed by the King's Troops." He confided that some New Hampshire patriots had made plans "to do" the business.[11]

II

The business was done indeed. On May 10, 1775—three weeks after the opening clash of the war at Lexington and Concord—a loose band of New Hampshire colonials led by Ethan Allen and Benedict Arnold attacked and seized Ticonderoga. Two days later Crown Point, a few miles to the north, also fell into American hands. The headlong rush carried the colonials into Canadian territory in the vicinity of St. John's.

The day Ticonderoga was seized, the second Continental Congress was reconvening in Philadelphia; and some days later that body was startled to learn of this first American offensive action of the war. However, in a resolution adopted May 18 Congress quickly justified the seizures by claiming knowledge of "indubitable evidence that a design is formed by the British ministry of making a cruel invasion from the province of Quebec upon these colonies." However, having no military plans at this point, Congress ordered that all captured stores taken at Ticonderoga and Crown Point be removed further south for their security.

Reviewing the event a few days later, Congress felt it might be wise to address the Canadians again, not only to justify the seizure of the two forts but also to calm any fears they might have concerning American intentions. On May 29, 1775, thereupon, Congress published another propaganda broadside, addressed this time *To the Oppressed Inhabitants of Canada,* in which it declared that the fate of the Protestant and Catholic colonies was strongly linked together; and it once more invited the Canadians to "join with us in resolving to be free." Argued Congress (excerpts):

By . . . your present form of government, or rather present form of tyranny, you and your wives and your children are made slaves. You have nothing that you can call your own, and all the fruits of your labor and industry may be taken from you whenever an avaricious governor and a rapacious council may incline to demand them. You are liable by the edicts to be transported into foreign countries to fight battles in which you have no interest, and to spill your blood in conflicts from which neither honor nor emolument can be derived. . . .

We are informed you have already been called upon to waste your lives in a contest with us. Should you, by complying in this instance, assent to your new establishment, and a war break out with France, your wealth and your sons may be sent to perish in expeditions against their Islands in the West Indies.

It cannot be presumed that these considerations will have no weight with you, or that you are so lost to all sense of honor. We can never believe that the present race of Canadians are so degenerate as to possess neither the spirit, the gallantry, nor the courage of their ancestors. . . .

Permit us again to repeat that we are your friends, not your enemies, and be not imposed upon by those who may endeavor to create animosities. The taking of the fort and military stores at Ticonderoga and Crown Point . . . was dictated by the great law of self-preservation.[12]

One thousand copies of this address, translated into French, were sent into Canada via agents.

At this initial stage of the war—with the siege of British troops in Boston not yet underway—Congress was defensive-minded and had no Canadian invasion plans. This attitude was particularly frustrating to at least one New Englander, fire-brand Ethan Allen, who in his eagerness to march north sought the support of the New York Provincial Congress. In a letter to that body on June 2, he declared: "I will lay my life on it, that with fifteen hundred men and a proper train of artillery, I will take Montreal." Allen argued there was an "unspeakable advantage in directing the war into Canada, that, instead of turning the Canadians and Indians against us (as is wrongly suggested by many), it would unavoidably attach and connect them to our interest. Our friends in Canada can never help us till we first help them, except in a passive or inactive manner."[13]

The northern colonials kept agitating for a Canadian expedition, but the Continental Congress was slow in making up its mind. In the meantime, several additional propaganda papers were being sent into Canada. One was a formal address from the New York Provincial Congress, dated June 2, 1775, which told the Canadian people that the key issue between Britain and her colonies "is whether they are subjects, or whether they are slaves" and beseeched the inhabitants "not to be imposed on" by British wiles.[14]

Another message on June 4 was sent by Ethan Allen to *Our Worthy and Respectable Countrymen and Friends, the French People of Canada*. In this appeal Allen sought to reassure the Canadians that the Americans had entered their country with not the least desire to injure or molest them or their property. American soldiers, he said, were under orders not to harm any Canadians "on pain of death." He declared that there was no real conflict between Americans and Canadians. "You are sensible," Allen said, "that war has already commenced between England and the Colonies. . . . But pray, is it necessary that the Canadians and the inhabitants of the English Colonies should butcher one another? God forbid. There is no controversy subsisting between you and them. Pray let old England and the Colonies fight it out; and you, Canadians, stand by and see what an arm of flesh can do."[15]

The effect of this American propaganda, which aimed at alienating the French Canadians from the British government, was great; and the British commander, General Carleton, soon found his position seriously undermined. Writing on June 7 to Lord Dartmouth (Britain's secretary of state for the colonies), Carleton complained that throughout Canada insubordination was growing, "the minds of the people [being] poisoned by the same hypocrisy and lies practiced with so much success in the other provinces, and which their emissaries and friends here have spread abroad with great art and diligence."[16] In his letter to Dartmouth, Carleton enclosed samples of recent American propaganda, including the address of the New York Provincial Congress of June 2, and a copy of a scrap of paper reportedly placed under the doors of French Canadian homes throughout the country, which warned: *Honi soit qui mal y pense, A lui qui ne suivra le bon chemin. Baston.*[17] ("Evil to him who evil thinks, who does not follow the good way. Boston.") *

On June 9—with British control over the province rapidly slipping away—Carleton issued a proclamation establishing martial law. In his proclamation Carleton attacked the "traitorous invasion" of Canada and denounced the Americans for "falsely and maliciously giving out" that they had come only to prevent the Canadians "from being taxed and oppressed," and

*To the Canadians the Americans were known as "Bostonians."

for spreading "false and seditious reports, tending to inflame the minds of the people and alienate them from his Majesty."[18]

III

In Philadelphia the American Congress slowly came around towards establishing a policy towards Canada. The opinion of the New England colonies carried the day, that is, the view that the American cause would be enhanced by an invasion of Canada.[19] The "great question," John Adams had said, was whether to push north with an army "sufficient to break the power of Governor Carleton, to overawe the Indians, and to protect the French. . . . It seems to be the general conclusion that it is best to go, if we can be assured that the Canadians will be pleased with it and join."[20]

On June 27, 1775—only a few days after Congress learned of the bloody Battle of Bunker Hill—it reached a decision. Instructions were issued to the newly appointed northern commander, Major General Philip Schuyler, to "immediately take possession of St. Johns, Montreal and any other parts" of Canada that he could. The attitude of the Canadians, however, remained of crucial importance. A previous condition, "a *sine qua non* of marching into Canada," wrote Samuel Chase to Schuyler, "is the friendship of the Canadians. Without their consent and approbation, it is not [to] be undertaken."[21]

In the months that followed—while Schuyler and his second-in-command, Irish-born Brigadier General Richard Montgomery, struggled to collect supplies and an army of 1,200 men—the British fought to counteract the impact of American propaganda. But it was already very late. "There is no persuading the country people here of their danger," wrote a British loyalist from Canada. "Emissaries of the rebels have made them believe that they are only come into the country to protect them from heavy taxes, which the Parliament designs to lay upon them. This, and the remembrance of what they suffered last war, makes them very desirous of observing a strict neutrality."[22]

Under the circumstances a strict neutrality was pro-American in effect, since it prevented General Carleton from calling out the Canadian militia to reinforce his meager forces (which totalled only 550 British regulars, scattered through five posts). Of this situation a British officer wrote from Quebec: "General Carleton is, I believe, afraid to order out the militia, lest they should refuse to obey," which would further undermine his authority. Added the officer: "In short, the Quebec bill is of no use; on the contrary, the Canadians talk of that damned absurd word liberty."[23]

In the last days of August 1775 General Montgomery began to move the hastily recruited American expedition slowly northward. As part of this invasion planning, on September 5 the ailing General Schuyler affixed his signature to a new propaganda message in French *To the Inhabitants of Canada.*

Addressing himself to his northern "friends and countrymen," Schuyler expressed his confidence that the Canadians would be pleased "that the Grand Congress have ordered an army into Canada, to expel from thence if possible, those British troops which, now acting under the orders of a despotic ministry, would wish to enslave their countrymen." The general assured the Canadians Congress would never have adopted such a severe measure if it had not been convinced "that it would be perfectly agreeable with you." Congress had judged Canadian feelings by their own: "They could not conceive that anything but the force of necessity could induce you tamely to bear the insult and ignominy that is daily imposed on you, or that you could calmly sit by, and see those chains forging which are intended to bind you, your posterity, and ours, in one common and eternal slavery." To secure both Americans and Canadians from such a dreadful bondage, declared Schuyler, was the only purpose of Congress.[24]

Copies of Schuyler's address travelled forward with the

army; and as the Americans pushed on, they were delighted to find the Canadians both friendly and helpful. Ethan Allen, who had gone ahead to Chambly, wrote from there: "The news of my being in this place excited many captains of the militia and respectable gentlemen of the Canadians to visit and converse with me, as I gave out I was sent by General Schuyler to manifest his friendly intentions towards them, and delivered the General's written manifesto to them to the same purpose."[25]

By mid-September, after several setbacks, Montgomery managed to put St. John's under siege. This siege turned into a very lengthy affair. As the days dragged on into weeks, Allen and John Brown were sent ahead to gather together several bodies of Canadians who were beginning to volunteer for American service in substantial numbers.

In October, Allen reached Longueuil across the St. Lawrence river from Montreal. Gazing at the peaceful town, his old dream of a great exploit seized him. Coming together with Brown's party, Allen concocted a plan to cross the river and make an immediate assault. On the night of October 24, 1775, the Montreal attack was set in motion; but somehow it miscarried. General Carleton, who was in Montreal checking defenses, rallied some English and Canadian citizens; and, together with 150 soldiers, he managed to surround Allen and forty of his men. Outnumbered, and with retreat cut off, Allen surrendered and was made a prisoner.

The capture of Ethan Allen, "the Notorious New Hampshire Incendiary," was less an important military defeat than a great propaganda blow against the Americans. It immediately affected the attitude of the Canadians; they began to think again about committing themselves to the American side. "The Canadians seemed to grow cool and fearful and some went off," reported one American, while another writer, a Montreal loyalist, exulted: "This little action has changed the face of things. The Canadians before were nine tenths for the Bostonians. They are now returned to their duty; many [are now] in arms for the King and the parishes, who had been otherwise."[26]

Fortunately for the Americans, the Allen incident was soon overtaken by more favorable events. On November 2, 1775—after a 55-day siege—the British commander at St. John's surrendered the post to General Montgomery, and this important event soon began to have a counter-effect. As the news spread through the many parishes south of the St. Lawrence, the Canadians once more began to rally to the Americans.

Montgomery pushed on towards Montreal as soon as he was able to reorganize his force. On November 11 he crossed over the St. Lawrence, landing above the town, where his column was greeted by four nervous citizens who came to inquire as to his intentions. Montgomery adopted a firm tone. In a written reply he expressed anxiety for the fate of Montreal, should it become necessary for him to open his batteries on the town. "When I consider the dreadful consequences of a bombardment," he said, "the distress that must attend a fire (at this season especially) when it is too late to repair the damage which must ensue, how many innocent people must suffer. . . ." After continuing in this threatening vein, Montgomery urged the citizens "to soften the heart of the Governor" and surrender the town and thus avoid disaster.[27]

But there was little need for this psychological game. General Carleton, estimating that his small force would be unable to defend Montreal, had already fled the town. The following day Montreal peacefully surrendered and was swiftly occupied by the Americans.

IV

During the period Montgomery was busy at St. John's and Montreal, further east the Americans had unleashed a second invasion of Canada aimed at capturing Quebec, the first town of the province. The plan for this second invasion was evolved in General Washington's headquarters at Cambridge, where the commander-in-chief was just beginning the long task of forming an army from the mixed provincial volunteers around Boston. By August 20 the Cambridge invasion plan was so far advanced that Washington was able to communicate it to Schuyler. The idea, wrote Washington, was "to penetrate into Canada by way of the Kennebeck River, and so to Quebec by a route ninety miles below Montreal."* Washington's plan was to detach a small volunteer force of 1,000 men from the army at Boston.[28] To lead the expedition Washington personally chose Benedict Arnold, the 34-year-old militia captain who had first come to public attention at Ticonderoga and Crown Point.

Arnold was given the rank of colonel and immediately threw himself into the job of preparing for the northern trek. Notice of the expedition appeared in Washington's general orders of September 5, 1775. The commander-in-chief, in preparing his formal instructions to Arnold, showed concern over the attitude of the Canadians. He cautioned Arnold to consider himself as marching, "not through an enemy's country but that of our friends and brethren." Severe disciplinary action was recommended against any soldier "so base and infamous as to injure any Canadian or Indian." The troops were also to be warned to "avoid all disrespect" to the Catholic faith of the Canadians.[29]

Washington also decided to address the Canadians directly to reassure them as to American intentions. His staff quickly drew up a new appeal *To the Inhabitants of Canada*. In this address Washington explained that the army under Schuyler had been sent to Canada "not to plunder but to protect you; to animate and bring forth those sentiments of freedom you have disclosed."

To cooperate with this design [Washington continued] and to frustrate those cruel and perfidious schemes which would deluge our frontier with the blood of women and children, I have de-

* Washington's figure is, of course, in error. Quebec is about 150 miles northeast of Montreal but properly "below" the latter city (i.e., the river flows "down" to the sea).

tached Colonel Arnold into your country, with a part of the army under my command. I have enjoined upon him, and I am certain that he will consider himself, and act as in the country of his patrons and best friends. Necessaries and accommodations of every kind which you may furnish, he will thankfully receive and render full value. I invite you therefore as friends and brethren to provide him with such supplies as your country affords; and I pledge myself not only for your safety and security, but for ample compensation. Let no man desert his habitation. Let no man flee as before an enemy.[30]

Arnold left Cambridge before the French-language copies of Washington's address were printed. These were forwarded to him on his march north, and he began a distribution of the broadside on reaching the first Canadian settlements. Arnold's experience with the Canadians was similar to that of the Americans in the west. On October 27 Arnold wrote to Washington from Chaudiere Pond that the Canadian attitude was friendly and that they "will very gladly receive us."[31]

Early in November, while anxiously awaiting word from Arnold, Washington learned that some of the provincial troops at Cambridge were planning to divert themselves with what he termed "the ridiculous and childish custom of burning the effigy of the pope." In his general orders dated November 5, Washington expressed amazement "that there should be officers and soldiers in this army so void of common sense as not to see the impropriety of such a step at this juncture, at a time when we are soliciting . . . the friendship and alliance of the people of Canada. . . . At such a juncture and in such circumstances, to be insulting their religion is so monstrous as not to be suffered or excused."[32]

On November 9 Arnold and his reduced column of 600 men, after a tortuous 45-day march, struggled out of the wilderness at Point Levi, across the river from Quebec. On the thirteenth, after locating some boats, they crossed the river and bivouacked on the Plains of Abraham, a mile and a half from the town. The

PAR SON EXCELLENCE

GEORGE WASHINGTON,

Commandant en Chef des Armées Des Provinces unies de L'Amerique Septentrionale.

AUX PEUPLES DE CANADA.

AMIS & FRERES,

LA Conteste denature entre les Colonies Ameriquaines, et Grande Bretagne est arrivé au point, que les Armes seules peuvent la decider. Les Colonies, se fiant à la Justice de leur Cause, & la pureté de leurs Intentions, sont obligé en Repugnance, de à cet Etre qui regle tous les Evenemens humains. Jusqu'à il a Beni leurs vertueux Efforts ; La Main de la Tyrannie est arreté dans le Cours de ses Ravages, & les Armes Brittaniques, qui sont Brillée avec tant de Eclat dans tous les Parties du Monde, se sont ternies, disgraçies et frustrees. Des Generaux de la plus haute Experience, et qui se sont vantez de subjuguer ce grand Continent, se trouvent resserrez entre les Murailles d'un seul Ville & de ses Fauxbourgs, souffrans toute la Honte & la Detresse d'un Siege. Tandis que les Enfans de l'Amerique animes par l'Amour de la Patrié et le principe de la Liberté generale, s'unissent de plus en plus, chaque Jour se perfectionnent en Discipline, repoussent avec Courage toutes les Attaques & meprisent touts les Dangers. Nous, nous rejouissons sur tout que nos Enemis sont trompez à votre Egard. Ils se sont flattes, ils ont osé dire que le Peuple de Canada ne turent nullement capables de distinguer entre les Douceurs de la Liberte, et la Misere de Servitude ; qu'on n'avoit qu'à flatter la Vanité d'un petit Nombre de votre Noblesse, pour eblouir les yeux des Canadiens. Ils ont cru par cette Artifice vous rendre faciles a touts leur Vues. Mais ils se sont heureusement trompez, au Lieu de trouver en vous, cette Bassesse d'Ame, & pauvreté d'Esprit, ils voient avec un Chagrin egal a notre joie que vous etes Hommes eclarés, genereux, et vertueux, que vous ne voulez ne renoncés à vos propres Droits, ni servir en Instrumens pour en priver les autres.

Venez donc, nos chers Confreres, unissons nous dans un Nœud indissoluble, courons ensemble au meme But. Nous avons pris les Armes en Defense de nos Biens, de Notre Liberté, de nos Femmes & nos Enfans—Nous sommes determines de les conserver, ou de mourir. Nous regardons avec Plaisir ce Jour, peu eloigné (comme nous esperons) quand touts les Habitans de L'Amerique auront le meme Sentiment et...

Incité par ces Motifs, et encouragé par l'Avis de plusieurs Amis de la Liberté chez vous, le Grand Congrés Ameriquain a fait entrer dans votre Province un Corps de Troupes sous les Ordres du General Schuyler, non a piller, mais a proteger, pour animer et mettre en Action les Sentiments liberaux que vous avez fait voir ; et que les Agents du Despotism s'efforcent d'eteindre par tout le Monde. Pur aider ce Dessein, & pour renverser le Projet horrible d'ensanglanter nos Frontieres par le Carnage des Femmes & des Enfans, J'ai fait marcher le Sieur Arnold, Colonel avec un Corps de l'Armée sous mes Ordres pour la Canada. Il est enjoint, et je suis certain qu'il se conformera à ses Instructions de se considerer et d'agir en tout, comme dans le Pais de ses Patrons et meilleurs Amis—Les Necessaires et Munition de toute Sorte que vous lui fournirez, il recevra avec Reconnoissance, et en payera la plein Valeur. Je vous supplie donc comme Amis, et Freres de pourvoir à touts les Besoins, et Je vous garantis ma Foi et mon Honneur pour un bonne et ample Recompense aussi bien que votre Sureté et Repos. Que Personne abandonne sa Maison a son Approche—Que Personne s'enfuit—La Cause de l'Amerique et de la Liberté est la Cause de tout vertueux Citoyen Ameriquain, quelle soit sa Religion, quelque que soit le Sang dont il tire son Origine. Les Colonies unies ignorent ce que c'est la Distinction hors celle que ce genre de la Corruption et l'esclavage peuvent produire—Allons donc, chers & generaux Citoyens, rangez vous sous l'Etendard de la Liberté generale que toute la Force et l'Artifice de la Tyrannie ne sera jamais capable d'ebranler.

G. Washington.

BY HIS EXCELLENCY

GEORGE WASHINGTON, Esquire

Commander in Chief of the Army of the United Colonies of North-America.

To the INHABITANTS of CANADA

FRIENDS and BRETHREN,

THE unnatural Contest between the English Colonies and Great-Britain, has now risen to such a Height, that Arms alone must decide it. The Colonies, confiding in the Justice of their Cause, and the Purity of their Intentions, have reluctantly appealed to that Being, in whose Hands are all human Events. He has hitherto smiled upon their virtuous Efforts—The Hand of Tyranny has been arrested in its Ravages, and the British Arms which have shone with so much Splendor in every Part of the Globe, are now tarnished with Disgrace and Disappointment.——Generals of approved Experience, who boasted of subduing this great Continent, find themselves circumscribed within the Limits of a single City and its Suburbs, suffering all the Shame and Distress of a Siege. While the troops Sons of America, animated by the genuine Principles of Liberty and Love of their Country, with increasing Union, Firmness and Discipline repel every Attack, and despise every Danger.

Above all, we rejoice, that our Enemies have been deceived with Regard to you—They have persuaded themselves, they have even dared to say, that the Canadians were not capable of distinguishing between the Blessings of Liberty, and the Wretchedness of Slavery; that gratifying the Vanity of a little Circle of Nobility—would be the Eyes of the People of Canada.—By such Artifices they hoped to bend you to their Views, but they have been deceived, instead of finding in you that Poverty of Soul, and Baseness of Spirit, they see with Chagrin equal to our Joy, that you are enlightened, generous, and virtuous—that you will not renounce your own Rights, or serve as Instruments to deprive your Fellow Subjects of theirs.—Come then, Brethren, unite with us in an indissoluble Union, let us run together the same Goal.—We have taken up Arms in Defence of our Liberty, our Property, our Wives, and our Children, we are determined to preserve them, or die. We look forward with Pleasure to that Day not remote (we hope) when the Inhabitants of America shall have Sentiment, and the full Enjoyment of the Blessings of a Government.

Incited by these Motives, and encouraged by the Advice of many Friends of Liberty among you, the Grand American Congress have sent an Army into your Province, under the Command of General Schuyler, not to plunder, but to protect you ; to animate, and bring forth into Action those Sentiments of Freedom you have disclosed, and which the Tools of Despotism would extinguish through the whole Creation.—To co-operate with this Design, and to frustrate those cruel and perfidious Schemes, which would deluge our Frontiers with the Blood of Women and Children ; I have detached Colonel Arnold into your Country, with a Part of the Army under my Command—I have enjoined upon him, and I am certain that he will consider himself, and act as in the Country of his Patrons, and best Friends. Necessaries and Accommodations of every Kind which you may furnish, he will thankfully receive, and render the full Value.—I invite you therefore as Friends and Brethren, to provide him with such Supplies as your Country affords ; and I pledge myself not only for your Safety and Security, but for ample Compensation. Let no Man desert his Habitation—Let no one flee as before an Enemy. The Cause of America, and of Liberty, is the Cause of every virtuous American Citizen ; whatever may be his Religion or his Descent, the United Colonies know no Distinction but such as Slavery, Corruption and arbitrary Domination may create. Come then, ye generous Citizens, range yourselves under the Standard of general Liberty—against which all the Force and Artifice of Tyranny will never be able to prevail.

G. Washington

A printer's copy in English and French of Washington's address to the Canadians, with editing marks by Major General Charles Lee. The French-language copies were distributed by Colonel Benedict Arnold during the ill-fated expedition against Quebec.

next day Arnold called upon the British lieutenant governor, Hector T. Cramahe, to surrender. An emissary carrying a flag of truce approached the walls with Arnold's demand for "the immediate surrender of the town, fortifications, &c., of Quebec to the forces of the United Colonies under my command; forbidding you to injure any of the inhabitants of the town in their persons or property, as you will answer the same at your peril."[33]

The British, however, had adopted a policy of nonrecognition of the American rebels; and gunfire from the walls sent Arnold's man into a fast retreat. The next day, thinking a mistake might have been made, Arnold sent another flag of truce but it also was fired upon. In a subsequent small diversion, he marched his troops "bravado-like" to within a short distance of the walls, where they "gave 3 huzzas" which was answered by some cheering from within the town, and then they retired. Obviously too weak to take Quebec by force, Arnold retired twenty miles up the river to await Montgomery and the American troops from Montreal.

Within Quebec there was a great deal of anxiety among the British, caused not only by the appearance of Arnold's troops outside the walls but also by the pro-American dispositions inside. Of this situation, a British officer of the Quebec garrison noted:

The success of the rebels under Mr. Montgomery induced many people in Quebec to show their sentiments, and, indeed, to act as if no opposition might be made against the rebel forces. A thousand different intimidating reports were industriously spread abroad concerning their numbers. Our enemies within the walls catched every favorable opportunity to work on the minds of such English and Frenchmen as were not confirmed in their principles. They spoke to their fears. Our force, said they, is nothing, theirs is great and grows daily. Be wise and remain neuter, that you may secure good treatment from those who will undoubtedly take the town sooner or later.[34]

These subversive activities put the British on the defensive, although they made efforts to counteract this American propaganda. The Americans, the British countered, were simply highwaymen, "rebel banditti" who had come into Canada looking only for loot and plunder. These arguments, however, were not very convincing: the Canadians were unmoved and continued to stand aside to watch the outcome of the struggle.

On November 19 an important event boosted British morale out of its depressed state. On that day General Carleton, who had "escaped from Montreal by paddling with his hands," slipped into Quebec to the "unspeakable joy of the garrison," which saw safety in his presence.[35] Carleton quickly took charge and one of his first moves was to try to purge Quebec of its pro-American elements. On November 22 he issued a proclamation ordering all those who would not serve actively in arms to defend the town, to evacuate in four days "under pain of being treated as rebels and spies." This order proved effective; a number of the disaffected and their families filed from the town in the next few days,[36] and the British garrison was thus indirectly strengthened.

It was not until December 2 that Montgomery arrived at Arnold's camp and took charge of operations. The combined American force stood at about 800 men, while the British defenders were able to call on more than twice that number (that is, including civilians). Montgomery was faced with a crucial decision, whether to "siege, invest or storm." The first two choices seemed impractical because the town had provisions to last eight months and the harsh Canadian winter had already begun. Montgomery's thoughts turned to the problem of storming the walls.

However, first he determined to try a propaganda assault. Aware that flags of truce would not be honored, Montgomery prepared letters to General Carleton and to the principal merchants of the town, calling for the surrender of the garrison.

He used an old woman, who begged admission to the town, to deliver the letters. But the British governor refused to receive them: he had the papers burned and sent the woman back with the word that he would receive no communication from a rebel.

Several days later Montgomery pursued his psychological warfare campaign via an ancient instrument. On the evening of December 12 he had copies of his letters fired into the town tied to Indian arrows. One letter to the inhabitants informed them of American surrender terms and painted the dreadful consequences of a refusal ("a city in flames, carnage, confusion, plunder"). The other letter was addressed to Carleton and threatened him with immediate death unless he gave up the city.[37] To back up his threats, Montgomery mounted several batteries on a height within 700 yards of the city walls.

However, there was no response to these tactics and on December 16 Montgomery issued a final, fierce surrender demand, dispatched again by messenger. In this document he pointed out to Carleton the weakness of his garrison, while noting that the American soldiers were "accustomed to success, confident of the righteousness of the cause they are engaged in, inured to danger and fatigue, and so highly incensed at your inhumanity . . . and the ungenerous means employed to prejudice them in the minds of the Canadians, that it is with difficulty that I restrain them. . . . Should you persist in an unwarrantable defence, the consequences be upon your own head. Beware of destroying stores of any sort. . . . If you do, by Heavens, there will be no mercy shown."[38]

Montgomery's latest messenger was promptly jailed. The letter was poor psychology to use on Carleton, a competent officer well aware of the importance of retaining Quebec. As long as Britain held Quebec, Canada would remain unconquered.

Propaganda and threats having failed, the sword alone could resolve the issue. During the early morning hours of December

31—in a blinding snowstorm—the people of Quebec were roused to meet the American assault. At first there was much confusion, until it became clear the two real American attacks were centered on the lower town. The British rallied, a number of Americans were caught in a trap and surrendered; others were slaughtered. In the fighting Arnold suffered a leg wound and General Montgomery fell mortally wounded. The Americans were beaten off.

When news of the failure at Quebec, and especially of the death of Montgomery, spread through the parishes of Canada, the American cause began to lose adherents. This was a quite natural reaction; it was a matter of self-preservation for the Canadians to choose, if they could, the winning side. Congress immediately recognized the impact the event must have on the Canadians. On January 24, 1776, after the unexpected news had reached Philadelphia, Congress drew up another address to the Canadians in an effort to counter the effects of the Quebec failure.

The best of causes [Congress said] are subject to vicissitudes; and disappointments have ever been inevitable. Such is the lot of human nature. But generous souls, enlightened and warmed with the sacred fire of liberty, become more resolute as difficulties increase; and surmount, with irresistible ardor, every obstacle that stands between them and the favourite object of their wishes.

We will never abandon you to the unrelenting fury of your and our enemies. Two battalions have already received orders to march to Canada, a part of which are now on their route. Six additional battalions are raising in the United States Colonies, for the same service. . . . The whole of these troops will probably arrive in Canada before the Ministerial army under General Carleton can receive any succours.[39]

Congress further urged Arnold to maintain the siege, and this was done. But the situation was somewhat ridiculous in that an American force of not more than 500 weary soldiers was besieging a garrison of about 1,600 men. Yet despite British military superiority, Carleton made no move to drive the Americans away. The British general's inactivity was partly the result of his complete disillusionment with the Canadians. Their "neutrality" coupled with American propaganda had had an impact on the British leader. He was content to sit safe within the walls of Quebec until reinforcements arrived from Britain.

The situation continued to deteriorate for the Americans. They had lost the aura of successful conquerors, and soon the presence and demands of the American troops in the country began to irritate the Canadians. In March 1776 a thoroughly alarmed Congress decided to dispatch a three-man commission to Montreal to obtain first-hand information on conditions. Named to the commission were Benjamin Franklin, Samuel Chase, and Charles Carroll. The commissioners were directed to reassure the Canadians that Congress would persist in the struggle against Britain, and that it was to Canada's interest "to cultivate a friendly intercourse with these colonies."[40]

The commission was also directed to set up "a free press" in Canada to publish "such pieces as may be of service to the cause of the United Colonies." To this end Congress agreed to pay the expenses of Fleury Mesplet, a French printer in Philadelphia, to remove himself, his family, and his printing press to Canada. (It was on Mesplet's press that Congress' three French-language propaganda broadsides of October 1774, May 1775, and January 1776 were printed.)[41] In still another move aimed at winning the allegiance of the Canadians, Congress persuaded the Reverend John Carroll, a Roman Catholic priest and a cousin of Charles Carroll, to accompany the commission to Canada. He was to try to influence the clergy to change over to the American side. The inclusion of the Reverend Carroll was considered by the American patriots to be "a master-stroke of policy."

Not until late April 1776 did the commissioners and their party reach Montreal, then under the military command of Arnold. They found the situation greatly deteriorated: the army had become extremely unpopular with the Canadians, having no hard cash to pay for supplies. Some of the Canadians had been forced to accept paper certificates in lieu of cash, and had been cheated and abused. On May 8, 1776, the commission wrote to Congress: "If money cannot be had to support your army here with honor, so as to be respected instead of being hated by the people, we report it as our firm and unanimous opinion that it is better immediately to withdraw it."[42]

Congress, however, could not easily give up its dream of uniting Canada to the colonies: it immediately ordered 300,000 dollars be sent northward and it requested the commission to publish another address to the Canadians, assuring them that Congress would give ample redress for any misconduct by any of the American soldiers.

Meanwhile, in Montreal, the Reverend Carroll met a wall of resistance in attempting to win over the French Canadian clergy. The clerics said they were quite satisfied with British rule and argued that the Quebec Act favored their national traditions. Further, they said they had not forgotten the address of Congress to the people of Britain which had denounced the Roman Catholic faith. Carroll was also unable to counter their statement that there was not a single colony in which the Roman Catholic church and clergy had such privileges as in Canada.[43]

The situation facing the Americans was well summed up by Moses Hazen, a former resident of Canada who had joined the patriot side. In a letter to General Schuyler from Montreal on April 1, Hazen wrote:

You are not unacquainted with the friendly disposition of the Canadians when General Montgomery first penetrated into the country; the ready assistance which they gave on all occasions, by men, carriages, or provisions, was most remarkable. Even when he was before Quebec many parishes offered their services in the reduction of the fortress, which were at that time thought un-necessary. But his most unfortunate fate, added to other incidents, has caused such a change in their disposition, that we no longer look upon them as friends but on the contrary waiting an op-portunity to join our enemies. That no observations of my own may remain obscure, I beg leave to observe that I think the clergy, or guardians of the souls and conductors of the bodies of these enthusiasts, have been neglected, perhaps in some instances ill-used. Be that as it will, they are unanimous, though privately, against our cause, and I have too much reason to fear many of them, with other people of consequence, have carried on a cor-respondence the whole winter with General Carleton in Quebec, and are now plotting our destruction. The peasantry in general have been ill-used. They have in some instances been dragooned with the point of the bayonet to supply wood for the garrison at a lower rate than the current price. . . . And in a more ma-terial point, they have not seen sufficient force in the country to protect them. These matters furnish very strong arguments to be made use of by our enemies. With respect to the better sort of people, both French and English, seven-eighths are Tories, who would wish to see our throats cut, and perhaps would readily assist in doing it.[44]

So drastically had American fortunes declined. The next important decision on Canada's future was made by the British. On May 6 five ships arrived at Quebec carrying troop reinforce-ments from England; and, thus bolstered, Carleton ordered out the greatest part of his garrison "to see what those mighty boasters were about." He found the Americans making a head-long retreat, and the five-months' siege of Quebec came to an abrupt end.

In the next few weeks, following an unsuccessful American effort to seize the strong point at Three Rivers, it became clear the whole American position in Canada was threatened. On

June 13 Arnold wrote: "The junction of the Canadas with the colonies is at an end. Let us quit them and secure our own country before it is too late."[45] Montreal was abandoned and the slow retreat began, first to Ile aux Nois and finally, in the early days of July 1776, to Crown Point, whence the invasion of Canada had begun ten months before.

v

Following the American retreat, Carleton's major task was to consolidate his position with the French Canadians. He wisely adopted a policy of leniency towards them, as well as towards "his Majesty's deluded subjects of the neighbouring provinces," and he offered medical aid to any who needed help plus the promise of "free liberty to return to their respective provinces" when their health was restored.[46] To the citizens of liberated Montreal, however, he hammered home the theme that "the people's greatest enemies" were the American colonists whose "flattering and perverted use of words" had undermined the governmental structure.[47] American propaganda had left its scars.

Carleton also thought to use Americans captured in the recent battles to spread British propaganda in the south. Early in August 1776 he paroled 147 American prisoners and sent them to New York in the hopes, he wrote, "that the confinement they have undergone may have brought them to a sense of their past crimes and that this proof given to the rebels still in arms that the way to mercy is not shut to them, the contrary being inculcated by their chiefs, and those who have an interest in fomenting the disorders of the country, may tend to work a favorable change in their minds."[48]

Carleton's show of clemency—his demonstration that the British did not hang their prisoners—had the desired effect. A few months later, as the British and American armies maneuvered at New York and in New Jersey, an American chaplain with the patriot forces tried to counter the influence of the prisoner release by warning the American troops that: "General Carleton's late conduct was only designed to deceive; his clemency is to be dreaded."[49] There was nothing ahead, he said, but victory or death. So must all soldiers be convinced.

But if the British in Canada thought they were now free from American propaganda, they were rudely awakened early in August 1776 when the Americans dispatched an officer northward carrying some new resolutions of Congress dealing with treatment of prisoners. Carleton was stirred to great anger by those papers, and his anger spilled over into his general orders of August 7, a copy of which was handed to the American emissary.

In this order Carleton directed his subordinate officers to inform all British personnel:

> . . . that letters or messages from rebels, traitors in arms against their King, rioters, disturbers of the peace, plunderers, robbers, assassins or murderers, are on no occasion to be admitted. That should emissaries of such lawless men again presume to approach the army, whether under the name of flag-of-truce men or ambassadors, except when they come to implore the King's mercy, their persons shall be immediately seized and committed to close confinement, in order to be proceeded against as the law directs; their papers and letters for whomsoever, even for the Commander-in-Chief, are to be delivered to the Provost Marshal, that, unread and unopened, they may be burned by the hands of the common hangman.[50]

Carleton plainly had had enough of American revolutionaries. "Let their crimes," he said, "pursue these faithless, bloody-minded men, who assert that black is white and white is black."[51]

Carleton had good reason to cry out against American propaganda, whose lingering effects were seen in the difficulty which his new subordinate, Major General John Burgoyne, had in trying to recruit Canadians for his regiment. Burgoyne, who had arrived with the British reinforcements, wrote to Lord George Germain (the new colonial secretary) and attributed his recruiting troubles partly "to the poison which the emissaries of the rebels have thrown into their mind."[52] As a result, only a handful of Canadians accompanied the British forces when they went on the offensive against the Americans on Lake Champlain in the fall of 1776.

In October, in an important naval battle near Valcour Island, Carleton's gunboats defeated an improvised American navy under Benedict Arnold. British control of the lake forced the patriots to abandon Crown Point. However, Arnold's resistance had so delayed the British that Carleton was forced to call a halt to operations for the winter. Thus the Americans retained Ticonderoga through the winter of 1776–77.

VI

It was during this long Canadian winter that the restless General Burgoyne returned to England, where he found his opinions and views about the American war in great demand. Ideas Burgoyne had in abundance, plus his own natural ambition which led him to submit to the King a paper entitled *Thoughts for Conducting the War from the Side of Canada.* In this paper he proposed an attack against Ticonderoga with a British force which he envisioned would include 2,000 Canadians and 1,000 Indian auxiliaries. After seizing Ticonderoga, the army would continue south by way of Lake George and the Hudson River Valley to Albany, New York. The main invasion would be supported by an auxiliary expedition marching on Albany by a western route.

The King and the ministry approved Burgoyne's plan and when he returned to Quebec in May 1777 it was as commander of a combined British-German expeditionary force. He superseded Carleton, who was ordered to remain behind as governor of Canada. Almost at once, however, Burgoyne's neat little plan began to go awry. He discovered the Canadians were still determined on neutrality; he was able to obtain only 150 of his hoped-for 2,000 men. Still it was an impressive army of 7,123 rank and file which, in June 1777, began its historic march which was to end ingloriously at Saratoga.

The details of that British disaster need not concern us here.* What is important from the viewpoint of this study is the great political and propaganda value which accrued to the American cause by Burgoyne's surrender. Not only did Saratoga bring French recognition of American independence and subsequent participation in the war, but that event gave a tremendous lift to American morale and revitalized American propaganda in Canada. From the time of Burgoyne's surrender to the end of the war, the British remained on the defensive in the north.

For example, the *Articles of Confederation,* which were adopted by Congress in November 1777, contained a paragraph which would allow Canada to join the new union by simply acceding to the confederation. On November 29 Congress appointed a committee to translate the *Articles* in French. This committee was also directed to prepare another address to the Canadians, and to develop a plan for distributing these new propaganda papers, hoping they would "conciliate the affections of the Canadians towards these United States."[53]

In December the committee brought in a partial report, but the following month, January 1778, Congress decided to do more than propagandize; it seized on a hastily conceived plan to undertake a new military "irruption" into Canada. The plan called for a contingent of French officers to join the northward march in the hope they would be able to persuade the Canadians to come over en masse to the American side.

---

* Other aspects of Saratoga are discussed in Chapters 2, 3 and 4.

Within a few months, however, reality reasserted itself when it became evident that neither supplies nor men were available and that it was too late in the season to organize an expedition. On March 13, having been informed of these problems, Congress ordered the plan set aside.[54]

One of the French officers who had been involved in this wild scheme was the youthful Marquis de Lafayette, who had gone to New York to undertake preparations for what he hoped would be a campaign of glory. After surveying the situation in Albany and noting the lack of all necessities, Lafayette reluctantly concluded that the expedition was impractical. However, news of his presence near the Canadian border added a further dimension to British fears.

In the months that followed, the entrance of France into the war naturally contributed to the apprehensions in British quarters over the security of Canada. Parliament acted to prohibit all intercourse between it and the southern colonies, and Carleton was given strict instructions to watch out for American emissaries and to seize any papers they might carry. Carleton needed no such directive. What he and his successors tried to do, as one historian has put it, was to build "a voice-proof wall on the frontier, with gates of bronze and no latch-string,"[55] in an effort to keep out the subversive Americans and their "unnatural" allies, the French.

But this feeble eighteenth-century attempt at an "Iron Curtain" had too many gaps in it to be effective. Indeed, in the fall of 1778 one of the most subversive propaganda appeals of the entire war was filtered into the Canadian countryside. The writer of this appeal was a Frenchman, Charles Henri Theodat, Comte d'Estaing, admiral of the French fleet sent to aid the Americans, who had dropped anchor in Boston in October.

During his stay in Boston d'Estaing was visited by some Canadian Indian chiefs of the Penobscot and Nova Scotia tribes. They had come, they explained, "to see with their own eyes" whether it was true that France had joined the American cause.[56] To the admiral it seemed that a golden opportunity had presented itself to use the Indians to carry back into Canada an appeal to the French Canadians. He thereupon drew up a declaration "in the name of the King of France," dated October 28, 1778, which was printed on his ship's press. Addressing the Canadians, d'Estaing declared (excerpts):

You were born French, you never could cease to be French. The late war . . . has wrested from you that which is most dear to all men, even the name of your country. To compel you to bear arms of parricides against it, must be the completion of misfortunes. . . .

As a French gentleman, I need not mention to those among you who were born such as well as myself, that there is but one august House in the universe under which the French can be happy and serve with pleasure . . . I shall not excite your regrets for those qualifications, those marks of distinction, those decorations, which, in our manner of thinking, are precious treasures, but which by our common misfortune the American French . . . are now precluded. These, I am bold to hope, and to promise, their zeal will very soon procure to be diffused among them. They will merit them, when they *dare to become the friends of our allies.*

I shall not ask the military companions of the Marquis de Levi, those who shared his glory, who admired his talents and genius for war, who loved his cordiality and frankness, the principal characteristics of our nobility, whether there be other names in other nations among which they would be better pleased to take their own.

Can the Canadians who saw the brave Montcalm fall in their defence, can they become the enemies of his nephews? Can they fight against their former leaders, and arm themselves against their kinsmen? At the bare mention of their names, the weapons would fall from their hands.

I shall not observe to the Ministers of the altars, that their evangelic efforts will require the special protection of Providence to prevent faith being diminished by example, by worldly interest, and by sovereigns whom force has imposed upon them, and whose political indulgence will be lessened proportionably as those sovereigns shall have less to fear. I shall not observe that it is necessary for religion that those who preach it should form a body in the State; and that in Canada no other body would be more considered, or have more power to do good than that of the priests. . . .

I shall not urge a whole people, that to *join* with the United States is to secure their own happiness; since a whole people, when they acquire the right of thinking and acting for themselves, must know their own interest; but I will declare, and I now formally declare in the name of his Majesty, who has authorized and commanded me to do it, that all his former subjects in North America who shall no more acknowledge the supremacy of Great Britain, may depend upon his protection and support.[57]

Admiral d'Estaing's subtle propaganda appeal—aimed at the clergy and nobility as well as the peasants—was followed in December 1778 by a letter from Lafayette to the Indian tribes of Canada, announcing France's adherence to America and urging them also to desert the British cause.*

News of these French appeals spread quickly. The British commander-in-chief, Sir Henry Clinton, when he heard of them, was certain that d'Estaing's broadside had "debauched" the Canadians.[58] So was Carleton's successor as governor of Canada, General Frederick Haldimand, who was convinced the appeals would be very seductive to Canadian hearts. Especially worrisome was the effect of the propaganda on the two elements of the population Britain had previously relied upon, the nobility and clergy. Reporting his apprehensions to London, Haldimand said that since it was learned France had entered the war, and in particular "since the address of Count d'Estaing and a letter of M. de la Fayette to the Canadians and Indians have been circulated in the province, many of the

* See Chapter 2, p. 80.

priests have changed their opinions, and in case of another invasion I fear would adopt another system of conduct."[59]

Both d'Estaing's address and Lafayette's letter were disseminated at a time when Congress was showing renewed interest in a northern expedition. This interest was stimulated by Lafayette, who conceived a new scheme for a combined French-American attack on Canada. To implement the plan, Congress agreed that Lafayette should return to France to seek the support of the French king. On October 22, 1778, Congress also sent instructions to Benjamin Franklin in Paris on the "Plan of an Attack Upon Quebec." The scheme called for cooperation of four or five thousand French troops, to sail in an invasion fleet up the St. Lawrence to seize Quebec, while at the same time an American force would move northward in two columns to capture Montreal and the British post at Detroit.

Washington, who had been by-passed by Congress in all the planning for the abortive "irruption" (January–March 1778), on this occasion was consulted; and he promptly threw cold water on the whole idea. Not only did he express doubts about the ability of America to support an invasion of Canada, but he also privately expressed concern over future political complications that might arise should France again obtain a strong foothold in Canada.

Washington's arguments against the expedition, presented both in private and public letters, carried the day in Congress. On December 5, 1778, the same day d'Estaing's Canadian address was read to the Congress at the request of the French minister, a congressional committee reported "the reasons assigned by the General against an expedition to Canada appear to the committee to be well founded, and to merit the approbation of Congress."[60]

Congress accepted the recommendation. Several weeks later a letter was addressed to Lafayette to inform him of the decision. Congress felt, the letter stated, "that the arms of America should be employed in expelling the enemy from her own shores before the liberation of a neighbouring province is undertaken."[61] Before this letter reached Lafayette, however, his ship had sailed for France. Not until five months later did he learn of the American decision, but by that time other stimulating projects (including the prospect of an invasion of England) were on his mind.

VII

For the remainder of the war the plan to win Canada was never far from the American consciousness, and each renewal of discussion—whether real or for deceptive purposes—gave sustenance to British apprehensions in the north. To General Haldimand it was particularly galling when Canadians and Indians slipped out of the country to go see the French fleet and returned to spread tales of French victories and French superiority. On many an occasion, Haldimand remarked to Lord Germain, he had seen the "secret pleasure" on the faces of the Canadians, even as they made their bows to him.[62] Meanwhile, American agents hovered on the frontier, agitating the people and disseminating additional copies of d'Estaing's address throughout the country.[63]

In May 1780, when Lafayette returned to America with the good news that a French army and fleet would shortly arrive, Washington undertook to utilize propaganda for strategic deception. In a conference with Lafayette the general suggested the French nobleman issue several proclamations to the Canadians. One, Washington said, should indicate that a French fleet and army would soon arrive in the St. Lawrence River to co-operate with the Americans in a northern campaign, and urge them to join the allied arms and assist in making Canada a part of the American confederation. The other proclamation "should be drawn on the supposition of the fleet and army being already arrived, and should contain an animating invitation to arrange themselves under the allied banners."[64]

To further confuse the British Washington thought it would be useful to slip into the American press some items to the effect that the impending French naval and land forces would join with the American army in "a combined operation against New York."[65] This latter operation was the plan Washington actually hoped to implement.

Lafayette quickly complied with Washington's request; and at least one proclamation is known to have been written, which Washington sent in great secrecy to Major General Benedict Arnold, the commander in Philadelphia, with the request that 500 copies be struck off. "The importance of this business," Washington wrote to Arnold, "will sufficiently impress you with the necessity of transacting it with every possible degree of caution. The printer is to be particularly charged not on any account to reserve a copy himself or to suffer one to get abroad."[66]

Unfortunately, Washington had placed his secret document into the hands of a man already playing the role of traitor.* Arnold sent a message to the British informing them of Lafayette's proclamation and of the impending French-American attack against Canada. In a sense this did not hurt Washington's plan and, in fact, seems to have furthered it. For example, as late as December 1780 (after Arnold's defection), General Clinton warned Haldimand:

By intelligence late received an attempt against Canada is so far set as to render naval transactions on this coast improbable. As the French . . . will compose the principal part of the armament I am inclined to credit the accounts I heard of a combination being formed in Canada by the inhabitants to join them. As [the invaders] . . . will probably be obliged to trust to the country for supplies of flour and other provisions, I submit to Your Excel-

* See Chapter 5, pp. 158–59.

lency whether it would not be of moment to take from the inhabitants every article of that sort except what may be absolutely requisite for the support of their families."[67]

Haldimand did not need Clinton's warning to stay alert, as the news in Canada was equally alarming; disaffection was running rampant and the Canadians, he said, were persuaded "that a French fleet will soon shew themselves" in the St. Lawrence.

There were, of course, no aggressive moves against Canada in 1780. However, the following spring a member of Congress, John Sullivan of New Hampshire, proposed to Congress that the army make a diversion in Canada which, if circumstances were favorable, might be turned into "a real attack." Sullivan asked Washington for an opinion. The General's letter of reply, which argued that the plan was impracticable, was intercepted by the British and published in the *London Gazette* on July 14, 1781. However, having received so many contradictory reports, it is not certain the British government was put entirely at ease.

By this late date, the peace negotiations were underway and Congress, in planning for them, instructed Franklin to try to obtain Canada and Nova Scotia in any settlement, if he could. Pursuing these instructions, Franklin in May 1782 suggested to the British representative that, if Britain "should voluntarily offer to give up this province," it would undoubtedly have "an excellent effect" on the American people. Further, argued Franklin, Britain would otherwise be forced to spend a great deal of money to govern and maintain its forces in Canada, which expense would be eliminated by giving it up to the United States.[68] The British were unmoved by such arguments. What they had managed to hold by force for seven years, they would keep.

The lesson of the struggle for Canada, if the Americans thought at all about it, was a simple one. It was that propaganda and diplomatic maneuvers were no substitute for "an arm of flesh." When General Montgomery fell mortally wounded in the snows of Quebec, the American cause in Canada, despite the friendly sentiments of the people, was lost.

2

★★★

The Campaign to Win the
Indians' Allegiance

Another major segment of people in North America besides
the French Canadians became a target for belligerent propaganda—the aboriginal Indians. Long before the outbreak of
fighting at Lexington and Concord on April 19, 1775, the
Americans realized their savage Indian neighbors along the
frontiers might play a crucial role in any armed conflict with
Great Britain. The Tory supporters of Britain very early had
invoked the threat of unnumbered tribes of savages fighting
under the banner of the King. The colonists, with a long history
of bloody frontier warfare with the Indians, recognized the
necessity of gaining the allegiance of the Indians, or at least
their neutrality.

Beginning in 1775 both sides were drawn into a complex
propaganda struggle for the Indian mind. In this struggle,
which involved economic and military as well as verbal propaganda, the British possessed certain advantages and the best
arguments. The result was tragic for both the American frontier
and the Indian nations themselves.

When the Revolution began, the important Indian tribes
were located in three general areas: (1) in northwestern New
York, hunting grounds of the great Iroquois confederation—

the Six Nations of Mohawks, Oneidas, Tuscaroras, Onondagas, Cayugas, and Senecas; (2) in the Kentucky-Ohio territory, lands of a loose western confederation which included Shawnee, Miami, Potawatami, Delaware, and other tribes; and (3) in the Virginia-Carolina-Georgia back country, home of the southern Indians, the Cherokees, Creeks, and Chickasaws.

Living in the midst of these Indians when the war began were British agents and Indian superintendents, serving as official representatives of the British government. In the Iroquois country the ruling family was the Johnsons. Sir William Johnson, the superintendent for Indian affairs, before his death in 1774 was a man of great influence with the Six Nations. His power was passed on to his son, Sir John, and to his son-in-law, Colonel Guy Johnson, the latter succeeding as superintendent. Elsewhere, at Detroit and in the southern territory, British officials such as John Stuart also were able to bring personal influence to bear on the Indians is an effort to insure loyalty to the British crown.

I

The propaganda struggle for the Indians' support is connected to a long-forgotten issue of American history: the question of who first employed the savages in military operations. In this the American patriots bear the onus. The Indians were first brought into action by the patriots on a limited scale at Boston. These were the semicivilized warriors of the Stockbridge tribe, a remnant of a once powerful people living in the Berkshire hills of Massachusetts.

In the tense days and weeks before the fighting broke out on the plains of Boston, the Massachusetts Provincial Congress sought the support of the Stockbridge Indians. A chief gave the tribe's reply on April 11, 1775.

Brothers [he told the patriots], whenever I see your blood running, you will soon find me about you to revenge my brothers' blood. Although I am low and very small, I will grip hold of your enemy's heel, that he cannot run so fast and so light, as if he had nothing at his heels. So then, if you please, I will take a run to the westward and feel the minds of the Six Nations, who have always looked this way for advice concerning all important news that comes from the rising sun. . . . If I find they are against you, I will try to turn their minds.[1]

But before the Stockbridge could act as propaganda agents for the Americans, and "feel the minds" of the Iroquois, the war had begun. True to their promise, a number of warriors signed up at once as minutemen. By April 30 these Indians were spotted by the British at the ferry near Boston. This was all the British commander-in-chief, Thomas Gage, needed to spur him to seek full-fledged support of the savages on the frontiers. As early as the fall of 1774 Gage had alerted the various British agents in Indian country to prepare for trouble. Now, in the spring of 1775, with the siege of Boston underway, he reported to London: "We need not be tender of calling upon the savages, as the rebels have shown us the example by bringing as many Indians down against us here as they could collect."[2] The British government quickly gave its official blessing to use of the Indians.[3]

In Philadelphia it was clear to Congress that the colonists were at a serious disadvantage in any competition to win support of the frontier tribes. Not only were the Indians attached to the persons of the British superintendents, who could remind them of their grievances against American encroachments on their hunting grounds, but Britain also controlled the supplies of goods and necessities with which to buy continued Indian loyalty. In view of these handicaps, the best the Americans could hope for was a pledge of Indian neutrality.

On July 12, 1775, Congress adopted a plan to keep the Indians neutral. After expressing fears England "will spare no pains to excite the several nations of Indians to take up arms against these Colonies," Congress approved the creation of three departments for Indian affairs, northern, southern, and middle. Five commissioners were named to the southern department, and three commissioners each for the other two. They were directed "to treat with the Indians . . . on behalf of the United colonies, in order to preserve the peace and friendship with the said Indians, and to prevent their taking part in the present commotions."[4]

The northern commissioners laid immediate plans to convene a council fire with the Iroquois confederation at Albany. To help them in their discussions, Congress approved a long American policy statement, studded with patriot themes, to be presented to the Indians. On August 26 and 28, 1775, in sessions attended by General Schuyler and the northern commissioners, Oliver Wolcott, Colonel Turbutt Francis, and Volkert P. Douw, the address of Congress was read and translated for the Indians.

In outlining the history of the dispute between America and the King's "wicked counsellors," Congress made the following key statements: "Brothers and friends! We desire you will hear and receive what we have told you, and that you will open a good ear and listen to what we are going to say. This is a family quarrel between us and Old England. You Indians are not concerned in it. We don't wish you to take up the hatchet against the king's troops. We desire you to remain at home, and not join either side, but keep the hatchet buried deep."[5] The patriots concluded with an attempt to anticipate and counter British propaganda. "This island,"* said Congress, "now trembles, the wind whistles from almost every quarter. Let us fortify our minds and shut our ears against false rumors. Let us be cautious what we receive for truth, unless spoken by wise and good men."[6]

On August 31 a Mohawk chief arose to give the Iroquois reply. Standing before the council fire, he declared that the British had also desired them to "sit still." Therefore, he said,

* A reference to North America.

the following was the decision of the Six Nations: "Not to take any part, but, as it is a family affair, to sit still and see you fight it out; we beg you will receive this as infallible, it being our full resolution."[7]

So it was the Iroquois pledged neutrality and Congress' Indian policy seemed to have borne fruit.

II

Although Congress had fixed its policy by August 1775, exceptions were made on an individual basis which made it seem the Americans were practicing deception. For example, Benedict Arnold during his march to Quebec in November 1775 persuaded some Canadian Indians to join his forces. In a meeting with these savages Arnold explained the American dispute with the King "and his wicked great men," and told them his force had entered Canada "to drive out the king's soldiers." He invited them to join, promising "one Portuguese per month, two dollars bounty and . . . provision, and the liberty to choose their own officers."[8] Whereupon fifty Indians signed up to march with the Americans.

In general, however, the Americans sought to influence the northern Indians to remain on the sidelines. A useful agent in these attempts was the Reverend Samuel Kirkland, a Protestant missionary who had lived among the Oneidas and Tuscaroras. In the fall of 1775 Kirkland persuaded an important Oneida chief to visit Washington's camp at Cambridge. Washington, who clearly understood the importance of making a good impression on the Indian leader, did all he could to make the visit agreeable.[9] But the best American propaganda in this instance was the sight of the British army shut up in Boston, surrounded by thousands of colonial militiamen.

Other Indians came to Washington's camp during this period, including leaders of the St. Francis and Caghnawagas of Canada. Washington found himself "a little embarrassed," as he put it in January 1776, when the visiting Caghnawagas offered to take up arms on America's behalf. In a letter to Schuyler Washington wrote that his embarrassment stemmed not so much "from the impropriety of encouraging these people to depart from their neutrality (accepting their own voluntary offer rather)," but because of the expense of supporting them. He added: "I am sensible that if they do not desire to be idle, that they will be for or against us. I am sensible also that no artifices will be left unessayed to engage them against us."[10]

In his reply Schuyler suggested Washington try "to get decently rid of their offer" in some way without offending them. He verified Washington's view on supplies: "The expense we are at in the [northern] Indian department is now amazing; it will be more so when they consider themselves in our service."[11] Washington finally resolved the problem by sending the Indians back to Canada with the promise he would call on them when help was needed.

By April 1776 Washington came to realize that as the American position deteriorated in Canada, it would be impossible to keep the Indians in a state of neutrality. In a letter to Congress, he asked whether it might not "be best immediately to engage them on our side , and to use our utmost endeavours to prevent their minds being poisoned by ministerial emissaries, which will ever be the case while a king's garrison is suffered to remain in their country."[12]

Washington's fears were justified, since the British were beginning an active campaign to secure the assistance of their "old friends and allies, the Indians of the Six Nations."[13] In May 1776 Colonel John Butler and other British agents collected some chiefs of the Iroquois at Niagara in an effort to persuade them to break their vows of neutrality and join the British standard. Initially, the Indians resisted, answering that they were determined "to maintain peace with both the King and the Bostonians, and receive no axe from either." One important influence working on their minds apparently was the news of the British evacuation of Boston several months earlier. In an effort to counteract the significance of that withdrawal, the British told the Iroquois leaders:

The King of England is very great and wise; he was never yet conquered. He has subdued both France and Spain. Pray, what can this handful in America do with such a King? The King is very subtle, he has deceived the Bostonians. . . . He ordered his forces continued at Boston till the Bostonians had collected all the cannon that could be found, from Philadelphia, New York, and even from Virginia, and brought them to that place. The Bostonians, having all their force and cannon collected, were about to destroy the town; but the King's officer commanding there forbade them, telling them he would leave it in a peaceful manner, as the purpose of his coming there was now answered. And now, brothers, you will soon hear that the King's ships have laid waste all their seaports, as they can make no resistance, having sent all their cannon and stores to Boston.[14]

Although the Indians may not have been impressed by these laborious arguments, Butler prevailed on them to send a delegation to talk with Colonel Guy Johnson, who had just returned from England with specific instructions to fully engage the Indians of the Iroquois confederation.

Meanwhile, Congress had not been idle. In April 1776 it turned its attention to a visiting delegate of Delawares of the middle department, headed by "Captain White Eyes." Hoping the Delawares could be used, Congress ordered a present of $300 plus two horses and saddles for Captain White Eyes. The Delaware chief was then urged to go among all the Indian nations to the westward, and to tell them "that we are determined to cultivate peace and friendship with them, and that we will endeavour, by making the best regulation in our power, to prevent any of our people wronging them in any manner, or taking their lands; and we will strive to put the trade between us on such a footing, as will secure the peace and promote the interest of all parties; and we expect that all the wise men of every Indian nation will use their influence for the same purpose."[15]

By June 1776, however, Congress' hopes of peace and friendship with the Indians began to dim. With the bad news from Canada came word that the British were actively trying to recruit the savages of the Six Nations. On June 3, thereupon, Congress decided to break away from its year-old policy of seeking Indian neutrality. On that day it authorized Washington to employ 2,000 Indians as auxiliaries to reinforce the northern army.[16]

III

In the now open competition between Americans and English for Indian support, both sides were aware that the greatest arguments that could be brought to bear on the savages were economic. From London Lord Germain wrote to General Carleton that a considerable supply of goods suitable for presents was on its way to America, "the better to enable you to prevail" on the Iroquois "to a general declaration in our favour."[17] The Americans, in desperate need of the same blankets, muskets, and knives which would buy Indian support, could only threaten the savages with dire revenge if they took up the hatchet on the British side.

For example, when word reached the Americans that the blood-thirsty Senecas were urging the Shawnese to attack the Virginia frontier, the Americans made many loud and frightening noises. As Jefferson reported (in August 1776): "We directed a declaration to be made to the six nations in general that if they did not take the most decisive measures for the preservation of neutrality we would never cease waging war with them while one was to be found on the face of the earth."[18]

This threat may have temporarily deterred the Indians. However, in the late summer of 1776 an incident took place at

British Detroit which bode no good for the patriots. It involved Captain White Eyes of the Delawares, and an American trader named William Wilson, who had gone into territory of the Wiandot tribe to spread the doctrines and messages of Congress. Wilson carried with him a written message to the Wiandots from Congress' agent in the middle department, George Morgan.

The Wiandots, who were under British influence, apparently notified the British lieutenant governor at Detroit, Henry Hamilton, who invited the two men to visit him for a friendly parley. Wilson and Captain White Eyes accepted. Once in Detroit, however, they found themselves the victims of an anti-American demonstration staged by Hamilton before a mixed gathering of savages. It began at the council meeting they were invited to, when Hamilton asked Wilson if he could see Morgan's message to the Wiandots. Wilson handed it over to the British leader, who read it slowly and then turned to the assembled Indians to denounce the Americans as "enemies and traitors to my king." While the Indians watched, Hamilton dramatically tore up the American address and the gift belt that had accompanied it, and threw the pieces about the council house.[19] Turning to Captain White Eyes, he ordered him to leave Detroit at once if he valued his life. So it was a much chagrined Delaware chief and American agent who speedily packed up and left the fort, their propaganda mission a failure.

The western Indians who had keenly observed Hamilton's little drama vowed to him that they were ready to act immediately against the Americans. Hamilton, however, held them back, having received instructions that the savages should be held in readiness to co-operate with British forces the following spring. He told the assembled Indians "to content themselves with watchfully observing the enemy's motions."[20]

Although in the north and central territories British policy in 1776 was to hold off the Indians until the campaigns of 1777, a different policy was pursued in the south. There John Stuart, the Indian superintendent, stirred up the Cherokees, Creeks, and Chickasaws to attack the frontier settlements in the summer of 1776. Stuart did not need to be very persuasive to win over these Indians, many of whom had long-standing grievances against the land-grabbing colonists.

The British plan in the south in 1776 called for synchronization of naval operations along the Carolina-Georgia coast with Indian outbreaks on the frontier. The sole propaganda operation undertaken in this connection involved an attempt to subvert the frontiersmen. In May 1776 the British disseminated a propaganda letter along the Carolina frontier which held out safety and salvation to any Americans who would rally to the government. The letter stated it was not the King's intention "to set his friends and allies, the Indians, on his liege subjects. Therefore, whoever of you are willing to join his Majesty's forces as soon as they arrive at the Cherokee nation, by repairing to the King's standard, shall find protection, and their families and estates be secured from all danger whatever."[21]

This letter also revealed British military plans, as follows: "Should any of the inhabitants be desirous of knowing how they are to be kept free of every kind of insult or danger, inform them that his Majesty will immediately land an army in West Florida, and march them through the Creek nation to the Chickasaws, where five hundred warriors from each nation are to join them, then come by the Cherokees, (who have also promised their assistance), and then take possession of the frontiers of North Carolina and Virginia."[22] This intelligence was interesting enough to cause excited preparations among the Americans to meet the impending attacks.

In July 1776 the first blow fell on settlers along the Holston River, when 700 savages advanced against Watauga Fort and Eaton's Station. Both attacks, however, were beaten off. This initiation of frontier warfare by the British and Indians was a gain for the patriot cause since, in striking the first blow, it turned southern opinion further against Britain and "the detestable villain, Stuart." Many Americans who had been lukewarm Tories turned Whig, according to one report from Charleston dated July 21: "A number of the heads of the Tories in this province, when they heard of the breaking out of the Indians, wrote to our governor and told him they never dreamt the King would descend to such lawless and diabolical designs; that they were now willing to do everything in their power to assist their brethren in America. These are men of influence on the frontiers, and will be very useful against the Indians."[23]

Meanwhile, the British forces were driven off by the Charleston patriots in late June 1776. The result on the frontier was that, after the Indians retreated, they left behind a fierce determination in American hearts to seek revenge. In the fall of 1776 this revenge was wreaked when several hastily organized columns of Carolina militia, plus a force of Virginians, marched into the Cherokee country, put villages and fields to the torch, and scattered the Indians.

In the north, when Washington heard the news of the American raid into Indian country, the commander-in-chief sought to spread the propaganda lessons before the eyes of a tribe of Canadian Indians. In a message to the chiefs of the Passamaquoddy tribe, Washington wrote in December 1776:

Brothers: I have a piece of news to tell you which I hope you will attend to. Our enemy, the King of Great Britain, endeavoured to stir up all the Indians from Canada to South Carolina against us. But our brethren of the Six Nations and their allies the Shawanese and Delawares, would not harken to the advice of the messengers sent among them, but kept fast hold of our ancient convenant chain. The Cherokees and Southern tribes were foolish enough to listen to them, and to take up the hatchet against us; upon which our warriors went into their country, burnt their houses, destroyed their corn, and obliged them to sue for peace and give hostages for their future good behavior.

Now, brothers, never let the King's wicked counsellors turn your hearts against me and your brethren of this country. . . .[24]

Washington was not alone in taking advantage of favorable events to spread friendly propaganda. On the British side John Stuart, in an effort to recoup his fortunes among the defeated Cherokees, spread the news of the defeats of Washington's army at New York and in New Jersey. Writing to the Indians early in 1777, Stuart said: "The King's army is victorious everywhere, and the rebels who bragged so much of their valor, fly before him like the deer before wolves and tigers. Their great army is dispersed and not finding protection in their strong forts and walls, have sought [safety] in inglorious flight. This we may reasonably expect will soon bring about a peace."[25]

The new year 1777 dawned on frontiers which were quiet. However, if Washington and the patriots had really believed the northern tribes had turned away from British persuasion, the year 1777—the "bloody year" in the history of the frontier —was to awaken them to the fact that most of the powerful Iroquois were lost to the American cause.

IV

The basic British plan for employing the Indians on a large scale in 1777 was to use them as auxiliaries with Burgoyne's army on the march from Canada, or to excite diversions on the frontiers. In the case of Burgoyne's army, there were to be two related operations. One group of Indians was to march under Lieutenant Colonel Barry St. Leger through the Mohawk Valley, while another group was to serve with Burgoyne's main force on the march against Ticonderoga and Albany.

Some 400 warriors joined up with Burgoyne's army, less than he had hoped for but enough to spread an alarm up and down the frontier, and to convince the English general of the usefulness of the Indians.[26] However, in this, as in other affairs, Burgoyne showed poor insight into the minds of the American frontiersmen, who were only led to greater resistance. Burgoyne's bombastic invasion proclamation of June 20, 1777, also was misconceived. Burgoyne had written: "I have but to give stretch to the Indian forces under my direction (and they amount to thousands) to overtake the hardened enemies of Great Britain. . . . The messengers of justice and wrath await them in the field; and devastation, famine and every concomitant horror that a reluctant but indispensable prosecution of military duty must occasion."[27]

If Burgoyne had expected to frighten the frontiersmen with these fine words, he was doomed to disappointment. Instead, a single killing involving his Indian warriors so inflamed the minds of the colonials that they rallied in large numbers from the farms and hamlets of New England. This incident was the murder and scalping of young Jane McCrea.

Miss McCrea, who lived in the Hudson Valley north of Albany, was the daughter of a New Jersey Presbyterian minister and was engaged to marry an American loyalist who had fled to Canada to join Burgoyne's army. Instead of leaving the troubled area, the girl decided to go to Fort Edward (south of Ticonderoga), hoping to greet her suitor there. But as the fort was abandoned, she stayed at the home of a Mrs. McNeil. On July 27, 1777—several days before Burgoyne's advancing army took over the fort—a scouting party of Indians came upon it, seized Mrs. McNeil and Jane, and started back towards the army. A dispute soon arose between two of the savages over who should be the girl's guard. One of the angry Indians finally shot her, scalped her, and stripped her clothing from her body.

Prior to this incident Burgoyne had tried to avoid such killings by issuing strict orders to the savages to spare aged men, women, children, and prisoners. On June 24 he had announced his "rules" for the campaign as follows:

I positively forbid bloodshed when you are not opposed in arms.

Aged men, women, children and prisoners must be held sacred from the knife or hatchet, even in the time of actual conflict.

You shall receive compensation for the prisoners you take, but you shall be called to account for scalps.

In conformity and indulgence of your customs, which have affixed an idea of honor to such badges of victory, you shall be allowed to take the scalps of the dead, when killed by your fire and in fair opposition; but on no account or pretence, or subtility, or prevarication, are they to be taken from the wounded or even dying.[28]

Now, only a few days after Burgoyne had laid down his rules, the British camp was startled to see a woman's scalp dangling from the hands of her murderer. Burgoyne immediately ordered the Indian's arrest; but when advised that all the other savages would defect if the man was punished, he was forced to pardon him.

News of the killing soon spread up and down the New York-New England frontier. And as the story travelled, Jane McCrea grew in beauty as the crime grew in horror. Murders of frontiersmen and women were common occurrences, but that of Jane McCrea captured the people's imaginations. To the Americans the choice was to wait quietly in their homes for the impending onslaught, or to march together against the enemy on a distant battlefield. They chose to march and soon hundreds of farmers and militiamen were trekking through the countryside to join General Horatio Gates' army.

Gates also played a significant role in spreading the story of Jane McCrea. In a letter to Burgoyne, which received wide publicity, Gates attacked the policy of using the Indians.

That the savages of America [said Gates] should in their warfare mangle and scalp the unhappy prisoners who should fall into their hands is neither new nor extraordinary; but that the famous Lieutenant General Burgoyne . . . should hire the savages of America to scalp Europeans and the descendants of Europeans, nay more, that he should pay a price for each scalp so barbarously taken, is more than will be believed in England until authenticated facts shall in every gazette convince mankind of the truth of this horrid tale. Miss McCrea, a young lady lovely to the sight, of virtuous character and amiable disposition, engaged to be married to an officer in your army, was with other women and children taken out of a house near Fort Edward, carried into the woods, and there scalped and mangled in the most shocking manner.[29]

The facts thus exaggerated somewhat by the Americans, the growing patriot legend of Jane McCrea proved to be but the forerunner of Burgoyne's troubles. In the weeks that followed came the disasters to British arms at Bennington and Fort Stanwix, and Burgoyne was left alone to march his army to its fate at Saratoga.

v

The failure of the British to take Fort Stanwix was the culmination of a series of events which saw the use of one of the most effective planted rumors of the entire war. The instigator of this operation was Major General Benedict Arnold.

It will be recalled Burgoyne had planned to send a column under St. Leger from Oswego, travelling east into the Mohawk Valley with the mission of meeting the main army at Albany. The force that began this march included between 800 and 1000 Indians under the famous Mohawk chief, Joseph Brant, and about 800 white men—British, American loyalists, and German mercenaries. St. Leger had received information that Fort Stanwix had only a weak garrison of about sixty men, and he did not anticipate trouble in seizing the fort. However, just before he arrived, the Americans received reinforcements which brought the garrison to a total of 750 men. St. Leger immediately invested the fort, paraded his mixed troops up and down before the palisades, and demanded its surrender. But the garrison, under the leadership of Colonel Peter Gansevoort, was determined to fight and the sight of the painted Indians only strengthened their resolve.

Meanwhile, news of the arrival of the British column in the Mohawk Valley, and the investiture of Fort Stanwix, began to spread panic among the settlers. Some who had been adherents of the patriot cause began to think of saving themselves by going over to the British. However, there were other patriots who were determined not to let the enemy pass. A force of 800 patriots, under Nicholas Herkimer, a brigadier general in the Tryon County militia, was hastily recruited and, on August 4, 1777, they marched west with the intention of relieving Fort Stanwix.

St. Leger received advance information of their coming, and he planned a trap for them at Oriskany Creek. To spring the trap he called upon the Indians under Brant and a portion of Sir John Johnson's troops. But he had not counted on the fighting determination of the Americans. In the vicious, hand-to-hand combat in the woods and ravines, both columns became hopelessly intermingled. Herkimer was mortally wounded in the struggle; but, when it was over, the Americans were in possession of the battlefield. However, they had suffered such heavy losses that they were unable to push on to Fort Stanwix.

While the battle had raged at Oriskany Creek, two hundred and fifty Americans suddenly issued out of Fort Stanwix in a surprise raid on the lightly guarded British camps outside. The raid was a complete success. Before returning to the fort, these Americans thoroughly looted the camps, taking everything they could carry away including most of the belongings of the Indians.

These unexpected mishaps caused much discontent among the Indians who were in the best of times, as Washington put it, "a not very persevering people . . . apt to be discouraged by the most trifling miscarriages."[30] On this occasion the miscarriages were serious. Instead of marching with a victorious army as they had believed, the Indians had found themselves in one of the bloodiest battles of the northern campaign. When, on returning to camp to tend their wounded and dead, they found most of their possessions gone, their morale sank even further.

It was in these circumstances that Benedict Arnold entered the scene. Arnold had been sent into the Mohawk Valley with a relief column of about 900 men. As he marched towards Fort Stanwix, he learned of the propaganda efforts of the British to frighten the people into joining the royal standard. Whereupon on August 20, 1777, he issued some American counterpropaganda, modelled after one of the British broadsides. Arnold proclaimed:

Whereas a certain Barry St. Leger, a British general in the service of the—George of Great Britain, at the head of a banditti of robbers, murderers and traitors, composed of savages of America and more savage Britons . . . have lately appeared on the frontiers of this state, and have threatened ruin and destruction of all the inhabitants of the United States.

They have also, by artifice and misrepresentation, induced many of the ignorant and unwary subjects of these states to forfeit their allegiance to the same, and join them in their atrocious crimes and parties of treachery and parricide. Humanity to these poor deluded wretches, who are hastening blindfold to destruction, induces me to offer them and all others concerned, whether savages, Germans, Americans or Britons, pardon; provided they do within ten days of the date hereof, come and lay down their arms, sue for protection and swear allegiance to the United States of America. But, if still blind to their own safety, they obstinately persist in their wicked courses, determined to draw on themselves the just vengeance of Heaven, and of this exasperated country, they must expect no mercy from either.[31]

This bold proclamation must have heartened the patriots almost as much as an Arnold proclamation of a later date was to anger them.* But Arnold was not yet finished with his

* See Chapter 5, p. 159.

psychological war. He also decided to spread a rumor in St. Leger's camp at Fort Stanwix that he was on the march with a great American army.

To carry this rumor into the enemy camp Arnold employed a mentally retarded Dutchman named Hon Yost Schuyler, who had been arrested within American lines with a British propaganda agent, trying to persuade the people to join the British. Both men were tried as spies, convicted, and sentenced to death. Hon Yost's mother and brother, however, on hearing of the sentence hurried to Arnold and pleaded for his life.

Arnold learned, meanwhile, that Hon Yost was held in great awe by the Indians for the very reason of his mental backwardness. He now agreed to spare the Dutchman's life but only if he would go to St. Leger's camp and spread a false story regarding the number of Americans on the march. To assure good faith Arnold said he would retain the brother as hostage. The family agreed that Hon Yost would go. To give plausibility to the deception, Hon Yost's coat was shot through with several bullets to support his story that he had escaped. In addition, Arnold called upon a friendly Oneida Indian to follow Hon Yost to verify the story to the British.

Thus it was that on August 22, 1777, around noon, Hon Yost suddenly appeared in St. Leger's camp with an excited story. He exhibited his bullet-riddled garments to the Indians, and babbled of the approach of a great American army whose soldiers numbered as the leaves of the trees. Then the Oneida entered the camp and verified Hon Yost's tale. As the story spread through the camp, the discouraged savages gathered the remainder of their belongings, looted some of the white men's, and the whole Indian body fled the scene. St. Leger tried to stop them, but panic leaped from red men to white and soon the English, Germans, and loyalists all took to their heels, not tarrying long enough to pack their tents and equipment. Arnold's rumor-mongering had succeeded beyond his wildest dreams.

The siege of Fort Stanwix lifted with such unexpected suddenness that the surprised Americans did not understand it. At 11 A.M. that morning the enemy had responded to a bombardment from the fort with an answering fire. At 3 P.M. several deserters approached the fort and told the defenders that "General St. Leger and his army was retreating with the utmost precipitation." Colonel Gansevoort sent out a party of sixty men who soon confirmed the account. It was not until 7 P.M. that the puzzle was solved, when Hon Yost slipped into the fort and related that Arnold was on his way "with two thousand men" (even then Hon Yost was exaggerating Arnold's force).[32] When Arnold's 900 men did arrive they were met by the cheers of the garrison.

So a simple rumor, striking minds at the perfect psychological moment, had sent the enemy flying.

VI

The bloody events in the north during 1777 had their counterpart on the Pennsylvania-Virginia frontier, where the British government also activated the tribes of the western confederacy. In May 1777 General Carleton received a London directive: "It is the King's command that you should direct Lieut. Governor Hamilton to assemble as many of the Indians of his district as he conveniently can, and placing proper persons at their head . . . employ them in making a diversion and exciting an alarm upon the frontiers of Virginia and Pennsylvania."[33] It was also suggested that Hamilton make a propaganda offer to the "considerable numbers of loyal subjects in those parts" to join his forces. He was authorized to promise 200 acres of free land to any American who came over. "These offers," said the directive, "it is hoped will induce many persons to engage in the King's service; which may enable Lieut. Gov. Hamilton to extend his operations so as to divide the attention of the rebels, and oblige them to collect a considerable force to oppose him, which cannot fail of weakening their main army and facilitating the operations . . . to be carried on against them in other quarters."[34]

Hamilton received his instructions at Detroit on June 16, and the following day he assembled a council meeting attended by members of the Ottawa, Huron, Chippewa, Potawatomi, Miami, Shawnee, and Delaware tribes. In the next two weeks Hamilton harangued the Indians, showed them "the hatchet," sang war songs, and described the methods they should use in making war on the frontier. As Burgoyne had done, Hamilton tried to impress upon the Indians that "they were men and were desired to make war against men, and not against women or children."[35] But, like Burgoyne, Hamilton was to learn that the savages had their own rules of warfare.

Hamilton also followed the suggestion to try to persuade some of the frontiersmen to come over. On June 24 he published a propaganda missive in which he invited the Americans to join his forces at Detroit. "I do assure all such as are inclined to withdraw themselves from the tyranny and oppression of the rebel committees," Hamilton wrote, "and take refuge in this settlement or any of the posts commanded by his Majesty's officers, shall be humanely treated, shall be lodged and victualled, and such as come off in arms and shall use them in defence of his Majesty against rebels and traitors, 'till the extinction of this rebellion, shall receive pay adequate to their former stations in the rebel service, and all common men who shall serve during that period, shall receive his Majesty's bounty of two hundred acres of land."[36]

To distribute this interesting appeal, Hamilton employed his Indian raiders. By August 1777 the proclamations began to appear on the Pennsylvania-Virginia frontier, left by the Indians on the doorsteps of abandoned homes or on the bodies of scalped settlers. This mixture of terror with an offer of salvation seemed to have some effect; and American officers in several frontier forts tried to suppress the propaganda sheets whenever they were found.

By November Hamilton's offer had been brought to the attention of Congress, along with other reports which noted "a dangerous spirit of disaffection has been excited and fomented among some worthless and evil-disposed persons on the . . . frontiers, who lost to all sentiments of virtue, honor, or regard for their country, have been induced to aid our remorseless enemy."[37]

But by this time important events elsewhere served to counteract the effects of the Hamilton-directed Indian raids. For example, the news of the failure of St. Leger's expedition was diligently spread by the Americans among the western Indians. General Edward Hand addressed the Delawares at Fort Pitt: "Brothers, the news papers will give you a full account of the great battles our armies have gained. The Indians who were so foolish as to join our enemies have found their mistake and those who have not run away are quite sick of their conduct. . . . The Oneidas and Tuscaroras have joined our army and are now in pursuit of the enemy. . . . What I have told you is true but do not . . . depend on words alone. If you send to the northward your messengers may see with their own eyes."[38]

News of the defeat of Burgoyne's army also was spread in the Indian territories. In particular, Congress in December 1777 delivered an address to the Six Nations, a strong statement which reminded the Indians how the patriots had entreated them "to remain neuter" instead of listening "to the voice of our enemies." The result of their "unprovoked treachery," said Congress, was nothing but shame and disgrace. "Your foolish warriors and their new allies have been defeated and driven back in every quarter; and many of them justly paid the price of their rashness with their lives."[39]

In this address Congress spoke with an especially fierce voice to those of the Iroquois confederation who had most strongly supported the British—the Cayugas, Senecas, and Mohawks. "Mark well what we now tell you," said Congress. "Let it sink deep as the bottom of the sea, and never be forgotten by you or your children. If ever again you take up the hatchet to strike us; if you join our enemies in battle or council; if you give them intelligence, or encourage them or permit them to pass through your country to molest or hurt any of our people, we shall look upon you as our enemies, and treat you as the worst of enemies. . . . The hand of the thirteen United States is not short. It will reach to the farthest extent of the country of the Six Nations."[40]

This address was dispatched to the northern commissioners with instructions to communicate it to the different Iroquois tribes. Congress seemed to be of two opinions concerning the defeated Indians. At first its hopes were raised so high by Burgoyne's surrender that it believed it might be possible to bring over the Six Nations en masse to the American side. But on second thought, Congress decided to try to restore friendship with them, and to induce them to return to neutrality.[41]

Early in 1778 the commissioners sent word to the Indians that a conference would be held at Johnstown. This meeting took place on March 9, 1778; and one of the commissioners later reported: "The number of Indians was something above 700 consisting of Oneidas, Tuscaroras, Onondagas, a few Mohawks, and three or four Cayugas but not a single Seneca attended. The latter had the insolence even to effect their surprise that while our tomahawks stuck in their heads, their wounds were bleeding and their eyes streaming with tears . . . we should think of inviting them to a treaty!"[42]

About all that the Johnstown meeting accomplished was a reaffirmation by the Oneidas and Tuscaroras of allegiance to the patriot side. The main body of the Iroquois remained anti-American. In a letter on the subject to Congress in May 1778, Washington offered his opinion that there was "very little prospect" of winning them over. "The advantage which the enemy possess over us in having the means of making presents more liberally than we can," Washington wrote, "has made a strong impression upon their minds, and seems to be more than a counter-balance for any arguments we can offer to conciliate their attachment."[43]

By June Congress reconciled itself to the fact that it had failed to win over the hostile tribes and, perhaps, had "confirmed the savages in an opinion industriously inculcated in them by the enemy that the forbearance of these states proceeds from their inability to revenge the outrages committed against them." The American Board of War subsequently recommended to Congress that an expedition be organized to march against the center of Indian agitation, British Detroit.[44] However, an expedition into Indian country was to await the passage of another year.

VII

During the first six months of 1778 Hamilton had continued the hit-and-run raids on the frontier, and both American prisoners and scalps began to flow into Detroit. In January alone (according to Hamilton's report to Carleton) the Indians brought in 73 prisoners and 129 scalps. Despite this, that very month Hamilton distributed another propaganda paper on the frontier which emphasized the "kind and humane treatment" theme. Dated January 5, this propaganda paper was in the form of a circular letter to the frontiersmen and contained a statement by eight American captives who assured their countrymen that they were receiving good treatment from both Indians and white captors. The letter offered "safe conduct" to all Americans on the frontier who would come to Detroit.[45]

This appeal was weakened by the very evidence of the scalps which came into Detroit, and eye-witness reports of them which filtered back to the American settlements only stirred the frontiersmen to greater resistance. Indeed, one of the British leaders at Detroit, Edward Abbott, came around to the view that the use of the Indians was doing the King's cause more harm than good. In a letter to Carleton on June 8, Abbott complained that "the employing Indians on the rebel frontiers has been of great hurt to the cause. . . . These poor unhappy people are forced to take up arms against their sovereign, or be pillaged and left to starve. . . ."[46]

Hamilton's bloody activities did not continue unanswered, and, in fact, led directly to one of the most important American expeditions of the war. Under the leadership of George Rogers Clark, this expedition changed the history of the Ohio Valley and led to the capture of Hamilton himself.

Clark, a backwoodsman who was serving as Virginia's military commander in Kentucky, had reached the conclusion that the best way to relieve the frontier was to strike deep into enemy territory, specifically into the Illinois country. He believed it possible to conquer the region before the British knew what had happened. Residents of the area consisted largely of settlers of French origin and these people, Clark hoped, might be receptive to American appeals.

Late in 1777 Clark returned to Virginia where he laid his plan before Jefferson, George Mason, and Richard Henry Lee. These leaders adopted the idea and undertook to persuade Governor Patrick Henry to support the Illinois expedition. Henry was won over, and shortly thereafter the Virginia Assembly authorized Clark to raise seven companies to be used ostensibly in defending Kentucky. In reality, secret orders were issued to him to attack and seize the town of Kaskaskia, Illinois, and perhaps Detroit.

So it was that in the summer of 1778 the frontier was startled by news that Clark and the Virginians were in Illinois country. On June 4, after a march across southern Illinois, Clark surprised and took Kaskaskia, not far from the Mississippi. To the surprised French inhabitants he proceeded to explain the causes of the war and to assure them they would be free men if they took the oath of allegiance to the United States. He clinched his arguments by announcing the news of the French-American alliance and by assuring the people their church would be protected by the new government. Clark's talk was persuasive, and the people of Kaskaskia took the oath of loyalty.[47] Not long thereafter the French residents of Vincennes, across the territory to the east, also were talked into swearing allegiance to the Americans.

When news of Clark's activities reached Hamilton at his Detroit headquarters, the British leader immediately grasped the implications of the American presence in Illinois. If nothing were done, rebel influence might spread north and east which would threaten the entire British position in the territory. Hamilton decided on a counter-blow, which he would personally direct; and in late 1778 he ordered an expedition against Vincennes. His march on Vincennes, which he reached in December 1778, proved successful. The inhabitants quickly capitulated to his force of 175 white soldiers and 60 Indians and resumed their allegiance to Britain.

Hamilton sought to consolidate his victory in a propaganda letter addressed on December 29 to "the People of Illinois." In this letter he warned the French "of the misfortunes to which they will be exposed by withdrawing themselves from the dominion of the King of England." He painted a forbidding picture of a combined force of Chickasaws, Cherokees, and other Indian tribes and a regiment of British regulars marching in the spring against the rebels. He reminded them that "the nations inhabiting the shores of the Lakes will all be devoted to whatever service I shall recommend to them." He concluded that it was up to the French inhabitants of Illinois: "If they suffer themselves any longer to be so far blinded by the promises of the Americans (hitherto so badly fulfilled) as to range themselves under their standard, they must prepare to abide by the consequences."[48]

While Hamilton devoted himself to consolidating his position, Clark at Kaskaskia reached a daring decision to undertake a winter march against the British at Vincennes. On February 6, 1779, rallying the French of Kaskaskia and the surrounding territory, Clark began an 180-mile trek across Illinois. His force, consisting of about 120 men, half of them French, reached the vicinity of Vincennes on February 22, their presence still unknown to the enemy. Near the town Clark picked up a number of French inhabitants and learned from them that Hamilton's strength included a force of 200 Indians.

Knowing his own strength was not one-fourth that of the combined British, Indians, and French of Vincennes, but also aware of the lukewarm allegiance of the French to Britain, Clark decided upon a bluff to neutralize the latter. Several of the Frenchmen he had captured, unaware of his strength, were dispatched to Vincennes to deliver the following note to the people:

Gentlemen, Being now within ten miles of your village with my army determined to take your fort this night and not being willing to surprise you, I take this step to request of such of you as are true citizens and willing to enjoy the liberty I bring you to remain still in your house, and those (if any there be) that are friends to the King, will instantly repair to the fort and join the hair buyer General and fight like men. And if any such as do not go to the fort shall be discovered afterwards, they may depend on being well treated and I once more request they shall keep out of the streets, for every [one] I find in arms on my arrival I shall treat him as an enemy.[49]

Clark's bluff succeeded. The people who gathered in the public square to hear the message were so surprised and fearful that none dared to go to the fort to tell Hamilton. Clark gave further play to their imaginations by ordering his men to begin their advance with colors flying. By marching them to and fro behind a slight elevation of land, which allowed only the flags to be seen from the town, he created the impression that a force of a thousand men was approaching.

At 8 P.M. that evening, under cover of darkness and led by five of his French prisoners, Clark's column entered the town. The surprise was complete. Before Hamilton knew what had happened, the Americans were in control of Vincennes and he and his troops were besieged in the fort. Clark wasted no time with preliminaries and immediately sent a threatening surrender demand to Hamilton.

The British leader found himself in a very weak position. A large part of his Indian allies had fled into the woods while inside the fort half of his defending force consisted of Frenchmen. Although he and the British soldiers were determined "to fight to the last extremity," the French "hung their heads," Hamilton later wrote, "and their sergeants first turned round and muttered with their men. Some said it was hard they should fight against their own friends and relations who they could see had joined the Americans and fired against the fort."[50] Faced with the probable defection of half his troops, Hamilton decided to surrender. The capitulation took place on February 24, 1779.

Hamilton's surrender was one of the most important blows struck against British prestige in Indian country in the entire war. That Hamilton, the proud English leader who had been almost deified by the western Indians, should be caught and placed in chains (as he was later on orders of the Virginia Assembly) was an astounding fact to the savage mind. Now the name of George Rogers Clark of the Big Knives (Virginians) was spread up and down the frontier. Clark clearly understood that everything he said to the Indians would carry great weight; and, in conferences with the Chippewas and other savages who had accompanied Hamilton, he threatened extermination to any who would not lay down their arms at once.

Clark also sent a strong speech to the tribes in the north in which he played to the hilt the role of conqueror. This speech deserves to be preserved in all its original flavor. Said Clark to the Indians (excerpts): "Its as you will I dont care whether you are for peace or war; as I glory in war and want enemies to fight us, as the English cant fight us any longer, and are become like Young Children begging the Big Knives for mercy and a little bread to eat; this is the last speech you may ever expect from the Big Knives, the next thing will be the Tomahawk. And you may expect in four moons to see your women & children given to the dogs to eat, while those nations that have kept their words with me will flourish and grow...."[51]

Clark's victory in the Ohio Valley had lasting effects, although American hopes for seizing Detroit were never to be fulfilled.

VIII

Congress, we have noted, had hoped the disaster to Burgoyne's arms would bring the Iroquois over to the American side, or at least their return to neutrality. But by the spring of 1778 evidence mounted that the Indians were about to strike again. In July the uneasy quiet was finally shattered when a combined British-Indian partisan force of about 900 men slipped into the Wyoming Valley of Pennsylvania, defeated the American militia, and laid waste the entire valley. More than 1,000 homes were destroyed, cattle and swine were driven away, and hundreds of scalps were taken. In August the Mohawk Valley shuddered under the impact of similar raids, led by Chief Brant and Captain Walter Butler. These raids continued into 1779.

The frontier inhabitants cried out for protection, and petitions flowed into Philadelphia. Congress, acting at last, called for an expedition into the Iroquois country. On February 25, 1779, orders were dispatched to Washington; and within two months the expedition had been organized and was on its way under the command of Major General John Sullivan. This punitive expedition, which lasted from May through September, ravaged the Indian countryside. By October Washington was able to report that "General Sullivan has completed the entire destruction of the country of the Six Nations; driven all the inhabitants, men, women and children out of it and is . . . on his return to join this army with the troops under his command." Washington hoped that this demonstration of American power, "to chastise them whenever their hostile conduct deserves it," would produce good effects.[52]

But Sullivan's expedition did not succeed in ending the Indian ravages. The Indian and loyalist forces were only driven back to the British post at Niagara, where they nursed their wounds and whence they launched revengeful and bloody raids against the frontier in 1780 and 1781.

During this period there were a number of related propaganda incidents. One involved the manifesto entitled, *Letter of the Marquis de Lafayette to the savages of Canada,* disseminated in December 1778. In this letter Lafayette had urged "his children" in the north to desert the British and join the Americans, France's new allies. "You know," wrote Lafayette, "that your fathers want to lead the thirteen states with one hand and Canada with the other in order to join them against our enemy, and the king has sent a declaration* to the Canadians to promise them his aid. But I realize that you would be very glad to receive confirmation of this news from me. . . . So my children, you will see us soon arrive in Canada with General Washington, the great war chief of the Americans, and we shall know who are our friends and who our enemies. . . ."[53]

To counter this propaganda about the French alliance, and the argument that Britain was unable to protect them, the British on a number of occasions put on a "show of force" for

* Admiral d'Estaing's proclamation.

the benefit of the Indians. In June 1779, for example, General Haldimand invited some western savages, as well as the Iroquois, to visit Quebec where they could see with their own eyes that it was the *British* fleet sitting in the bay. Haldimand cautioned the Indians not to listen "to mischievous birds that whisper into your ears all manner of bad news and falsehoods to disturb your well-being and unanimity in order to bring you strife and trouble."[54]

However, on all sides the British authorities were beset. From Nova Scotia the British agent there reported to General Clinton in August 1779 that the Indians were much alienated and he warned: "As their attachment to the French interest is yet very strong and their regard for the rebels much strengthened by their alliance with France, it requires the greatest attention and address to keep them quiet." He added he feared they might take up arms should "any French squadron or ship" appear on the coast.[55]

Besides taking advantage of the potent French alliance, the Americans invoked an old technique to insure the loyalty of certain of the tribes. This was to present the chiefs army commissions, which brought the Indians the same pay and subsistence as other American soldiers. At least one such commission was offered in the rank of major to a chief of the St. Francois tribe of Canada;[56] but usually these commissions went no higher than the rank of captain.[57]

Throughout the war Washington followed a policy of paying every courtesy to Indian visitors to his army. This had as its purpose, he once explained to General Schuyler: "To give them an idea of our force and to do away with the false notions they might have embibed from the tales which had been propagated among them."[58] An account of such a visit was recorded by James Thacher in May 1779.

Our brigade [wrote Thacher] was paraded for the purpose of being reviewed by General Washington and a number of Indian chiefs. His Excellency, with his usual dignity, followed by his mulatoo servant Bill, riding a beautiful gray steed, passed in front of the line and received the salute. He was accompanied by a singular group of savages, whose appearance was beyond description ludicrous. Their horses were of the meanest kind, some of them destitute of saddles. . . . Their personal decorations were equally farcical. . . . But his excellency deems it good policy to pay some attention to this tribe of the wilderness, and to convince them of the strength and discipline of our army, that they may be encouraged to be friendly or deterred from aggression, if they should become hostile to our country.[59]

In the summer of 1780, when the French expeditionary force under General Comte de Rochambeau arrived at Newport, Rhode Island, it also played host to visiting Indians. Rochambeau showed his savage visitors great hospitality and sent them away with presents, to serve in the back country as willing volunteers for the dissemination of allied propaganda.

During the last years of the war the uncompromising attitude of the Americans towards the Indians was well illustrated by a directive Jefferson sent to Clark in January 1780. "We would have you," Jefferson wrote, "cultivate peace and cordial friendship with the several tribes of Indians (the Shawanese excepted). Endeavour that those who are in friendship with us live in peace with one another. Against those who are our enemies let loose the friendly tribes. The Kikapous should be encouraged against the hostile tribes of the Chickasaws and Choctawas and the others against the Shawanese. . . ."[60]

Both Englishmen and Americans understood by this time that the Indian mind was impressed almost solely by two things: armed strength and economic power. The patriots showed enough strength on the frontier to prevent the Indian raids from having any significant effect on the main strategy of the war. But British economic power also continued to count for a great deal and was used very effectively in gaining and holding the loyalty of many of the tribes. In the end, however, since not enough military power was available or used to put down the rebellion, Britain's employment of the Indians only widened the split between the colonists and the mother country.

3

★★

The Incitement of
Negro Insurrection

There was yet another important group of people in America, besides the Indians, whose possible use towards subduing the rebel movement caught the imagination of British officials in 1775—the large slave population, estimated at between 500,000 and 600,000 persons.[1] The presence of these "intestine enemies," the bulk of them in the southern colonies, seemed, as in the case of the Indians, a potential weapon the British might well seize upon to bring the colonists "back to their senses."

The subject of the slaves came up during a House of Commons debate on October 26, 1775, when one of the supporters of the ministry, Governor William Lyttelton, compared America to a chain, the upper part strong and the lower part weak. Governor Lyttelton "explained this by saying the northern colonies or upper part of the chain were strong, populous, and of course able to make resistance; the southern colonies, or lower part, were weak, on account of the large number of Negroes in them. He intimated if a few regiments were sent there the Negroes would rise, and imbrue their hands in the blood of their masters."[2]

Earlier in the year, Dr. Samuel Johnson had published in

England his political tract, *Taxation No Tyranny,* in which he referred to a proposal that the slaves be set free, an act, he suggested, "which the lovers of liberty must surely commend."[3] When these words reached America in the spring, the always present colonial fears of a slave uprising came alive. Indeed, on June 19 the North Carolina delegates in Congress, in a letter of warning to their home committees of safety, cited the Johnson statement.[4]

Even in the northern colonies—in New York, Pennsylvania, and New Jersey, where the slave population was relatively small—hints of concerted action by the slaves set nerves on edge in the first year of the war. However, it was in the south that the greatest potential threat lay and, in November, John Adams recorded in his diary the opinion of two gentlemen from Georgia, who said that if the British landed one thousand well-provisioned troops in the south, and proclaimed freedom to all slaves who joined them, "twenty thousand Negroes would join . . . in a fortnight."[5]

In the colony of North Carolina in the summer of 1775 such fears led the various committees to adopt a series of precautionary measures. In June and early July special armed patrols were organized to seek out any Negroes who might possess weapons. The "patrollers" of Pitt County were authorized "to shoot any number of Negroes above four, who are off their masters plantations and will not submit."[6]

In June Josiah Martin, the royal governor of the colony, fearful of being seized by the rebels, had fled aboard a British sloop in Cape Fear River. From this place of safety Governor Martin reported to his superiors in London and, in a letter, indignantly referred to "a most infamous report" being circulated that he had "formed a design of arming the Negroes and proclaiming freedom to all such as should resort to the King's standard."[7] His denial of the rumor was weakened, however, by his subsequent words, in which he referred to the high proportion of blacks to whites in neighbouring Virginia and in Maryland, "a circumstance," he said, "that would facilitate the reduction of those colonies."[8]

While Martin's thoughts lingered on that prospect, the Americans in Pitt County on July 8, 1775, discovered "a deep laid, Horrid Tragik Plan" for a slave insurrection that very night. A full report of the movement, dated July 15, by the chairman of the County Committee of Safety, Colonel John Simpson, gave credit for its exposure to a slave belonging to a Mr. Bayner and another belonging to a Captain Thomas Respess. According to the testimony of these Negroes, the "intended insurrection" was to be put "into execution that night."[9]

Immediately, the Committee of Safety sounded the alarm and appointed one hundred men to patrol the countryside. The show of force was successful. The next day, July 9, the committee met and examined the evidence that had been gathered. This evidence, largely based on Negro testimony, named a Captain Johnson of White Haven as the leader of the movement, and a Negro slave named Merrick, who had "propagated the contagion." On July 10 the committee ordered that several Negroes caught in the "patrollers'" net be given eighty lashes and have their ears "crap'd." Additional evidence was accumulated, in the form of arms and "considerable ammunition" seized from the Negroes.

In the days that followed, the committee was busy "examining and scourging" the slaves. According to Simpson's report, "from whichever part of the county they come they all confess nearly the same thing": that on the night of the eighth they were all to fall on and destroy the families where they lived, then to go from house to house burning as they went, and finally they were to retreat into the back country where they would receive a welcome by persons appointed by the British.[10]

While news of the "horrid" plan was disseminated, early in August a letter Governor Martin had written several weeks before came to the attention of the Committee of Safety at New Bern. In this letter, written to a Lewis DeRosset, the refugee governor denied that he had ever "conceived a thought" of encouraging the Negroes to revolt. "And," he said, "I will further add my opinion that nothing could ever justify the design, falsely imputed to me, of giving encouragement to the Negroes, but the actual and declared rebellion of the King's subjects, and the failure of all other means to maintain the King's government."[11]

But the King's subjects were already in rebellion! Thus in the opinion of the New Bern committee, the Governor's words contained, "in plain English, and in every construction of language, a justification of the design of encouraging the slaves to revolt." Whereupon, the committee ordered Martin's letter be published in the press to expose his "public avowal of a crime so horrid and truly black a complexion. . . ."[12]

For even thinking of tampering with the slaves, Governor Martin, who eventually retired from the scene, found himself abused. However, true infamy in the eyes of the southerners in this connection was not to be Martin's. This honor was reserved for the King's governor of Virginia, John Murray, Earl of Dunmore, who issued an "emancipation proclamation" in November 1775 which set in motion the most threatening movement of all against the south.

I

The events which led to Dunmore's proclamation also were related to the patriot agitation in Virginia, which in April 1775 led him to seize twenty kegs of gunpowder from the public magazine at Williamsburg. This action stirred the Virginians to attempt the forcible return of the powder. Dunmore, however, insisted he would not give up the powder; and he warned the Virginians that if any injury or insult were offered him, "by the living God" he would free and arm the slaves, and would not hesitate at burning rebels' houses to ashes and spreading devastation wherever he could reach.[13]

The threat to free the Negroes and put arms into their hands "startled the Insurgents,"[14] and everywhere the Virginians reached for their weapons. From Philadelphia Thomas Wharton wrote of Dunmore to his brother: "Could he act so diabolical a part he is not fit to hold the reins of government."[15] However, the leaders of Virginia—Washington, Edmund Pendleton, and Richard Henry Lee among them—urged moderation on their excited countrymen, and they succeeded in preventing any immediate movement. The lull they won was short-lived: early in May, when news was received from the north of the skirmishing outside Boston, Patrick Henry aroused his followers for a march to repossess the powder.

Now Dunmore sought to pacify his unruly subjects, and he agreed to pay for the seized powder, which agreement succeeded in halting the march. However, being uncertain of the outcome, Dunmore set cannon before the palace in Williamsburg, obtained reinforcements from a British man-of-war, the *Fowey*, and armed his own slaves and some Indians he had been holding hostage. This mixed crew settled down to defend the palace against the Virginians, who never came.

In June, when the atmosphere seemed calmer, Dunmore recalled the Virginia Assembly into session to transact some important public business. Immediately the body got out of hand. With the fever of rebellion arising, Dunmore, fearful like his counterpart in North Carolina that he might be seized, fled with his wife and children aboard the *Fowey*, lying in the harbor at York.

From his refuge aboard the warship, Dunmore meditated how he might crush the rebel movement. As news reached him that the Virginians were forming military units and undertaking general war preparations, he pursued a plan long-conceived to raise a combined force of Indians, loyalists, and Negroes which, together with his small group of marines and soldiers, he hoped would be sufficient to restore the King's authority in the colony. His plan, broached to his superiors in London on May 1, was approved.[16]

The late summer of 1775 saw both sides arming for battle. While the patriots strained to find weapons and powder to equip their new militia units, Dunmore was accumulating a small fleet of ships at Gosport, about a half-mile from Portsmouth, and laying plans for the campaign. The need for provisions for his growing force, however, increased apace; and his British seamen, who formerly had been able to freely restock in the colonial ports, were forced into plundering expeditions. In the process they began to entice the slaves from the nearby plantations.

Although chagrined by these activities, the Americans were still unprepared when autumn came to confront Dunmore's forces. In October the rebels were startled when Dunmore's men swooped down on Norfolk and seized the American press there. Writing about this incident to Lord Dartmouth, Dunmore said he had taken the press because "the public prints of this little dirty borough of Norfolk has for some time past been wholly employed in exciting, in the minds of all ranks of people, the spirit of sedition and rebellion by the grossest misrepresentation of facts, both public and private."[17] Now, he said, he was going to have "a press for the King" on board his ship.

If the Virginia rebels were upset by this conversion of their press into a King's newspaper, they were even more angered by successive raids on October 13, 17, 19, 20, and 21, during which the rampaging governor seized arms, cannon, and other supplies. The thoroughly alarmed Virginia Committee of Safety could no longer wait: it ordered a regiment to the Norfolk area, under William Woodford.

In the days that followed there were new clashes. During one key skirmish on November 7 Dunmore's forces, 150 men and a small following of Negroes and loyalists, routed about 300 Virginians and captured a number of prisoners. This victory

By his Excellency the Right Honourable JOHN Earl of DUNMORE, his Majesty's Lieutenant and Governour-General of the Colony and Dominion of Virginia, and Vice-Admiral of the same:

A PROCLAMATION.

AS I have ever entertained Hopes that an Accommodation might have taken Place between *Great Britain* and this Colony, without being compelled, by my Duty, to this most disagreeable, but now absolutely necessary Step, rendered so by a Body of armed Men, unlawfully assembled, firing on his Majesty's Tenders, and the Formation of an Army, and that Army now on their March to attack his Majesty's Troops, and destroy the well-disposed Subjects of this Colony: To defeat such treasonable Purposes, and that all such Traitors, and their Abetters, may be brought to Justice, and that the Peace and good Order of this Colony may be again restored, which the ordinary Course of the civil Law is unable to effect, I have thought fit to issue this my Proclamation, hereby declaring, that until the aforesaid good Purposes can be obtained, I do, in Virtue of the Power and Authority to me given, by his Majesty, determine to execute martial Law, and cause the same to be executed throughout this Colony; and to the End that Peace and good Order may the sooner be restored, I do require every Person capable of bearing Arms to resort to his Majesty's S T A N-DARD, or be looked upon as Traitors to his Majesty's Crown and Government, and thereby become liable to the Penalty the Law inflicts upon such Offences, such as Forfeiture of Life, Confiscation of Lands, &c. &c. And I do hereby farther declare all indented Servants, Negroes, or others (appertaining to Rebels) free, that are able and willing to bear Arms, they joining his Majesty's Troops, as soon as may be, for the more speedily reducing this Colony to a proper Sense of their Duty, to his Majesty's Crown and Dignity. I do farther order, and require, all his Majesty's liege Subjects to retain their Quitrents, or any other Taxes due, or that may become due, in their own Custody, till such Time as Peace may be again restored to this at present most unhappy Country, or demanded of them for their former salutary Purposes, by Officers properly authorised to receive the same.

GIVEN under my Hand, on Board the Ship William, *off* Norfolk, *the* 7th *Day of* November, *in the* 16th *Year of his Majesty's Reign.*

D U N M O R E.

G O D SAVE THE K I N G.

George Washington wrote of Lord Dunmore, the author of this "emancipation proclamation": "Nothing less than depriving him of life or liberty will secure peace to Virginia."

so stimulated the governor and his supporters that he decided the moment had come to issue his "emancipation proclamation." That same day, November 7, he published a proclamation establishing martial law in the colony and calling upon "every person capable of bearing arms to resort to his Majesty's standard, or be looked upon as traitors to his Majesty's crown and government." The most important sentence, however, was his announcement giving freedom to "all indented servants, Negroes and others" who were able and willing to bear arms for the King.[18]

In a subsequent letter to General William Howe, Dunmore reported that, as a result of his proclamation, the slaves were "flocking in from all quarters." Openly gathering them in as fast as he could, the governor assigned them to a Negro corps (called Lord Dunmore's Ethiopian Regiment), under white officers. By the end of November he had nearly 300 black soldiers all decked out in uniforms. To add insult to injury, and to mock the rebels' slogan, *"Liberty or Death,"* he had emblazoned across the breast of each Negro's uniform the slogan *"Liberty to Slaves."*[19]

These actions infuriated the Virginians. If any hopes had remained that the English might yet win back the allegiance of influential southerners, the Dunmore proclamation killed them entirely. Wrote Richard Henry Lee: "Lord Dunmore's unparalled conduct in Virginia has . . . united every man in the colony. If administration had searched through the world for a person best fitted to ruin their cause, and procure union and success for these colonies, they could not have found a more complete agent than Lord Dunmore."[20]

Washington was both worried and outraged when news reached him at Cambridge of the activities of the "arch-traitor to the rights of humanity, Lord Dunmore." Writing to Lee, Washington warned: "If, my dear sir, that man is not crushed before spring, he will become the most formidable enemy America has; his strength will increase as a snowball by rolling, and faster, if some expedient cannot be hit upon to convince the slaves and servants of the impotency of his designs." Washington suggested that simply forcing Dunmore back aboard his ships was not sufficient: "Nothing less than depriving him of life or liberty will secure peace to Virginia."[21]

A propaganda effort along the lines Washington suggested had already been made. In an article in the *Virginia Gazette* on November 25, an anonymous rebel writer, after attacking Dunmore, addressed himself directly to the Negroes and warned they would probably be sold in the West Indies and perish either "by the inclemency of the weather, or the cruelty of barbarous masters." The writer added: "Be not then, ye negroes, tempted by this proclamation to ruin yourselves. We have given you a faithful view of what you are to expect; and declare before God in doing it, we have considered your welfare as well as that of the country. Whether you will profit by the advice, we cannot tell; but this we know, that whether we suffer or not, if you desert us, *you* most certainly will."[22]

Still reports were heard of "great numbers" of slaves joining Dunmore. The English tenders, reported one writer, were "plying up the rivers, plundering plantations and using every art to seduce the Negroes."[23] In an attempt to halt this defection, the Virginia Assembly issued a warning of death to any Negro who joined the governor. To those slaves who immediately would forsake the governor, the Virginians offered a full pardon; and they also appealed to everyone "to explain and make known this offer of mercy to those unfortunate people."[24]

The promise of punishment for slave fugitives was no idle threat. When two unlucky Negroes hailed a rebel vessel in the belief it was a British tender, and offered to aid the governor, they were brought in and sentenced to death as an example to others.[25]

In the meantime, the Virginia militia under Woodford had reached the vicinity of Great Bridge, several miles from Norfolk, where in December they began to dig in behind some earthworks. Dunmore, fearing the growth of rebel strength, ordered an attack, which took place on December 9. In a short but brisk exchange of fire at Great Bridge, the British lost sixty men killed or wounded, including some Negro soldiers. Forced to retire from the field, the British force retreated to Norfolk where it gathered itself back aboard Dunmore's fleet of ships.

For the Virginians this short battle was decisive. The elated militia quickly followed up by occupying the all but abandoned town of Norfolk. They were not yet rid of Dunmore, however. On January 1, 1776, his ships opened up a bombardment of the town, while his landing parties began to set torches to waterside buildings. As this destruction got underway, the American militiamen seemed to find the prospects of looting the town irresistible; they began to run amuck, setting fires of their own in the process. By the time the flames had subsided, two-thirds of Norfolk was in ashes, and another mark was chalked up against Great Britain. (Two years later an investigation by Virginia revealed that whereas Dunmore's forces had destroyed only 19 buildings, the Americans were responsible for the destruction of 863!)[26]

Dunmore still lingered off the Virginia coast, watching the Americans and being watched by them. He had not given up his hopes of success in raising a winning force. In March 1776, in another letter to Lord Dartmouth, he wrote: "Your lordship will observe by my [earlier] letter . . . that I have been endeavouring to raise two regiments here—one of white people, the other of black. The former goes on very slowly, but the latter very well, and would have been in great forwardness had not a fever crept in amongst them, which carried off a great many very fine fellows."[27]

Spring came and still the governor lingered, his small navy trying various means to bring over more Negroes. Thus an American captive aboard one of Dunmore's ships later reported that, when three Negroes in a canoe rowed out to the vessel, the British captain, seeking their aid, promised them freedom "when this disturbance was over, which he expected would be very soon, and then each of them should have a plantation of the rebels' land."[28]

In April, in an effort to prevent and hinder such activities, the Virginia Committee of Safety ordered that all Negroes above the age of thirteen be removed from the eastern counties of Norfolk and Princess Anne further inland, away from the British forces.

For many of the slaves who had earlier defected to Dunmore, the only reward was sickness and death. In June the governor again reported to London that the fever was proving "a very malignant one," and had carried off many of his troops, "especially the blacks." Had it not been "for this horrid disaster," he insisted, "I am satisfied I should have had two thousand blacks, with whom I should have had no doubt of penetrating into the heart of this colony."[29]

The game had finally ended for Dunmore, and he sailed away to join the main British force converging on New York. Behind him, however, he left many bitter memories which continued to fester in the minds of the Virginians. Thus it was that in their convention in May 1776, the Virginia rebels approved the historic recommendation to their delegates in Congress to seek separation and independence from Great Britain. Among the reasons cited for this perhaps inevitable motion was Dunmore's "piratical and savage war against us," including his "tempting our slaves by every artifice to resort to him, and training and employing them against their masters."[30]

Dunmore's activities also became an indictment of King George in June, when the Virginia Assembly adopted a new constitution and government. The preamble to the constitution, written by Jefferson, charged the King with encouraging the Negroes "to rise in arms among us." In Philadelphia this issue also was on Jefferson's mind when the young Virginian sat down to write the *Declaration of Independence*. In the rough draft of the *Declaration* he submitted to Congress, Jefferson attacked the King for "captivating & carrying" the Negroes into slavery; for opposing attempts to end the "execrable commerce," and finally for "exciting those very people to rise in arms among us, and to purchase that liberty of which he has deprived them, by murdering the people on whom he also obtruded them: thus paying off former crimes committed against the liberties of one people, with crimes which he urges them to commit against the lives of another."[31]

This political attack against the throne on the grounds of supporting slavery did not stand in the final version of the *Declaration*, since too many Americans were involved in that "execrable commerce." When the delegates of South Carolina and Georgia objected to the statement, Congress struck out the entire paragraph.

II

As a result of Dunmore's debacle, the threat of a general Negro insurrection receded, although fear remained. General Charles Lee, while on his way south in the spring of 1776, wrote to Robert Morris and recommended Congress have three or four regiments from the middle colonies on the alert, ready to reinforce the southern front in case a slave revolt should materialize.[32]

When the situation did not deteriorate, both sides turned their attention to the recruitment of small numbers of Negro soldiers. On Long Island the British organized a regiment of Negroes totalling about 200 men, while at the siege of Newport in August 1777, a newly raised Rhode Island all-Negro regiment under Colonel Christopher Greene distinguished itself in repelling three successive attacks by Hessian troops.[33] By August 1778, according to a special return by Alexander Scammell, adjutant general of the American army, 755 Negroes were serving in uniform, the largest group in New England detachments.[34]

This comparatively small number was an indication of the general American reluctance to use slave recruits. As early as 1775, when the Continental Army was forming, Washington had asked a council of general officers whether they should "enlist any Negroes in the new army" or whether there should be a distinction "between such as are slaves and those that are free?" The council agreed unanimously "to reject all slaves, and, by a great majority, to reject Negroes altogether."[35]

This decision, announced shortly thereafter in general orders to the Army, discriminated against some able free Negroes who had already fought bravely in early battles around Boston. In reconsidering the question, Washington on December 31, 1775 wrote to Congress: "It has been represented to me that the free Negroes who have served in this Army, are very much dissatisfied at being discarded. As it is to be apprehended that they may seek employ in the Ministerial Army, I have . . . given license for their being re-enlisted. If this is disapproved by Congress, I shall put a stop to it."[36]

In Congress the southern delegates earlier had opposed, and continued to oppose, the use of any Negroes in the army, whether slave or free. Congress supported Washington in this particular instance, and resolved on January 16, 1776: "That the free Negroes who have served faithfully in the army at Cambridge may be re-enlisted therein, but no others."[37] Subsequently, Congress gave the responsibility to the states whether they should enroll Negroes in their militias; and, as the war dragged on and recruitment of white American soldiers became more difficult, the Negroes began to appear more frequently in the American ranks. According to one estimate, at least 4,000 Negroes eventually saw service on the American side.[38]

Although British hopes of a general slave insurrection had been aborted, they continued to consider the Negroes as an asset to their cause. As Joseph Galloway remarked in a report to London in January 1778: "The Negroes may be all deemed so many intestine enemies, being all slaves and desirous of freedom, and would, was an opportunity offered them, take up arms against their masters."[39] Even without an uprising, the large slave population in the south aided the British cause, "by reason of the great proportion of [southern] citizens necessary to remain at home to prevent insurrections among the Negroes," and to prevent their desertion to the British side.[40]

By the year 1779 the entire problem of the slaves suddenly became more pressing following the entry of British forces into Georgia, the capture of Savannah from the Americans, and the subsequent complete subjection of that state to Great Britain. Across the border to the north South Carolina officials, correctly surmising they were the next target on the British schedule, hurriedly dispatched a call for help to Congress.

The British successes in the south caused a change of attitude in the minds of some Americans towards the Negroes, and gave impetus to a plan proposed by Lieutenant Colonel John Laurens of South Carolina to free and arm the slaves for the defense of the south. As early as 1776 the young southern liberal, who had imbibed a dislike of slavery, urged that the Negroes be permitted to earn their freedom by fighting in the patriot cause.

Now, with the entire south in danger, he renewed his proposal to his father, Henry Laurens, former president of Congress (November 1777–December 1778) and an important figure in that body. The elder Laurens, although doubtful it would be accepted, agreed to push his son's plan in Congress. To his surprise, he found that the emergency had brought him the support of General Isaac Huger, who had been dispatched from South Carolina to get northern aid, and that of the other South Carolina delegate, William Henry Drayton.

Henry Laurens also sought the opinion of General Washington. In a letter to the commander-in-chief on March 16, 1779, Laurens wrote: "Had we arms for 3000 black men as I could select in Carolina, I should have no doubt of success in driving the British out of Georgia and subduing East Florida before the end of July."[41] Washington, however, did not think much of the idea. "The policy of arming our slaves," he wrote to Laurens, "is, in my opinion, a moot point, unless the enemy set the example; for should we begin to form battalions of them, I have not the smallest doubt . . . of their following us in it, and justifying the measure upon our own ground. The upshot then must be, who can arm fastest, and where are our arms?" Washington added that if only a few slaves were given their freedom to fight, and the others were left in slavery, the latter might become greatly dissatisfied with their status.[42]

Alexander Hamilton, on the other hand, threw his support behind the Laurens' plan. In a letter to John Jay, president of Congress, Hamilton said he did not see how a sufficient defensive force could be collected in the south without using the Negroes. He was certain, he said, "that the Negroes will make very excellent soldiers, with proper management. . . . It should be considered that if we do not make use of them in this way, the enemy probably will; and that the best way to counteract the temptations they will hold out, will be to offer them ourselves. An essential part of the plan is to give them their freedom with their swords. This will secure their fidelity, animate their courage, and, I believe, will have a good influence upon those who remain, by opening a door to their emancipation."[43] These views of Hamilton were, of course, opposed to those of Washington.

Since the need for a decision was urgent, Congress appointed a committee to consider the matter and it received arguments, including a "representation" made by young Laurens. In his arguments, Laurens referred to the strength of the British force in the south (3,500 regulars, 1,500 others expected) which, he said, constituted more than South Carolina could handle, even if they did not arm the Negroes.

With only six "very weak" battalions in Carolina for defense and no possibility of obtaining reinforcements from neighboring states, the "only resource" left to the patriots, said Laurens, was the Negroes. Therefore, he recommended that Congress purchase these people from their owners (at $1,000 per slave) and place them into service, the condition of that service to be "emancipation at the end of the war."[44] Laurens further argued:

It is well known that in times of invasion a large body of slaves is generally regarded as a mass of internal enemies. But commotions on their part are always less to be apprehended in proportion as the military force of the country is more respectable and the successes of the invaders become more doubtful. Besides, a reinforcement of such troops as are here proposed would give a decided turn to affairs, change the nature of the war from defensive to offensive, and in all human probability enable us to expel the enemy from Georgia in the course of the campaign.[45]

The formal proposal made to the committee by the delegates of South Carolina was that Congress pay for the release of 3,000 slaves in South Carolina and Georgia, and help arrange for putting them into military service. On March 29, 1779 the committee, noting the fact the southerners themselves were behind the measure and in view of the critical situation in the south, approved the Laurens plan. Congress also unanimously endorsed it, declaring: "That every Negro who shall well and faithfully serve as a soldier to the end of the present war, and shall then return his arms, be emancipated and receive the sum of fifty dollars."[46]

However, having adopted a plan with such far-reaching implications for the institution of slavery, Congress further ordered that it should not go into effect without the consent of the two states concerned. Shortly thereafter, Colonel Laurens hurried to Charleston to present the proposal to the South Carolina Assembly. His reception was cold. Most of the southerners there were bitterly opposed to any plan so hostile to slavery and it was defeated.*

In the meantime, the British devised an intriguing propaganda plan aimed at bringing the Negro slaves over en masse to the British camp. On June 30, 1779 the British commander-in-chief, General Clinton, issued the following proclamation:

Whereas the enemy have adopted a practice of enrolling Negroes among their troops, I do hereby give notice that all Negroes taken in America, or upon any military duty, shall be purchased for a stated price, the money to be paid to the captors.

But I do most strictly forbid any person to sell or claim right over any Negro, the property of a rebel, who may take refuge with any part of this army: and I do promise to every Negro who shall desert the rebel standard, full security to follow within these lines any occupation which he shall think proper.[47]

This well-conceived proclamation, calculated to make "fair game" of all Negroes in America except those who joined the British, brought a round of denunciation from the Americans, who now linked Clinton in their propaganda with "the noted Negro thief, *Lord Dunmore*."[48]

But with British forces operating successfully in the south between 1779 and 1781, the proclamation seems to have played an important part in bringing thousands of slaves over to the British camp.† Some of the Negroes were promptly organized into military units, and in Georgia at least one group of British-trained fugitive slaves, calling themselves the "King of England's Soldiers," continued to harass the people living on the Savannah River even after the end of the war.[49] The final total

* Three years later the scheme was revived by Laurens, received much more support, but in the end again was rejected.

† After the peace treaty a group of slaves n New York City refused to return to their former status, as the Americans demanded, insisting on their rights "under the Clinton proclamations." The British supported them in this, and hundreds of Negroes sailed away when the British fleet withdrew.

of slaves who fled the plantations will never be known; one estimate is that South Carolina lost 25,000 slaves, and that seven-eighths of the Negroes of Georgia went over to the British.[50] Jefferson believed that, during Cornwallis' invasion of Virginia in 1781, the state lost 30,000 slaves.[51]

These Negroes were in an unenviable position, once Britain had lost the war. Aside from their fear of their former masters, those who survived smallpox and camp fever discovered that some English officers did not consider binding Clinton's promise of freedom. Hundreds and perhaps thousands of the Negroes again found themselves part of the "execrable commerce," resold for profit in the West Indies. Others, who could not be evacuated when the British withdrew from the south, turned fugitives, as did the "King of England's Soldiers."

Once more it would seem that when the final decisions were in, the British appeal to these "intestine enemies" had, on balance, done the King's cause little good. Like the English appeal to the Indians, the involvement of the Negroes only served to embitter the conflict and to strengthen the determination of northern and southern leaders to stand together.

4

★★

The Campaign to Subvert
the Hessians

If one of the results of Dunmore's proclamation of Negro "emancipation," and the ministry's agitation of the Indian tribes, had been to push the Americans faster down the road towards independence, the King's decision in 1775 to hire foreign troops also strengthened patriot conviction that reconciliation with the mother country was impossible. At the time of the King's decision, few British officials questioned the desirability of using foreign mercenaries to reinforce the British army, and the government almost routinely approved the recommendation of General Gage, made in October 1774, that: "If force is to be used at length, it must be a considerable one, and foreign troops must be hired."[1]

The practice of hiring mercenaries was an ancient and honorable one in the eighteenth century, and therefore it was not strange that the royal court turned to the powers of Europe in an effort to find reinforcements. The King's representatives first tried to obtain the services of 20,000 Russians from Catherine the Great. When she declined, and efforts to obtain a regiment from Holland also failed, the British government turned to the principalities of Germany, whose rulers were more than glad to trade German manpower for English sterling.

Rumors that Britain was seeking mercenaries from Russia and the German states soon reached America. In besieged Boston the then Major General Henry Clinton, on hearing of the negotiations, wrote a recommendation that Russian soldiers be obtained rather than Germans. In a letter to the adjutant general of the British army on 1775, Clinton expressed the fear that the German soldiers would desert, whereas the Russians would not because "they have no language but their own; they cannot desert."[2] Clinton clearly foresaw an American psychological warfare campaign against the Germans. Since their language was well known to the colonists, many of whom were of German origin, direct appeals could be made to the mercenaries.

If this important factor was given serious consideration by the British government, it did not impede efforts to bring in German troops. Between January 9 and February 5, 1776, three treaties were negotiated with the Duke of Brunswick, the Landgrave of Hesse Cassel, and the Hereditary Prince of Hesse Cassel for about 17,000 troops. Treaties with other principalities later brought the total number of foreign troops to about 30,000 men.

On February 29, 1776, the first treaties were submitted to Parliament. A member of the Whig opposition, Captain James Luttrell, promptly pointed to the same weakness which Clinton had detected. In a speech in the House, Luttrell noted that there were some 150,000 Germans then living in the colonies and that Britain, by employing German mercenaries, was simply providing "an excellent opportunity for our hired troops to desert, because they most likely will be offered lands and protection."[3] Several months later Ambrose Serle, secretary to Admiral Howe, also commented on the adverse effect the use of foreign troops would have in tending "to irritate and inflame the Americans infinitely more than two or three British armies upon such an occasion."[4] But such misgivings did not halt Parliament's approval of the treaties.

I

During the spring of 1776 several important documents crossed the Atlantic to the colonies. One was a letter from Lord Germain, who informed the new British commander-in-chief, General William Howe, of the impending arrival of German reinforcements, some of whom were destined for Canadian service.[5] Other documents came from "several eminent gentlemen" in London, who advised their American friends as follows: "If offers of settlement &c., are prepared to fling into the camp in German, when the Germans arrive it must have a great effect." This suggestion from the Whigs of England was adopted by the Americans and became one of the central techniques used in the ensuing patriot propaganda campaign.

The documents from the eminent gentlemen of London were carried to Boston by one George Merchant, an American who had been captured by the British at Quebec, taken to England, and then released there. Apparently contacted by the English Whigs, Merchant took immediate return passage to America, carrying hidden in his clothing copies of the British treaties for the German troops. These papers, which confirmed the rumors of the hiring of mercenaries, moved Benjamin Franklin to comment: "The German auxiliaries are certainly coming. It is our business to prevent their returning."[6]

Congress—after studying the treaties—on May 21, 1776 created a five-man committee which was ordered to extract and publish the papers. It was also directed to recommend a suitable reward for Merchant and to prepare an address "to the foreign mercenaries who are coming to invade America."[7] Named to the committee were John Adams, William Livingston, Thomas Jefferson, Richard Henry Lee, and Roger Sherman. For some unknown reason, the committee completed only the first two assignments. No action was taken on the address, although a draft of an eloquent appeal to the invaders was prepared by a non-committee member, George Wythe.[8]

Not until August, when the Hessian troops had already arrived aboard British transports off Staten Island, did Congress take further action. It directed a new committee, composed of Jefferson, James Wilson, and Richard Stockton, "to devise a plan for encouraging the Hessians, and other foreigners* employed by the King of Great Britain, and sent to America for the purpose of subjugating these states, to quit that iniquitous service."[9] On August 14 the committee brought in its report. Congress adopted it in the form of a resolution which became the first American propaganda broadside directed to the German troops.

In this broadside Congress explained to the Germans that American policy had long been to provide protection to all who were willing to settle in the country, regardless of background or religion, and that such a policy would be continued. In view of the "cruel and unprovoked war," said Congress, in which Britain had applied for help to "certain foreign princes who are in the habit of selling the blood of their people for money," Americans had thought that the German troops "would choose to accept of lands, liberty, safety and a communion of good laws and mild government, in a country where many of their friends and relations are already happily settled," rather than to fight an unjust war against an innocent people. Thus Congress announced that:

. . . these states will receive all such foreigners who shall leave the armies of his Britannic majesty in America, and shall choose to become members of any of these states; that they shall be protected in the free exercise of their respective religions, and be invested with the rights, privileges and immunities of natives, as established by the laws of these states; and, moreover, that this Congress will provide for every such person 50 acres of unappropriated lands in some of these states, to be held by him and his heirs in absolute property.[10]

* Other Germans. The mercenaries became generally known as Hessians, the largest element, but they included Waldeckers, Brunswickers, etc.

Translated into German, copies of this resolution were dispatched to Washington at his New York headquarters. The general was much impressed with these propaganda papers. "I am persuaded," he wrote, "[that it] would produce salutary effects if it can be properly circulated among them. I fear it will be a matter of difficulty."[11] The next day, in order to insure their better dissemination, he requested Congress supply him with a larger quantity of the papers.[12]

The problem of disseminating these propaganda broadsides to the German troops was resolved by Washington through the use of agents, one of whom apparently was a 56-year-old German immigrant named Christopher Ludwick, who later became "Superintendent of Bakers" of the Continental Army.[13] On August 26 Washington wrote to Congress: "The papers designed for the foreign troops have been put into several channels, in order that they might be conveyed to them, and from the information I had yesterday, I have reason to believe may have fallen into their hands."[14]

The papers indeed had come into the hands of the Germans. Major Carl Baurmeister of the Hessian forces, in a confidential letter to the Landgrave dated September 2, 1776, reported that: "Congress intended to distribute in the Hessian camp several thousand printed leaflets, dated August 14th, informing us in high-sounding phrases of their just cause and promising property to deserters. A few came into the possession of the brigade on Staten Island. . . . So far I have been unable to obtain one of these handbills; if I do I shall enclose it in some future letter."[15]

This first propaganda appeal to the Germans was soon followed up with a second broadside. The new appeal resulted from a suggestion made by an American colonel, James Wilson, who had seen the first broadside in the American camp at Amboy. Wilson wrote to John Hancock, president of Congress, expressing surprise that no distinction had been made between the German officers and privates. He said several persons—"one

Im Congreß, den 14ten August, 1776.

Sintemal es hiebevor die weise Landesordnung dieser Staaten gewesen ist, den Schutz ihrer Gesetze über alle die zu verbreiten, welche sich unter ihnen niederlassen, von welchem Volk oder Religion sie seyn mögen, und sie zum Genuß der Wohlthaten Bürgerlicher und Religions-Freyheiten aufzunehmen; so machen der aus diesem Verfahren entstandene Nutzen, sowol als die heilsamen Wirkungen desselben, es der Mühe werth selbige in folge.den Zeiten fortzusetzen.

Und da nun Seine Brittannische Majestät, um unsere Freyheit und Glückseligkeit zu vernichten, einen grausamen Krieg ohne einige Reizung dazu gegen uns angefangen hat; und weil gedachter König nicht im Stande ist Britten genug aufzubringen seine blutdürstigen Maaßregeln zu vollziehen, so hat er um die Hülfe gewisser fremder Fürsten, deren Gewohnheit es ist das Blut ihres Volks um Geld zu verkaufen, angehalten, und grosse Anzahlen Ausländer erhalten und hier herüber führen lassen. Da man sich nun vorstellet, daß solche Ausländer, wenn sie von vorgemeldeter Uebung dieser Staaten benachrichtiget werden, lieber Ländereyen, Freyheit, Sicherheit und den Genuß guter Gesetze und gelinder Regierung in einem Lande wo bereits viele von ihren Freunden und Verwandten glücklich ansäßig sind, annehmen würden, als den Mühseligkeiten und Gefahren eines langen und blutigen Krieges bloßgestellet zu seyn, der gegen ein Volk geführet wird, welches keines andern Verbrechens schuldig ist, als nur, daß es seine Freyheit nicht für Sclaverey verwechseln will; und daß sie dieses um so viel bereitwilliger thun werden, wenn sie erwägen, daß, nachdem sie ein jedes Gebot des Christlichen Glaubens und der Sittenlehre werden geschändet haben, durch gewaltsame Ueberfälle und Versuche diejenigen, die sie oder ihr Land niemals beleidiget, zu verderben; ihre einzige Belohnung, wenn sie ja dem Tode und der Gefangenschaft entgehen, seyn wird, unter die willführliche Gewalt ihres Fürsten zurück zu kehren, um durch ihn wieder verkauft zu werden die schändliche Arbeit eines oder des andern Feindes der Rechte des Menschlichen Geschlechts zu verrichten.

Und sintemal das Großbrittannische Parlament, vermittelst einer letztherigen Acte, gut gefunden, unsere Truppen nicht nur bloß einzuladen unsern Dienst zu verlassen, sondern auch verordnet hat, unsere zur See weggenommene Leute zu zwingen gegen ihr Land zu dienen: So ist daher

Beschlossen, Daß diese Staaten, alle solche Fremdlinge, welche die Armee Seiner Brittannischen Majestät in America verlassen, und erwählen wollen Glieder einiger dieser Staaten zu werden, aufnehmen wollen; daß sie in der freyen Uebung ihrer respectiven Religionen geschützt, und mit den Rechten, Freyheiten und Befreyungen der Ingebornen dieses Landes, wie selbige durch die Gesetze dieser Staaten vestgesetzet sind, begabet werden sollen. Und dieser Congreß will überdas eine jede solche Person mit Fünfzig Acker Land das sonst keinen Eigner hat, in einigen von diesen Staaten versehen, um durch ihn und seine Erben als ein vollkommenes Eigenthum gehalten und besessen zu werden.

Auf Verordnung des Congresses,

John Hancock, Präsident.

Bezeugt
Charles Thomson, Secretär.

Staatsarchiv Marburg, Bestand 4 h 410 Nr. 1 Seite 370

This first congressional propaganda offer to the German mercenaries promised fifty acres of free land to any soldier who deserted the British army. Later American broadsides included offers of cows, pigs, and oxen as well as free land.

of them a German well acquainted with the manner and disposition of his countrymen"—had expressed concern on this account and he wondered whether "it is not yet too late to offer additional rewards to officers in proportion to their rank and pay."[16]

Congress agreed Wilson's suggestion was pertinent. On August 27 a three-man committee composed of Jefferson, John Adams, and Franklin brought in another report which Congress subsequently adopted. In this second broadside, Congress offered the following new incentive to the German officers who would defect: "To a colonel, 1,000 acres; to a lieutenant colonel, 800 acres; to a major, 600 acres; to a captain, 400 acres; to a lieutenant, 300 acres; to an ensign, 200 acres; to every noncommissioned officer, 100 acres."[17] Any officers who brought off a number of soldiers with them were promised additional rewards.

The next day Franklin sent copies "of both sorts" of broadsides to General Gates for distribution. "Some of them," wrote Franklin, "have tobacco marks on the back so that tobacco being put in them in small quantities, as the tobacconists use, and suffered to fall into the hands of these people, they might divide the papers as plunder before their officers could come to the knowledge of the contents, and prevent their being read by the men."[18]

Franklin well understood that in a propaganda operation of this type, the officers would be more difficult to subvert. The real targets were the enlisted men.

II

It was unreasonable to hope for immediate results from these early propaganda efforts, especially after the combined British-German forces easily cleared the field of the Americans in the battle on Long Island on August 27. However, from Canada the Americans received the encouraging news that the German troops serving with Carleton's forces were desertion-minded. On August 4, 1776, two Canadian militia captains told General Gates that "great numbers" of the Germans were deserting daily, and they claimed on one occasion seventy Brunswickers had made off together.[19]

This report was verified several weeks later by a 22-year-old deserter, one Anthony Hasselaband, who went over to the Americans and reported that he and nineteen others had fled Montreal on June 24.[20] Among the reasons Hasselaband cited were the great dissatisfaction among the Germans over the lack of pay and failure of the British to provide provisions promised them.

There was, however, a more important reason why many of the German enlisted men were dissatisfied, stemming from the manner in which they had been "recruited" for the British service. A typical instance was that of Johan Gottfried Seume, a theological student who had been travelling through Germany on his way to Paris when recruiting officers of the Landgrave of Cassel placed him under arrest. Seume later wrote that he found himself among other miserable "companions in misfortune," strangers of all kinds who, he said, "were arrested, imprisoned, sent off. They tore up my academic matriculation papers, as being the only instrument by which I could prove my identity."[21] Thus there was created in these German soldiers dissatisfactions that would prove fertile soil for American propaganda.

Some of the Germans captured by Washington's scouting parties in the New York area verified the story that they had been torn from their country by force. On October 26, 1776, after twelve Waldeckers were captured near White Plains, these men expressed a willingness to join the American side. Wrote Washington's aide, Tench Tilghman: "They say if their fellow-soldiers knew how kindly they would be treated, and how plentifully and happily they might live, they would lay down their arms and come among us. We shall contrive to make good use of these fellows."[22]

The use of such prisoners-of-war to spread American propaganda had been on Washington's mind for some time. As early as May 1776 he had toyed with the idea of raising some companies of American Germans "to send among them when they arrive" in order to stir up a spirit of disaffection and desertion.[23] But in October, with the German prisoners in his hands, Washington decided to use them to carry patriot propaganda into the enemy camp.

The first step was to turn the new prisoners over to Christopher Ludwick, who escorted them to Philadelphia where they were treated with great hospitality as an informal prisoner "re-education" program began.[24] The next step was to send the now enlightened Germans back to the British camp in exchange for American prisoners. To disguise his purpose, Washington suggested to the Board of War that it send him all British prisoners it could spare, to be exchanged with the Germans. "The return of the latter," he said, "I think will be attended with many salutary consequences, but should it be made without that of a large proportion of other troops, it will carry the marks of a design and occasion precautions to be taken to prevent the ends we have in view."[25]

However, the British were not unaware of American intentions. Frederic Mackenzie, a British officer, wrote on November 11: "General [Archibald] Robertson is of opinion that the men have been gained over by the rebels, whose intention it is now to send them among their countrymen, that they may endeavour to persuade them to desert. . . . Should they come back, it will be prudent to keep a strict watch upon them in order to discover if they attempt to corrupt their fellow soldiers."[26]

Despite this, the American strategy—of treating German prisoners well and returning them to the British camp—proved successful. Baurmeister took note in his journal of two German *jagers* (riflemen) who had been captured on October 23 and then released: "They could not praise enough the good treatment they had received. They had even been given companions who could speak German and who promised them great rewards if they would enter the rebel service and urge their countrymen to do likewise."[27]

Unfortunately for the American cause, the overall military picture had darkened so considerably by November 1776 that few Germans deserted. Instead, on the sixteenth the German forces captured Fort Washington, and four days later Fort Lee also fell. Washington's army fled into New Jersey with the King's army not far behind. During these unhappy days Congress, seeking to invigorate its propaganda program, appointed a committee to translate into German one of the treaties between London and Hesse. It was hoped that a dispersion of copies of this document, with its blood money provisions (for soldiers killed or wounded), might work for the American interest.[28]

The most important American propaganda during this period proved, however, to be Washington's blow against the Hessians at Trenton. This desperate action on December 25 not only brought to a halt the disastrous succession of American defeats, but it also placed in American hands some 948 Hessian prisoners. Now indeed the patriots could undertake a large-scale "brain-washing" program.

On December 28 a congressional committee, in a letter of congratuations to Washington on his victory, suggested to the general that the capture of the Hessians was a favorable opportunity to acquaint them "with the situation and circumstances of many of their countrymen, who came here without a farthing of property and have, by care and industry, acquired plentiful fortunes."[29] The committee also suggested that the officers be separated from enlisted men, and the latter be turned over to the Pennsylvania Council of Safety for further disposition.

Washington immediately wrote to the Council of Safety, urging that the German prisoners be well treated and suggesting that the various congressional propaganda broadsides be distributed among them.[30] The prisoners, meanwhile, were marched to Philadelphia where they were paraded through the streets on December 30, 1776, for the edification and encouragement of the populace.

The following day the council addressed the public concerning the prisoners.

There arrived yesterday in this city [said the Council] near one thousand Hessian prisoners, taken by his Excellency, Gen. Washington in his late fortunate and successful expedition to New Jersey. The General has recommended to this Council to provide suitable quarters for them, and it is his earnest wish that they may be well treated, and have such principles instilled in them whilst they remain prisoners, that when they return on being exchanged they may fully open the eyes of their countrymen in the service of the king of Great Britain, who at present are not a little jealous of their English fellow soldiers.

These miserable creatures now justly excite our compassion. They have no enmity with us. According to the arbitrary customs of the tyrannical German princes, they were dragged from their native country and sold to a foreign monarch, without either consulting their inclinations or informing them of the place they were destined for, or the enemy they were to contend with. Their pay a mere pittance, they were necessitated and encouraged to plunder. It is therefore nothing strange that they have been guilty of great irregularities, tho' inferior to the brutal behaviour of the British troops. But from the moment they are rescued from the authority of the British officers, we ought no longer to regard them as our enemies, at least whilst their conduct will justify our favorable opinion. 'Tis Britain alone that is our enemy. . . . The most favorable opportunity now offers to weaken the force of our enemies, by making their auxiliaries our friends and we earnestly entreat you to embrace it by surpassing any resentment that might naturally arise on recollecting their late hostility, and treating the much injured and deceived Hessians now in our power in the most friendly manner as a people we would wish to unite with ourselves in improving the fertile forests of America, extending its manufacture and commerce, and maintaining its liberty and independency against all attacks of foreign and arbitrary power.[31]

The council, in another letter to the committee at Lancaster, Pennsylvania, where many of the prisoners were to be sent, repeated Washington's recommendations "to have them well informed of the reasons for the war, and good principles instilled in them."[32]

In the months that followed a new situation arose which, to Washington, seemed to threaten the American propaganda effort. This situation revolved around the captivity of Major General Charles Lee, second-in-command under Washington, who had been captured by the British on December 13.* The British considered Lee, who had held a commission as a lieutenant colonel in the British army, a deserter. He was kept under close guard and plans were made to ship him to England to stand trial for treason.

However, Congress, considering Lee to be one of America's top military leaders, ordered Washington to obtain his immediate exchange as a prisoner-of-war, by returning five Hessian officers captured at Trenton and a British lieutenant colonel. Rumors of Britain's intentions towards Lee had reached Congress, and it further directed that, if the British persisted in considering Lee a deserter and refused to give him up, the five Hessian field officers and the lieutenant colonel were to be detained "and sacrificed as an atonement for his blood should the matter be carried to that extremity."[33] Washington was to notify General Howe of this American policy.

The commander-in-chief, however, saw many things wrong with Congress' order, and on March 2, in a letter to Robert Morris, Washington complained: "Does Congress know how much the balance of prisoners is against us? That the enemy have, at least, 300 officers of ours in their possession, and we

* See also Chapter 5, p. 163.

not fifty of theirs. . . . Do they know that every artifice is now practicing to prepossess the Hessians with an idea of our mal-treatment of their countrymen (in our possession), that we are treating of them as slaves; nay, that we mean to sell them? And will not the close confinement of their . . . officers be adduced as strong evidence of this? Congress, therefore, should be cautious how they adopt measures."[34]

However, Congress was adamant in its instructions that the Hessian officers and British lieutenant colonel be exchanged provided "the enemy will relax in their treatment of Genl. Lee and acknowledge him to be a prisoner of war."[35] On the British side General Howe was as much worried over the question as was General Washington. He feared that if Lee was indeed sent to England to stand trial, Congress would carry out its threats against the Hessians and this, in turn, "would occasion much discontent" among the German mercenaries. Unwilling to make a decision, Howe passed the problem along to London, which finally agreed (September 1777) to designate Lee as a legitimate prisoner-of-war.[36] Lee was finally released in a pris-oner exchange in March 1778.*

III

Although the British had driven the Americans from Phil-adelphia in September 1777, the war dragged on with no sign of victory; and discouragement set in, even among the formerly exuberant German officers, one of whom now wrote: "It is truly to be desired that this miserable war will soon end."[37]

As the winter of 1777–78 began, the Americans received a number of reports to the effect that certain German officers were willing to change sides if enough inducements were held out. One such report reached Washington's ears in January 1778.[38] Whether these stories were responsible for the renewed

* Lee eventually disgraced himself in the Battle of Monmouth and was court-martialed.

propaganda offer made by Congress in April is uncertain; but in that month a new promise was held out "To the officers and soldiers in the service of the King of Great Britain, not subjects of the said King."

This was the longest message yet addressed to the Germans. In it Congress again emphasized that Americans were fighting "a just and necessary war," and that they were certain the Germans were reluctant soldiers. "We not only forgive the injuries which you have been constrained to offer us," said Congress, "but we hold out to your acceptance a participation in the privilege of free and independent states. Large and fertile tracts of country invite and will amply reward your industry."[39]

These free lands, continued Congress, amounted to twenty to thirty thousand acres, set aside specifically for men who defected from the British side. Every German captain who came over with forty men, before the first day of September 1778, was promised 800 acres of good woodland, "also four oxen, one bull, three cows, and four hogs." If he came over with his lieutenant, the latter would receive 400 acres of woodland, two oxen, two cows, and four hogs. A sergeant who accompanied his captain would receive 200 acres, and his share of livestock, while each private who also defected would get 50 acres and livestock.

Officers or noncommissioned officers who came off together or separately were also promised rewards. Congress further announced: "Such of the officers and non-commissioned officers as choose to enter into the military line, shall receive an additional rank in detached corps, which shall be formed of native Germans of those who now reside in America; which corps shall not be employed but with their own consent in any service than that of guards at a distance from the enemy, or in garrison upon the western frontiers."[40]

One thousand copies of this appeal were published in German. A printer at Lancaster, Francis Bailey, produced the broadsides, 500 copies of which were immediately dispatched to Washington for distribution.[41]

This new broadside was disseminated just before the British evacuation of Philadelphia, an evacuation forced on them in June 1778 by France's entrance into the war. Howe's successor as commander-in-chief, General Sir Henry Clinton, decided to make the withdrawal to New York by land. Although it was generally successful, the British-German forces suffered hundreds of desertions during the march. Baurmeister, in a report dated July 8, 1778, estimated the Hessians alone (that is, excluding other Germans) had lost 200 men, which he attributed not to the fatiguing march "but rather to our long stay in Philadelphia and the many kinds of temptations, which need not be very alluring to blind the common soldier and make him break his oath."[42] These temptations included American girls with whom many German soldiers had fallen in love. During the British retreat Washington voiced the opinion that the enemy might lose "near one thousand men" through desertions, but the final figure was closer to 600, most of them Germans.[43]

IV

Several weeks later Congress' propaganda offer of April 1778 brought in the first two officers known to defect from the German regiments—Lieutenants Carl Frederick Fuhrer and Carl Wilhelm Kleinschmidt. These two men appeared at Washington's new camp at White Plains, New York. In an interview with the commander-in-chief, they said they had served as first lieutenants in the Hessian corps, that they had been among the prisoners taken at Trenton, and had been lately exchanged.

Washington wrote to Congress about the two defectors on August 9. He reported they had asked to enter the American service and had claimed there was a number of other German officers of the same disposition. "It appears to me," said Washington, "that important advantage may attend the encouraging a disposition of this nature if it really exists, which is far from impossible, from the influence it will necessarily have on the soldiery by increasing that spirit of desertion and discontent which already prevails among them."[44]

Washington suggested Congress authorize the two officers to raise a corps for themselves, "by inlisting such German inhabitants, and such of the prisoners and deserters from the foreign troops as may be willing to engage." This corps could be a kind of experiment, he said, that might be increased as circumstances dictated. Washington added that the two Germans had expressed confidence such a plan would succeed, but that they expected some "augmentation of rank." He recommended this be granted, but that it not be carried too far.[45]

While waiting for Congress' reaction, a week later Washington received a letter from the Hessian General Wilhelm von Knyphausen (Lieutenant Fuhrer was of his regiment), apparently containing derogatory information concerning the two men.[46] Kleinschmidt, according to another report, had deserted "on account of his debts."[47]

Congress sent Washington's letter to the Board of War, which brought in a recommendation on August 29, 1778, that "a new corps of troops be raised by the name of German volunteers, to consist of such deserters from the foreign troops which have been or shall be in the service of the king of Great Britain."[48] The board suggested the corps be enlisted for three years or the duration of the war, and that its personnel receive the same bounty and clothing given regular army troops. It further recommended that Fuhrer and Kleinschmidt be raised to the rank of captain, dependent on their success in enlisting at least thirty men in a three-month period beginning September 3, 1778.[49] Congress quickly approved the plan.

The two new captains seemed to have entered their work with great enthusiasm; and within several months the British became aware that "the light-minded officers, Fuhrer and Kleinschmidt, are persuading many to take service" with the

Americans.[50] One of these new recruits may have been Lieutenant Charles Juliat, a third German officer, who showed up
within the American lines and also asked to serve with Washington's army.

Juliat's petition was sent to the Board of War. The board,
apparently feeling that Fuhrer and Kleinschmidt were sufficient personnel to get the new corps started, recommended
that he be permitted to serve as an infantry volunteer with
Count Casimir Pulaski's legion.[51] However, it soon became
clear the new deserter was undependable. Although he accepted the board's recommendation, Juliat found his position
and circumstances not to his liking. In early November 1778 he
re-defected back to the British camp.[52]

If Juliat had been a deliberate British plant, he could not
have more effectively torpedoed the activities of Fuhrer and
Kleinschmidt. The Americans began to have second thoughts
about the German volunteers and, early in December, concluded it would be "impolitic to trust them." Thereupon, the
Board of War recommended to Congress that the plan for the
new German corps be set aside. Congress accepted the recommendation and ordered that Fuhrer and Kleinschmidt be informed "that it is inexpedient to employ them at this time."
The auditors at Philadelphia were ordered to pay them their
expenses, plus one month's extra pay and subsistence.[53]

The two officers were in an unenviable position. No longer
trusted by the Americans and facing drastic punishment if they
returned to the British side, they must have found their
prospects discouraging. In the next few years they made several
appeals to their old German commanders (one in February
1779 and one in October 1780) asking for reinstatement. On
this latter occasion, Baurmeister wrote: "The pitiable deserted
Lieutenants Fuhrer and Kleinschmidt . . . have sent in very
humble requests to be pardoned and received in our lines
again."[54] However, unlike Juliat, who was pardoned and served
again with the British forces during the war, the two men seem

to have become permanent displaced persons. On October 1, 1781, according to Von Krafft, portraits of the two men, and that of a third German officer deserter, one Von Masco, were affixed to a gallows in New York as deserters,[55] and the two names vanish from the record.

They were, however, not the only German officers who deserted. At least three others, including a chaplain, changed sides during the war.[56]

v

One of the important tactics adopted by the patriots in their propaganda campaign—an "illegal" tactic—was to try to cause desertions from among prisoners-of-war. This applied in particular to Burgoyne's "Convention Army,"* whose 2,700 German soldiers became a tempting target for American propaganda.

When Burgoyne surrendered in October 1777, the prisoners were marched to Massachusetts, the German prisoners being segregated in barracks on Winter Hill, near Cambridge, while the English prisoners occupied nearby Prospect Hill, in barracks built by the Americans during the siege of Boston. During their year's stay in Massachusetts (before the prisoners were marched to Virginia to sit out the war), the soldiers of the "Convention Army" were encouraged to flee their captivity and join the Americans.

To counter American propaganda in the camps, the German commander, General Friedrich Adolph von Riedesel, harangued the enlisted men in an effort to prevent desertion. On April 4, 1778, in a circular letter read to the men, he posed the question:

* Under the terms of the surrender (in deference to Burgoyne called a "Convention") Gates agreed that Burgoyne's army would be marched to Boston and returned to their homeland, on the guarantee they would never be employed again on American duty. This agreement was never fulfilled by Congress, which feared they would simply relieve other British troops who in turn would be employed in America.

Which is better, to be false now and desert and, after the war, be a slave, or to live here with the officers and soldiers for a short time in misery, and return afterward as an honored and brave soldier to his own people, and be able in peace and quiet to recall one's good actions? I therefore exhort all the brave soldiers, considering them my comrades and loving them as my children, to reflect and act as becomes a good soldier and give up all thoughts of desertion; and should there be evil disposed men in the corps, I hereby admonish all the good ones to keep a vigilant eye on these, in order that the already achieved glory of the whole corps may not be dimmed by such shameful desertions.[57]

Riedesel was struggling against formidable odds. The Americans had pressed into their service "good for nothing Germans" (i.e., German-Americans) who were able to talk many a Convention soldier into defecting. In addition, late in April 1778, according to historian Von Eelking, "the presumption of the Americans soon degenerated into impudence." This presumption was the distribution of copies of Congress' latest offer of lands and livestock to any who would desert. Wrote Von Eelking: "They not only busily circulated the proclamation, dressing it up in the most tempting language, but they posted it on houses by the roadside, and even in the camp upon the barracks and the houses of the sentinels."[58]

Both the German and English officers protested against this "illegal" activity and Riedesel ordered that the broadsides be removed from the barracks. The following month, the Americans came up with a new propaganda leaflet to counter British arguments that all deserters were being forced to enter into state militias. Published in German, this leaflet contained a resolution of Congress of May 22 which recommended to the various states that "all those who have deserted, or shall desert during the present war from the English army or navy, shall be free from militia service."[59] All these efforts produced many desertions, both English and German, from the Convention

Army, with one writer listing the latter at 160 men as of April 1.[60]

While some Americans were eager to enroll these deserters in the militia service, Washington had learned from bitter experience that they rarely could be trusted. A typical Washington comment was contained in a letter to Colonel Theodore Bland in July 1779. "With respect to the deserters from the Convention Army," Washington wrote, "I must entreat that you will use every possible means to have them recovered, and to prevent any farther desertions. There is not the smallest confidence to be placed in the professions of the soldiery and let them be as solemn as they will, and even sanctified by an oath, they will seize the first opportunity to escape to the enemy."[61] Such men not only re-defected, but often carried off with them American arms and other expensive pieces of equipment.

However, several years later, when some Hessian deserters approached the French minister in Philadelphia in July 1780 and asked to join the French expeditionary army in America,[62] both Washington and Congress agreed to this step.[63] As the war neared its end, and as recruiting of Americans for the Continental Army became extremely difficult, Washington changed his mind about using German prisoners-of-war. In April 1782 he agreed that ten of these men might be profitably incorporated into every American company.[64]

Washington made his recommendation to the Secretary of War, and the plan was approved by Congress. Soon thereafter the German prisoners at Lancaster and Reading were visited by a German-speaking clergyman who announced to them that the King of Great Britain had refused to pay their subsistence any longer as prisoners-of-war, and that their own princes had abandoned them. Therefore, he said, Congress was now offering them a choice: either enlist in the American army or pay for their past maintenance. If they had no money to pay (and they had none), various farmers were willing to advance the sum if they bound themselves to labor for such farmers for three years. In any event, they must take the oath of allegiance to the United States.[65]

The clergyman advised the Germans to enter into military service rather than to submit to the farmers. He pointed out that every man who enlisted would receive eight dollars bounty, "and one hundred acres of good land in America after the war."[66] However, this combination of threats and promises did not produce any immediate results. On August 8, 1782, two American officers appeared and repeated the proposition, and this time they laid down an ultimatum: The Germans *must* accept one or the other choice—indent themselves over to the farmers, or serve with the American forces. On this occasion there were some results, some men went off to the army and at least thirty-nine men signed to serve on the American frigate, the *South Carolina* (subsequently captured by the British).[67]

Meanwhile, the propaganda war against the Germans still serving in the field was renewed by various southern state governors. In Virginia Governor Thomas Jefferson, who entertained some of the German officer prisoners in his home and used those occasions to spread American doctrines, renewed the original offer of Congress. In a proclamation which reproduced almost the identical language of the 1776 appeal (which he probably wrote), Jefferson on February 2, 1781 added the following statement:

I have therefore thought fit by and with the advice of the Council of State to issue this my proclamation hereby notifying more generally the said engagement of Congress, and further promising to all such foreigners who shall leave the armies of his Brittanic majesty while in this state and repair forthwith to me at this place, that they shall receive from this Commonwealth a further donation of two cows, and an exemption during the present war from all taxes . . . and from all militia and military service: and moreover that they shall receive a full compensation for any arms and accoutrements which they shall bring with them, and deliver to the commanding officer or any of the posts holden by our forces, taking his receipt for the same.[68]

In Georgia, where Savannah was still held by British and German troops, Governor John Martin in February 1782 also issued a proclamation in German, offering 200 acres of land, a cow, and two swine to every noncommissioned officer or private who would desert the British service.[69]

The American propaganda campaign continued into the last days of the war. Following the peace treaty of 1783, there was an increase in the numbers of Germans who fled the British side, especially from the regiments captured at Yorktown. During the march northward, an estimated 752 Germans defected (plus hundreds of British soldiers) from those regiments. "These desertions," wrote Baurmeister, "are due only to the scattering of printed invitations and previous persuasion on the part of the inhabitants, who have resorted to every possible inducement."[70]

Just before the British evacuated New York, Baurmeister received American permission to travel to Lancaster and Reading to seek out his countrymen and explain that a general pardon and amnesty had been issued by their commanders. He found many former prisoners in various situations: some were living on farms, were married and had children; others were indented for three years and working in iron mines and small manufacturing shops. Of 162 Brunswickers he located in one area, only 39 professed any desire to return to Germany, while none of 13 Hesse-Hanauers he talked to wanted to return.[71]

VI

The American psychological warfare campaign against the mercenaries was the most successful one of the Revolution. Of the 30,000 German soldiers hired out by King George during the war, only 17,313 or about 58 per cent returned to

Germany.[72] That left about 12,000 unaccounted for. Relatively few of these 12,000 died in battle, and, while a great many more succumbed to illness or accident, thousands more deserted and joined the patriots to improve "the fertile forests of America, extending its manufacturing and commerce, and maintaining its liberty and independency."

5

Propaganda and Military Operations

In the direct clash of American and Englishmen, the military capabilities of both sides was a recurring propaganda theme, repeatedly invoked to frighten the enemy or to sustain morale. As early as the winter of 1774–75, before the war began, one of the arguments between loyalists and patriots centered on the general question: Could the colonists ever hope to stand up against the trained regular soldiers of Great Britain? The party loyal to Britain argued against a final showdown, insisting that the colonists would have no chance in a war with English troops, and that such an event would bring only disaster to America.

The patriot party took the other side of the question, especially such men as Charles Lee, who spoke out strongly against the loyalist claim of English superiority in arms. As a former British lieutenant colonel, and soon to become a major general in the American army, Lee reminded the patriots of the beginnings of the French and Indian War in 1755. "Some of the most esteemed British regiments were sent over to this country," he said. "They were well dressed, they were well powdered, they were perfect masters of their manual exercise, they fired together in platoons—but fatal experience taught us, that they knew not how to fight."[1] So did Lee recall the shades of General Braddock!

Lee published his views in February 1775 as an answer to some of the loyalist opinion disseminated by Dr. Myles Cooper. His arguments had great influence with the patriot side, especially his reminder of American expertness with firearms, "whereas the lower and middle people of England are, by the tyranny of certain laws, almost as ignorant in the use of a musket as they are of the ancient catapults."[2]

Here was one of the beginnings of the propaganda of the dreaded American marksmen, whose presence in the parapets and battle lines caused British military planners a great deal of trouble. In June 1775 one of the first acts of Congress was to issue a call to American riflemen to join the Continental Army forming around Boston. On June 18 John Hancock wrote to Joseph Warren that ten companies of frontier riflemen from Pennsylvania, Maryland, and Virginia had been ordered to proceed immediately to Boston. "This is a good step," said Hancock, "and will be an excellent additional strength to our army. These are the finest marksmen in the world. They do execution with their rifle guns at an amazing distance."[3]

Within a very short time more than 1,000 volunteer riflemen, dressed in the frontier hunting shirt and Indian-style breeches, were on their way to Boston. American newspapers went into excited panegyrics over them. For example, a writer in the Pennsylvania *Journal* told his readers on August 23:

These men have been bred in the woods to hardships and dangers from their infancy. They appear as if they were entirely unacquainted with, and had never felt the passion of fear. With their rifles in their hands they assume a kind of omnipotence over their enemies. One cannot much wonder at this when we mention a fact which can be fully attested by several of the reputable persons who were eyewitnesses to it. Two brothers in the company [of riflemen] took a piece of board five inches broad and seven inches long, with a bit of white paper about the size of a dollar nailed in the center, and while one of them supported this board perpendicularly between his knees, the other, at a distance of upwards of sixty yards, and without any kind of rest, shot eight bullets through it successively, and spared a brother's thigh![4]

The riflemen began arriving in large numbers at the American camp at Cambridge in August 1775, and surgeon James Thacher noted in his journal: "They are now stationed on our lines, and their shot have frequently proved fatal to British officers and soldiers who expose themselves to view, even at more than double the distance of common musket-shot."[5] In the parapets at Bunker's Hill the British learned to keep their heads down.

However, the presence of the riflemen at Cambridge was not all profit for the patriots. Washington's new recruits were, like most frontiersmen, undisciplined and unruly. Struggling to establish some kind of order in the new army, Washington soon found the strong-willed southern riflemen too disruptive to be tolerated. They jumped in and out of the American lines on Prospect Hill, fired without orders, and often at such great distances as to waste scarce powder. In September Washington was forced to court-martial an entire platoon of thirty-three riflemen, who were fined twenty shillings each for "disobedient and mutinous behavior."[6] Since many of them began to desert to the British about this time, their reputation began to sink.

Nevertheless, their recognized ability with the rifle was a propaganda asset the Americans continued to invoke. In Virginia, for example, after a skirmish at Hampton between patriot forces and Lord Dunmore's troops, in which the latter was defeated, the Virginia *Gazette* boasted that in the engagement "a rifle-man killed a man at a distance of 400 yards." The paper added ominously: "Take care, ministerial troops."[7]

The claim of 400 yards may be exaggerated. General Lee, who was ordered south by Congress in 1776 to help the patriot defenders of Charleston, urged the local commander there to insist the riflemen stop firing at such great distances. "It is a certain truth," said Lee, "that the enemy entertain a most fortunate apprehension of American riflemen. It is equally certain that nothing can diminish this apprehension so infallibly as a frequent, ineffectual fire."[8] Lee recommended that no man should fire at a distance greater than 150 yards. "In short," he advised the southerners, "they must never fire without almost a moral certainty of hitting their object."[9]

In July 1776 Washington also sought to take advantage of British fears of the riflemen when the problem arose of clothing his soldiers. Washington recommended to the troops that they adopt the rifleman's hunting shirt with the long breeches. Not only was that costume cheap and utilitarian, he said, but also it constituted a dress "justly supposed to carry no small terror to the enemy, who thinks every such person a complete marksman."[10]

The British, before they discovered they also had an important and effective weapon of terror in the bayonet, sought to match the American riflemen with German *jagers*. About 1,000 of these men, trained to use rifle-barrel guns in boar hunting in the German forests, were among the mercenaries hired by Britain.

It was not until after the first battle of Long Island on August 27, 1776, that the Achilles heel of the riflemen was suddenly uncovered. During the fight the English and German generals noted the basic weaknesses of the rifle—it took too long to reload, and it had no bayonet. The American riflemen could scarcely get off several shots before the advancing columns of British and German infantry were on them with the bayonet.

The disadvantages of the rifle versus the musket-with-bayonet also have been described as follows:

The musket and bayonet were the weapons for the line of battle, where the target was not an individual, but another line, and when the lines closed the bayonet was ready for use. Firearms were very sensitive to the weather; after long-continued or heavy rain they were useless, and lack of a bayonet was then fatal. To take advantage of the rifle, fire must be opened at a longer range, and its accuracy utilized in aiming at individuals. It could not be used with the musket in the line of battle, for the smoke then prevented the riflemen from seeing his target, thus nullifying the principle advantage of the weapon.[11]

When these faults had been revealed, the rifle suddenly became a handicap. General William Howe, in preparing his British troops for the next battle, reminded them "of their evident superiority" with their bayonets and he recommended that they place "an entire dependence" on that weapon.[12] As the campaign progressed, so confident did the British leaders become in their superiority that they ordered many an attack *with muskets unloaded,* leaving the troops no alternative but to use their bayonets against the terror-stricken American militia.

Propaganda, that parasite on success, now was invoked to tell the British story of superiority with a weapon which, in battle after battle, struck fear in the hearts of the untrained Americans and sent them flying. The colonists' growing inhibitions over the bayonet became an important psychological handicap which Washington and his officers worked hard to overcome. However, it was not until 1778—when bayonet practice was introduced into the Continental Army by the German volunteer, Baron von Steuben—that progress was made in this direction.

One of the most revealing statements made in connection with this problem came from General Anthony Wayne, who exclaimed in a letter to Richard Peters in February 1778:

I don't like rifles. I would almost as face an enemy with a good musket and bayonet without ammunition, as with ammunition without a bayonet. For although there are not many instances of bloody bayonets, yet I am confident that one bayonet keeps off another—and for the want of which the chief of the defeats we have met with ought in a great measure to be attributed. The enemy knowing the defenceless state of our riflemen rush on; they fly, mix with or pass through the other troops and communicate fears that is ever incident to a retiring corps. But it would be still better if good muskets and bayonets were put into the hands of good marksmen and rifles entirely laid aside. For my own part I never wish to see one, at least without a bayonet. I don't give this as mere matter of opinion or speculation, but as matter of fact to the truth of which I have more than once been an unhappy witness.[13]

With the strength of his belief, "Mad" Anthony, during the successful storming of the British fort at Stony Point in July 1779 (discussed below), had his men attack with unloaded muskets, "placing their whole dependence on the bayonet."[14] This victory was a sure sign the Americans were slowly mastering their fears.

Although the musket with bayonet remained the main infantry weapon throughout the Revolution, the rifle still retained its usefulness. This was well demonstrated in January 1781 when famed Dan Morgan of the Long Rifles managed to utilize both rifles and muskets in a successful engagement. In the important battle of Cowpens, Morgan deployed his riflemen in the front line with orders to fire two volleys at "the men with the epaulets," and then to retire to the second line of militia. The second line was told of this plan to prevent panic at the sight of the retreating riflemen. The second line also was ordered to fire "low and deliberately" and then to retire when hardpressed to the rear of the main American formation, where they would reform as a reserve.

Morgan's battle plan worked. The successive American withdrawals drew in the British troops under Lieutenant Colonel Banastre Tarleton, while the riflemen's fire took a deadly toll. At the critical moment in the battle the main American formation was ready with muskets and bayonets. At last the patriots seemed to have solved the problem of utilizing both weapons in a single engagement.

Nevertheless, eight months later, in September 1781, while

Washington's army was on its march to the historic denouement with Cornwallis at Yorktown, the commander-in-chief used the occasion to encourage his troops "to place their principle reliance on the bayonet, that they may prove the vanity of the boast which the British make of their particular prowess in deciding battles with that weapon."[15]

Although the rifle had declined in importance as a weapon of the line until Morgan's demonstration, it still was much feared in the hands of American partisan units. "Their riflemen are terrible," complained a German officer. Indeed, Jefferson also expanded on that idea in a letter to a friend in Europe in 1778. Jefferson ascribed higher British casualties (more than double American losses, he said) as due to "our superiority in taking aim when we fire, every soldier in our Army having been intimate with his gun from his infancy."[16]

So went the propaganda of the rifle and the bayonet.

I

This "weapons propaganda" was but one aspect of the general war of broadsides and bayonets waged during the eight years, 1775–83. The English resort to the bayonet—to armed force—was, of course, their final argument in the dispute, which they believed would persuade the rebels to lay down their arms and submit to the King's rule.

However, during the first year of the war the English were under the severe handicap of being almost entirely on the military defensive in America. It was the Americans who produced what might be called the first propaganda broadside of the Revolution aimed at the enemy's troops. Their target was the 100-man Royal Irish Regiment stationed in New York in the spring of 1775.

Within days after news reached New York of the fighting at Lexington and Concord, an "English American" published a broadside addressed *To the Regular Soldiery of Great-Britain*

now on Service in the British American Colonies. It was a long
political exposition of the colonial viewpoint, dated May 1,
1775, which ended with an open invitation to the soldiers to
desert:

As the service on which you were sent here is dishonorable and
injurious to your country, we have reason to think it is highly disagreeable to you. Therefore, in the name of the British colonies
in general, I am authorized to assure you and all the British soldiery at present in America, that if you will quit the service and
join your American brethren in opposing the wicked designs of
the Ministry (or if you please, you shall not be required to draw
your swords or take any active part in the contest) You shall be
kindly received as brothers and friends and provided with a com-
fortable subsistence among us. You shall be sent with a proper
escort to any part of the continent where you choose to retire—
together with your wives, children and effects—or these shall be
sent after you. You shall be protected against the Army and the
military laws of Great Britain, which have no legal force in America.[17]

When reports of this and other American subversive efforts
reached Boston, General Gage ordered the regiment withdrawn
from the city. Early in June 1775 an embarkation of the unit
took place, but not without incident. According to Lieutenant
Governor Cadwallader Colden, reporting to Lord Dartmouth
on June 7 on the regiment's departure: "As soon as the troops
marched from the barracks, several people began to harangue
them, exhorting them to desert, and assuring them of sufficient
protection. Two or three of these fellows had the hardiness to
turn off with the arms from the ranks, and were immediately
carried away by the people."[18] These soldiers were probably
the first troop desertions from either side during the Revolution.

The Royal Irish Regiment joined Gage's besieged forces in
Boston, where during the summer of 1775 at least two other
American propaganda papers were distributed among the

British troops. One was entitled, *An Address to the Soldiers,* and was a reprint of a document produced in London by a Whiggish "Old Soldier," who had addressed the troops as follows: "You are about to embark for America to compel your fellow-subjects there to submit to Popery and Slavery. . . ."[19] The other was a leaflet disseminated from rebel-controlled Prospect Hill, which contained the following comparison:

PROSPECT HILL	BUNKER'S HILL
I. Seven Dollars a Month.	I. Three Pence a Day.
II. Fresh Provisions, and in Plenty.	II. Rotten Salt Pork.
III. Health.	III. The Scurvy.
IV. Freedom, Ease, Affluence and a good Farm.	IV. Slavery, Beggary and Want.

Dissemination of this leaflet to the British troops was accomplished by American patrols operating at night to avoid detection and to get the leaflets into the hands of the rank and file before the officers could destroy them. The leaflets were wrapped around bullets "to make them fly well" and heaved into the British entrenchments on Bunker's Hill.[20]

In Boston the British commander-in-chief, General Gage, struggled to counter American propaganda through various means, including a broadside issued on June 12, 1775, in which he denounced the whole rebel movement. In this tract, published a few days before the battle of Bunker's Hill, Gage attacked the leaders of the rebellion as individuals who had no interest in truth but who had disseminated "the grossest forgeries, calumnies, and absurdities that ever insulted human understanding."

The American press, the English general complained, "has been invariably prostituted to the most contrary purposes." And not only those "flagitious prints" but also "the popular harangues of the times" had taught men "to depend upon activity in treason for the security of their persons and prop-

New-York, May 1; 1775.

To the Regular Soldiery of Great-Britain, now on Service in the British American Colonies;

Friends and Countrymen,

THE Bufinefs and Profeffion of a Soldier, when properly applied—to its true and lawful Defign, is highly ufeful, neceffary, and honourable. A Soldier, duly acting in his Function, may be confidered as a Guardian to Society, a Supporter of Peace and Safety, a Defender of Law and Juftice, Liberty and Property, and, in fhort, a common Friend, who has devoted his Life to the public Service of his Country, and is by that Country, for that Purpofe, armed with Weapons of War, and trufted with more Power than his Fellows— tho' ftill under the Reftraints of Law, and to be directed by the civil Power.

But, if a Soldier, inftead of acting for the Benefit of the People where he is ftationed, taking Directions from them, and defending them in their Rights and Privileges, acts againft them, is fupported by, and takes Directions from their Enemies and Oppreffors, and invades or endangers their Rights and Liberties,—Then the Bufinefs of a Soldier changes its Nature, his Employment is no longer honourable, or juft——He is to be confidered as a dangerous Engine of Oppreffion and Violence, a common Peft and Difturber, neither fit to be fupported nor permitted in any Society who have the leaft Pretentions to Spirit, or common Prudence.

My Friends and Countrymen, of the Regular Soldiery, It depends upon you, to prove by your Conduct, on this important and trying Occafion, in which of the two before defcribed Characters, you will appear, with refpect to us.

By your Military Order, or Inftitution, as Soldiers of the BritifhCourt, you are entitled toRefpect and Honour; but by the difgraceful, odious, and unlawful Service to which you are ordered, by the wicked Miniftry of the Britifh Court, you are placed, with Refpect to us, in

an equal Weight in paffing, or rejecting a Law, with thofe of the moft worthy Reprefentatives, of the moft confiderable City, or County in England. The Number of Members for thefe pitiful Boroughs, amounts to a great Majority of the whole Houfe. The Minifter, by a villanous embezzlement and Mifapplication of the public Money, improperly committed to his Care, is enabled to advance larger Sums than private Perfons can, in purchafing the Votes of thofe mercenary Electors; and by that Means, he has the Difpofal of the Seats in Parliament, of Members for all thofe Places. Thefe Seats he beftows upon needy Men of abandoned Principles, who will vote according to his Directions; and thus he gives, or withholds the Form of Law, to whatever he pleafes. By other Practices equally vile and criminal, in the Difpofal of Places, &c. he has a fimilar Influence in the Houfe of Lords; and thus the Forms of Adminiftration, totally fuppreis the Operations of the Conftitution.

II. An affumed Power in the Reprefentatives, (collectively) that was not conferred by, nor vefted in their Conftituents, either fingly, or collectively. This pretended, myfterious Power, fpringing from a Source unknown, and undefined in its Limits and Extent, has often fhewn itfelf in very dangerous Effects, threatening nothing lefs than Deftruction to its original Caufe (or the natural Rights of thofe thro' whofe choice it is pretended to be derived.) Thus, the Election being once made, and Reprefentatives chofen to act for one year, in making wholfome Laws and Regulations for the common Good, and for the security of Liberty and Property—This new formed Body, immediately affume the Power of extending their Exiftence to the Space of feven Years, or as long as they pleafe; of ftripping their Con-

ADDRESS to the Soldiers in the Continental Army, 1780.

THE time is at length arrived, when all the artifices, and falfehoods of the Congrefs and of your commanders can no longer conceal from you, the mifery of your fituation; you are neither Clothed, Fed, nor Paid; your numbers are wafting away by Sicknefs, Famine, Nakednefs, and rapidly fo by the period of your ftipulated Services, being in general expired, this is then the moment to fly from flavery and fraud.

I am happy in acquainting the old countrymen, that the affairs of Ireland are fully fettled, and that Great-Britain and Ireland are firmly united, as well from intereft as from affection: I need not now tell you who are born in America, that you have been cheated and abufed; and you are both fenfible, that in order to procure your liberty you muft quit your leaders, and join your real friends who fcorn to impofe upon you, and who will receive you with open arms; kindly forgiving all your errors.

You are told that you are furrounded by a numerous militia, this is alfo falfe—affociate then together, make ufe of your firelocks and join the Britifh Army, where you will be permitted to difpofe of yourfelves as you pleafe.

Papers of Continental Congress, National Archives; Broadside Collection, Library of Congress

Two examples of "desertion" appeals to the soldiers of each side. The upper broadside was disseminated in the spring of 1775, the smaller leaflet in the spring of 1780.

erties; till, to complete the horrid profanation of terms and ideas, the name of God has been introduced in the pulpits to excite and justify devastation and massacre."[21] So were the minds of men prepared for treason, Gage charged, especially by such persons as Samuel Adams and John Hancock whom he now excluded from a general pardon offered "to all persons who shall forthwith lay down their arms, and return to the duties of peaceful subjects."[22]

The publication of Gage's proclamation had been approved in London,[23] but, under the circumstances of British forces isolated in Boston, it could have little effect and soon it became the subject of ridicule in the patriot press. Even in the House of Commons a member of the opposition party managed to get in a dig at "Gage's foolish and contemptible proclamation."[24]

A somewhat similar propaganda mishap occurred in May 1776, when General Clinton appeared off the coast of North Carolina with a British fleet and force of soldiers and made motions to invade that state to restore the King's government. From his flagship Clinton sent a proclamation to the Americans in which he denounced "a most unprovoked and wicked rebellion" which had usurped, he said, the powers of government and had erected "a tyranny in the hands of Congresses and Committees of various denominations." Clinton warned he had authority to march against all men in arms as enemies of Britain. However, "from the principle of humanity," he first offered free pardons to all who would lay down their arms and submit to British rule.[25]

After having taken such an uncompromising stand, Clinton failed to impose his will with the bayonet. Instead, in a change of plans, he sailed away to make his unsuccessful assault on Charleston, South Carolina, in June 1776, and the only effect of his proclamation to the North Carolinians was to solidify their ranks.

The first co-ordinated British effort to talk or force the Americans into laying down their arms did not begin until the arrival of the Howe brothers off the coast of America in the summer of 1776. The brothers, Lord Howe, admiral of the fleet, and General William Howe, successor to Gage, had been named "commissioners for restoring peace to his Majesty's colonies and plantations." Their campaign was initiated by Lord Howe as soon as his flagship, the *Eagle,* arrived off Massachusetts bay on June 20, when the admiral promptly dispatched three sets of documents to the mainland: (1) letters to the refugee royal governors; (2) a "Declaration" announcing the appointment of his brother and himself as commissioners, authorized to grant pardons to all who would speedily "return to their duty"; and (3) personal letters from Englishmen to their American friends, "placing the character of the Howes in the most amiable point of view, and recommending reconciliation with G. Britain."[26]

These latter papers were sent to the rebel camp under a flag of truce, and Washington forwarded them to Congress. Among the personal letters were several addressed to members of Congress, including one to Benjamin Franklin which he presented to the assembly. Congress' reaction to these papers was to order the "Declaration" published, in order to "let the people see upon what terms reconciliation is proposed to them." The truth of the matter was, commented one delegate, "the door is shut. . . . The sword must determine our quarrel."[27]

On this occasion the British were quite prepared to implement their words with the sword. Between June and August 25, 1776, hundreds of English transports arrived in lower New York Bay, disembarking a grand army of 32,000 soldiers (including German mercenaries)—"the greatest expeditionary force Great Britain had ever sent out from its shores."[28] To oppose these trained professional troops the Americans managed to muster some 19,000 colonists.

The British commander-in-chief, General Howe, turned to the printing press before beginning military operations on Long Island. On August 23 he issued an appeal to the "loyal inhabitants of this island" who had been "compelled by the leaders in rebellion to take up arms against his Majesty's government." To any such person who would desert the American side and present himself at British army headquarters, Howe promised his protection. And, if the Americans chose to join the King's standard under arms, they would be given every encouragement.

Soon after this broadside was put into circulation, the first battle took place, sustaining the loyalist argument of the winter of 1774–75: the Americans were sent into headlong retreat. General Howe had demonstrated British military superiority with ease, his army killing or capturing 1,000 of the rebels. Since the time seemed opportune to talk to the Americans again, the Howes sent one of their newly acquired prisoners, Major General John Sullivan, to Congress with a request for a parley. They suggested the meeting be between the admiral and a "private" group of Americans.

Congress at first balked at such unofficial talks, fearful of what John Adams called English "Machiavelian maneuvres."[29] However, it was clear that if Congress refused even to confer, the loyalists and moderate Americans might paint that body as "obstinate and so desirous of war and bloodshed" that it had refused even to listen to Lord Howe's peace proposals.[30] To prevent such a possible appeal directly to the people, Congress finally agreed to send a three-man delegation to meet with the admiral. It named to the group John Adams, Franklin, and Edward Rutledge.

II

This interview took place on September 11, 1776, on Staten Island. As it began the American fears quickly evaporated that Lord Howe might somehow talk them out of their revolution. Howe was firm in his approach, but mild and quite un-Machiavelian. The principal stumbling block to reconciliation with Britain, he said, was the two-month-old *Declaration of Independence,* which had made it "absolutely impossible for me to treat, or even confer upon that ground, or to admit the idea in the smallest degree."[31] But the Americans would not and could not retreat from independence. The conference predictably ended in failure.

Having been unsuccessful at verbal persuasion, the Howe brothers unsheathed the sword again; and, in the next few days, the British army demonstrated its superiority on Manhattan at Kips' Bay and Harlem Heights. In the first skirmish Washington's militiamen fled in panic; and, in the second, although they did somewhat better, they were again forced from the field.

On September 19, while the English and German forces regrouped and fortified new positions, the Howes issued a new appeal over the heads of Congress to "his Majesty's well-affected subjects" and "the inhabitants at large." This propaganda broadside declared (excerpts):

> Although Congress, whom the misguided *Americans* suffer to direct their opposition to a re-establishment of the constitutional government of these provinces, have disavowed every purpose of reconciliation not consonant with their *extravagant and inadmissable claim of Independence,* the King's Commissioners think fit to declare that they are equally desirous to confer with his Majesty's well-affected subjects upon the means of restoring the public tranquillity, and establishing a permanent union with every colony as a part of the British empire. . . . It is recommended to the inhabitants at large to reflect seriously upon their present condition and expectations, and judge for themselves whether it would be more inconsistent with their honor and happiness to offer up their lives as a sacrifice to the *unjust and precarious cause* in which they are engaged in, or return to their allegiance, accept the blessings of peace, and to be secured in a free enjoyment of their liberties and properties.[32]

By this appeal to the colonists the British leaders seemed to have hoped they could ignore Congress. As for the King's "well-affected" subjects, these loyalist elements had already been drawn to British-controlled New York in large numbers to confer with the Howes on ways and means of crushing the rebellion.

The Howes' appeal of September 19 did not go unchallenged by the rebels. A counter-proclamation—almost a word-for-word parody of the British broadside—soon made its appearance; it insisted that the King's commissioners really wished "to confer with his Majesty's subjects (if any so weak and abandoned are to be found) upon the means of establishing a permanent tyranny over every colony, and fix them the everlasting slaves of the British empire."[33]

The political situation thus had not changed when, on October 12, General Howe put his army into motion again. And again Washington's forces were unable to meet the challenge. As they retreated to the north, Fort Washington and Fort Lee (named in honor of the commander-in-chief and his second in command) were besieged and fell into British hands. The loss of Fort Washington in particular was a hard blow to the American cause. Captured with it were 230 officers and 2,600 soldiers, together with a great amount of guns, cannon, shells, and other equipment. By mid-November, with the American militia enlistments fast expiring and his army suffering many desertions, Washington fled into the Jerseys, carrying with him "the remains of a broken army." The enemy followed closely at his heels.

If ever the moment was ripe for an English propaganda offensive, the last days of November and early December 1776 was the time. As the rebel cause began to lose adherents, General Howe issued a new appeal to all Americans to come in and renew their allegiance to the King. In a tract published on November 30, he ordered those rebels in arms to disband and return to their homes. Other rebels, "assembled together under the name of General or Provincial Congresses, Committees, conventions, or other associations by whatever name or names known," were directed to cease all such "treasonable actings and doings." Further, Howe established a deadline—sixty days from the date of this proclamation—for the people to come in and obtain their "full and free pardon of all treason."[34] Those who failed to do so by that date, it said between the lines, would face the traitor's gibbet.

Now, indeed, British propaganda took effect. As one English historian has put it: "New Jersey rose to this bait almost en masse."[35] A contemporary observer wrote: "A great many came to headquarters in Trenton, were accepted, and dismissed with a [paper] protection."[36]

The early weeks of December 1776 saw the rebel cause at its lowest. In their extremity the Americans turned to an ancient propaganda technique in the effort to rally the people to greater defensive efforts. This was the atrocity story, which painted the British and German soldiers in brutish colors. In its march through the countryside, the British army had been involved in a certain amount of looting, pillaging, and desecrations. By the time American propagandists finished with these incidents, they had been somewhat expanded, especially as to sexual assaults. "The enemy," wrote a friend to Jefferson, "like locusts sweeps the Jerseys. . . . They to the disgrace of a civilized nation ravish the fair sex, from the age of ten to seventy."[37]

A more detailed description of some of these incidents, published in December by orders of the Pennsylvania Council of Safety, was contained in an anonymous letter from an "officer of distinction in the American army" to a friend.

Since I last wrote you this morning [said the officer] I have had an opportunity of hearing a number of the particulars of the horrid depredations . . . of the British army. . . . Besides the sixteen young women who had fled to the woods to avoid their brutality, and were there seized and carried off, one man had the cruel mortification to have his wife and only daughter (a child of ten years of age) ravished; this he himself, almost choked with grief, uttered in lamentations to his friend, who told me of it, and also informed me that another girl of thirteen years of age was taken from her father's house, carried to a barn about a mile, there ravished and afterwards made use of by five more of these brutes.[38]

The theme of British-German sexual depravity was to be repeated by the Americans on numerous occasions, leading finally to an outraged cry of indignation in the Tory press: "The charge of 'deflowering defenceless women' is one of those deliberate, malicious falsehoods which are circulated by the rebels, purely to incense the inhabitants against the British troops."[39]

In late December 1776 a more positive note was injected into American propaganda by one of the most famous writers of the period. A few days before the battle of Trenton, *The American Crisis* by Thomas Paine came into Washington's hands. Paine, who earlier had written the influential pamphlet, *Common Sense*, was then serving as a volunteer in the American army. The opening words of his new appeal still reverberate in American ears:

These are the times that try men's souls. The summer soldier and the sunshine patriot will, in this crisis, shrink from the service of his country; but he that stands it now, deserves the love and thanks of man and woman. Tyranny, like hell, is not easily conquered; yet we have this consolation with us, that the harder the conflict, the more glorious the triumph.[40]

Washington quickly perceived the effect Paine's words would have on his discouraged soldiers. He had the drums sounded, and the men assembled to hear their officers read from the pamphlet. "It was," comments one writer, "as wine to the weary patriots, giving them strength to endure the bitter winter winds that swept the Delaware and whipped them as they stumbled through the snow and sleet . . . to Trenton."[41]

The success of Washington's attack at Trenton was a turning point in the war. Although General Howe at first dismissed it as of limited military significance, as it was, he soon became unhappily aware of Trenton's real meaning—in the area of patriot morale and confidence. In January 1777 he wrote to Lord Germain: "It is with much concern that I am to inform your Lordship, the unfortunate and untimely defeat at Trenton has thrown us further back than was at first apprehended, from the great encouragement given to the rebels. I do not now see a prospect of terminating the war, but by a general action."[42]

This revealing statement is the key to Howe's early military strategy. He had not been thinking in terms of a general action: he simply had been applying military pressure to give substance to earlier British arguments, hoping the combination would persuade the Americans to cease their resistance. But, with Trenton, the "bubble of British invincibility" was punctured. The effects of all the British military successes between August and December had been practically swept away. They were indeed not even back where they started, since the rebels had tasted an important victory and knew they could win, if conditions were right. Now it would take a great many more bayonets, and a great many more broadsides, to prove to the rebels that Trenton was an accident of war. It would take "a general action."

III

A new phase of the propaganda war began in January 1777. Washington had been given unprecedented powers by Congress to deal with the crisis, and he proceeded to issue his own counter-proclamation to the people. This broadside was aimed at Americans who, he said, had been influenced "by inimical motives, intimidated by the threats of the enemy, or deluded by a proclamation issued the 30th of November last, by Lord and General Howe," and who had taken oaths of allegiance to the throne. Washington ordered all such persons—in order to enable the patriots to distinguish "between the friends of America and those of Great Britain"—to travel immediately to his headquarters, or to any other general officer of the army, and surrender such British certificates and take the oath of allegiance to the United States. Those who refused to do so within thirty days were "to withdraw themselves and their families within the enemy's lines."[43]

This proclamation, which had the effect of clearing American-controlled territory of loyalist elements, brought Washington unexpected criticism from delegates in Congress. The New Jersey delegates in particular expressed alarm that the commander-in-chief was setting a dangerous precedent by assuming "the legislative and executive powers of government in all the states." Abraham Clark, one of the New Jersey men, argued: "We set out to oppose tyranny in all its strides, and I hope we shall persevere."[44] In February a congressional committee was appointed to examine this complaint. It found that Washington's proclamation had not interfered "with the laws or civil government of any state, but considering the situation of the army was prudent and necessary,"[45] and the matter was dropped.

Although military operations had come to a halt for the winter, in both camps propaganda planning went on. In March and April 1777 Howe's staff produced several new desertion appeals which were effective in causing defections from Washington's army. The first appeal was dated March 17 and promised rebel soldiers who surrendered to the British army before May 1, that they would receive not only full pardons but also that every man who brought in his weapons would be paid their full value. Further, any deserter who wished would be allowed to join a provincial corps being formed in the British army.[46] The second appeal, dated April 21, promised 200 acres of land to every noncommissioned officer, and 50 acres to every private, who enlisted in the provincial corps and served for two years or for the duration of the war in North America.[47]

Early in May, in a letter to Congress, Washington reported that these British propaganda appeals had had "an unhappy influence on too many of the soldiers; in a particular manner on those who are not natives.* . . . I could wish some means could be devised to cause more frequent desertions of their troops. Congress may think of some expedients. A larger bounty might have some effect."[48]

To counter British efforts and to prepare the American people for the impending "general action," Congress published a lengthy address on May 29, 1777, *To the Inhabitants of the United States*. In this paper Congress reviewed the background of the struggle which began, it said, "because you would not be slaves." Said the Congress (excerpts):

Commissioners, at the head of *fleets* and *armies* were sent to restore *peace* to America. After their arrival they issued a proclamation containing a promise of pardon. A pardon implies a precedent crime. What crime was it which the pardon so graciously proffered was meant to extinguish? That of refusing to surrender your birthright and to be bound, in all cases, by the acts of the British parliament. To receive a pardon was to acknowledge that asserting the essential rights of freemen was criminal; and to promise never to assert them any more. . . .

No middle line can now be drawn. Absolute and unconditional submission to their power is the end, long intended. . . . Absolute and unconditional submission! These are terms to which your ears have been unaccustomed. It behooves you fully to understand their meaning. . . . The horrors of *Asiatic* slavery rush into your views. . . . You would be numbered among slaves. . . .[49]

Further, Congress warned, the people should remain on guard against "the secret arts and machinations of emissaries" sent among them. Such persons, said Congress, "gain and transmit intelligence; they invent and propagate false and injurious reports; they create and foment jealousies between states and individuals; they magnify the power, numbers, and resources of the enemy; they undervalue yours. By these means, the

* American-born. There were many Irishmen and English-born soldiers in the American army.

timid are dismayed; and the honest but unsuspicious are mis-informed and misled."[50]

This address, a timely and effective piece of counterpropa-ganda, was issued just before two British armies began to move. In the north Burgoyne in June began his march from Canada, while the British army under Howe sailed away mysteriously from New York, finally reappearing at the Head of Elk, Mary-land, where they disembarked for the march against Phila-delphia.

The day he landed in Maryland, August 27, 1777, Howe published another propaganda paper whose purpose (as he later described it in a letter to Germain) was: "To quiet the minds of the people at large in Pennsylvania and the counties to which it has relations . . . as well as . . . to disunite their army."[51] In this broadside, Howe renewed his offer of pardon "to all such officers and private men" in the rebel army who surrendered "to any detachment of his Majesty's forces."[52]

Washington described the appeal immediately as another obvious effort "to seduce the people to give up their rights and to encourage our soldiery to desert."[53] However, at this time military operations rather than propaganda were uppermost in Washington's mind, as he hurried his forces to block the British advance on Philadelphia. On September 11 the ma-neuverings of the two armies led to the Battle of Brandywine, where Washington's forces were once more thrashed and forced to retreat. Shortly thereafter, the British army marched un-molested into rebel-deserted Philadelphia.

Howe had hoped the capture of the rebel capital would be a turning point in the struggle. Unfortunately for this hope and the English cause, the American loss was counterbalanced by Burgoyne's defeats. In August 1777 Congress learned that a force of New England militiamen under John Stark had de-feated part of Burgoyne's army at Bennington, Vermont. This news was immediately published by Congress in leaflet form and sent to Washington for distribution to his troops. Thanking

Congress for the papers, Washington responded: "I doubt not but they will answer the good end which is intended by them. Every piece of good news circulated in this manner through the camp, will certainly inspirit the troops."[54]

Several weeks later Washington made use of further good news from the north to prepare his soldiers for the coming battle. In general orders read to the troops, Washington cited the northern victories over Burgoyne and then challenged his soldiers: "The army, the main American army, will certainly not suffer itself to be outdone by their northern brethren. . . . Let it never be said that in a day of action you turned your backs on the foe. Let the enemy no longer triumph."[55]

The next day, on October 4, the "main" American army marched out to do battle with the British at Germantown. For a time it looked as if it would win, but the British rallied and Washington's army again was swept into retreat, losing about 1,000 men in dead, wounded, and prisoners. However, the Americans had done so well in this battle that morale was not seriously undone.

After the Battle of Germantown, and before Washington brought his battered army to the bleak ground at Valley Forge, only the shining success over Burgoyne brought comfort to the patriots. While Howe's army went into winter quarters in Philadelphia, where a round of dancing and parties began, Washington and his men settled at Valley Forge to wait out the harsh winter of 1777–78.

IV

The festive atmosphere in British-occupied Philadelphia seemed almost to have been deliberately invoked by Howe to demonstrate the rewards of loyalty and rebellion. Several times during the winter the British, addressing themselves to the suffering rebel soldiers at Valley Forge, renewed the offers of pardon and other benefits if they would give up their struggle.

These offers had great effect: by March 25, 1778, according to figures compiled by Joseph Galloway, Howe's superintendent-general of police, 1,134 soldiers and 354 sailors deserted the American armed forces and fled to Philadelphia, where they took the oath of allegiance to Great Britain. The bulk of these defectors, however, were foreign-born, most of them natives of Ireland, England, or Scotland.[56]

Still, their desertion substantially weakened Washington's force and the success seems to have stimulated British and loyalist planners; several weeks later they launched another subversive effort against the American army. This latter operation involved the publication in the loyalist *Evening Post* in Philadelphia of a document purporting to be an official resolution of Congress, which declared that American militiamen who had enlisted or were drafted to serve for limited periods, nevertheless would be detained beyond the stipulated times.

When this report reached Valley Forge, Washington moved at once to deny it. In his general orders of April 23, 1778, Washington declared that the report "is as false as it is wicked and is intended to induce those who have already inlisted or have been drafted to desert and to intimidate others from engaging into the service of their country."[57] He further declared:

Our enemies, finding themselves unable to reduce us by the force of their arms, are now practicing every insidious art to gain time and disunite us, but the General hopes that men who have struggled with every difficulty and encountered every danger are not to be conquered by artifices which are so easily exposed. It is necessary to give warning to such weak men as might otherwise be deluded by the traitorous promises of the enemy that, under pretence of sending deserters from this army passage free to Great Britain or Ireland, there to be set at large, they confine them on ship board with a view either to force them into their service as seamen or transport them as recruits to some garrison.[58]

Within a few days these propaganda incidents were forgotten in the excitement over the important and stirring news which Congress sent to Washington: France had recognized the independence of the United States! On May 2 a great celebration broke out in the American camp. In British Philadelphia the same news threw a dark shadow over all English prospects in America.

Prior to receipt of the news of France's decision, Washington had received from the British governor of New York City, William Tryon, a draft of Lord North's "conciliatory bills." These bills, a belated attempt by the British government to prevent the signing of the French-American alliance, offered important concessions to the Americans to restore old ties—everything, in fact, but complete independence. To sell these new proposals peace commissioners were appointed and ordered to America to negotiate with the rebels "to reunite the British empire."

Washington, after studying the papers sent him by Tryon, dispatched them to Congress with his comment that they were obviously "meant to poison the minds of the people and detach the wavering, at least, from our cause." He urged Congress to investigate and expose the new British move.[59]

Washington's negative reaction was reflected in the actions of Congress. On April 22 that body adopted a resolution which declared that, if the papers were authentic, they indicated a loss of British confidence in their ability to conquer America. In any event the concessions (which included doing away with all taxation) were no longer important since Congress could not hold any conference or meet with any commissioners "unless they shall, as preliminary thereto, either withdraw their fleets and armies, or else, in positive and express terms, acknowledge the independence of the said states."[60] To demonstrate its confidence, Congress ordered the British proposals be printed "for the public information," despite the fact they seemed to have been "industriously circulated by the emissaries of the enemy in a partial and secret manner."[61]

The same day Congress acted, Washington received "an extraordinary and impertinent request" from Governor Tryon, who asked that copies of the bills be disseminated among the officers and men of the American army. On the twenty-sixth Washington replied to Tryon that he would indeed circulate the bills among his soldiers, "in whose fidelity to the United States I have the most perfect confidence." He enclosed a copy of a newspaper showing Congress' resolve to publish the bills anyway, and also some American propaganda papers, requesting these be disseminated among the soldiers of the British army! That was a game two could play.

The new effort at conciliation had gotten off to a bad start for the British. When the new peace commissioners—the Earl of Carlisle, William Eden, and George Johnstone—arrived at Philadelphia in early June 1778, they learned to their dismay that the British army was evacuating the city and that Congress already had taken a firm stand against the new proposals. The unhappy commissioners were forced to join the retreat to New York. Later they tried to use various secret agents, such as one John Berkenhout, to go to Philadelphia to sound out influential Americans on the British proposals, but these efforts proved unsuccessful and some of the agents were jailed. Other subversive operations also failed.* The rebel leaders seemed impervious to British arguments.

In a final desperate effort to succeed in their mission, the commissioners attempted to take their case directly to the American people. Beginning on October 3, they launched a large-scale propaganda operation (called by one commissioner "a last dying speech"). By land and by sea they sent great numbers of a *Manifesto and Proclamation* to all members of Congress, to members of state assemblies and conventions, to ministers of the gospel, to governors of various states, to officers of the Continental Army, to chief justices and judges of the American courts, and to the people in general.

In their *Manifesto* the commissioners reminded the people

* See Chapter 6, pp. 173–174 ff.

that Congress had, in the beginning, asked only for redress of grievances and had denied any desire to become independent. But now that it was being granted all it asked, it had enlarged its demands and was insisting on independence. Congress, declared the commissioners, had no authority "either to reject our offers without the previous consideration and consent of the several assemblies and conventions of their constituents, or to refer us to pretended sovereign treaties, which they know were delusively framed in the first instance, and which have never yet been ratified by the people of this continent."[62]

The commissioners then proceeded to fling offers in all directions: to the local assemblies, suggesting direct negotiations; to the "free inhabitants" under arms, suggesting they join the British army; to the ministers of the gospel, suggesting Britain was their best guarantee of religious liberty and Protestantism. Having flung their net so wide, the commissioners' tone, towards the end of their "dying speech," became threatening:

The policy, as well as the benevolence of Great Britain, have thus far checked the extremes of war, when they tended to distress a people still considered as our fellow-subjects, and to desolate a country shortly to become again a source of mutual advantage: but when that country professes the unnatural design not only of estranging herself from us, but of mortgaging herself and her resources to our enemies, the whole contest is changed. . . .

Under such circumstances, the laws of self-preservation must direct the conduct of Great Britain: and if the British Colonies are to become an accessory to France, will direct her to render that accession of as little avail as possible to her enemy.[63]

The final decision in the dispute was up to the American people, said the commissioners, who concluded their address with an offer of full pardons to any colonist who applied under the terms of the *Manifesto* for forty days from the date of the document, or until November 11, 1778.[64]

Congress' first reaction to this propaganda appeal was to

forbid dissemination of the papers, a reversal of its previous confident attitude towards the conciliatory bills. On October 16 it ordered all authorities to seize and suppress the "seditious" papers whenever and wherever they were found. Washington had some misgivings about Congress' reaction. In a letter he voiced a fear that "the avenues and channels in which [the papers] may be conveyed are so various and numerous that no exertions will be found sufficient entirely to prevent the evil." The commander-in-chief also felt that the attempt to suppress the British offer might, in the end, have more bad effects than a free circulation of them, made "with proper strictures."[65]

The general also quickly noted the "implied threat" in the *Manifesto* to change the war "to one of a more predatory and destructive kind." The British may have done this, he suggested, "only in terrorem; but it is possible that it may be intended as a serious principle of practice."[66] As one reaction to this threat, Congress on October 10 warned the people "there is every reason to expect" that Britain would "as the last effort, ravage, burn and destroy every city and town on this continent they can come at." Congress recommended to Americans, living in exposed areas which might be attacked, to immediately build huts thirty miles from their homes, where they could take refuge in an emergency. It further suggested that if such burnings did take place, the patriots retaliate by setting fire and destroying the properties of refugee loyalists.[67]

Several weeks later, on October 30, Congress decided to issue its own threatening "manifesto." Taking note of the British intimations of more widespread devastation, it announced the firm resolve of Congress "that if our enemies presume to execute their threats, or persist in their present career of barbarity, we will take such exemplary vengeance as shall deter others from a like conduct."[68] Printed copies of this resolution were sent to Washington; and, after setting his agents in motion, he reported to Congress on November 6 that the British in New York City would soon "be possessed of some of the copies and of the news papers that contain them."[69]

By the end of the year 1778 it had become clear to the commissioners that their *Manifesto* and all their efforts had failed. Their propaganda answered by counterpropaganda, their emissaries arrested, and their proposals ignored, the commissioners finally gave up the struggle and returned, in December, to England.

v

Having been so unsuccessful in their campaigns in the north, failing equally in the central states despite Howe's early military successes, the British now turned hopefully to the "weak" end of the American chain, to the southern states, where a new phase of the war now began. This phase dates from the capture of Savannah, Georgia, on December 29, 1778, by Lieutenant Colonel Archibald Campbell and a combined British-German and loyalist force of 3,500 men.

Prior to this victory, a view which had currency in British circles in New York was that if just one province could be subdued, and a royal government restored, "then everyone believes all provinces would prefer peace to war."[70] The capture of Savannah and the routing of the patriot militia seemed to bring about a complete submission of Georgia. At last Great Britain had its subdued province.

In consolidating its position in the south the British army utilized once again the propaganda broadside. One paper, dated January 4, 1779, formally announced "to all his Majesty's faithful subjects of the southern provinces, that a fleet and army . . . are actually arrived in Georgia for their protection, to which they are desired to repair without loss of time, and by uniting their force under the royal standard, rescue their friends from oppression, themselves from slavery."[71] On January 11 a second paper offered a reward for the capture of the "ring-leaders of sedition, and some skulking parties from the rebels of Carolina."[72] A third document also was issued, a combination oath of allegiance and "safe conduct pass," to be signed by Americans who submitted.

This literature, backed by British military supremacy, proved highly effective and Colonel Campbell reported with satisfaction to Lord Germain that "the inhabitants from all parts of the province flock with their arms to the standard, and cordially embrace the terms which have been offered."[73] On March 4 the British re-established a civil government, and on March 24 further announced that Georgia was formally "at the peace of his Majesty."[74]

While the British army thus consolidated its hold on Georgia, in July 1779 several important military and propaganda events occurred in the north. The first involved a punitive raid into Connecticut on the third anniversary of the American *Declaration of Independence*, by a British force of 2,600 men. The raiders, who plundered and burned as they marched, simultaneously disseminated a propaganda *Address to the Inhabitants of Connecticut*. The document warned the people that they lay entirely at the mercy of the British forces, whose control of the seas allowed them to land at will, and posed the question: "Why then will you persist in a ruinous and ill-judged resistance?"[75]

These papers were distributed by Admiral Sir George Collier and Major General Tryon at the suggestion of General Clinton. Tryon later reported to Clinton that the effect of the broadsides could not be determined "till there are some further operations and descents upon their coasts. Many copies . . . were left behind at Newhaven and at Fairchild."[76]

But if the reaction of at least one congressman was any indication, the raid had an effect "directly contrary" to what was intended. Americans, said James Duane, could never "be worked to submission by cruelty and devastation. Their aversion to their destroyers will become deeper rivetted; and their efforts to defend themselves more strenuous and decisive."[77]

Congress was so angered by the event that a committee of retaliation was created "to take the most effectual means to carry into execution the manifesto of October 30, 1778, by burning and destroying the towns belonging to the enemy in Great Britain and the West Indies." A directive was drafted to Franklin in Paris, instructing him to hire incendiaries "to set fire in the capital of the British Dominions, particularly the royal palace, and to such other towns in Great Britain as may be most expedient, and that as soon as some great object of this sort can be accomplished, you do in a proper manifesto avow the same as having been done by the order of Congress."[78]

It is not certain this directive ever was sent to Franklin, but similar instructions on retaliatory measures did reach him; and certain invasion plans and others were co-ordinated with the French.*

Several weeks after the Connecticut raid General Anthony Wayne restored the Americans' good humor with his capture of the British fort at Stony Point. What particularly encouraged the patriots was the cold efficiency with which Wayne's troops attacked with the bayonet, killing some sixty and capturing the entire garrison—543 men. Exulting over this victory, the New Hampshire *Gazette* wrote on July 27: "Nothing can exceed the spirit and intrepidity of our brave countrymen in storming and carrying . . . Stony Point. It demonstrates that the Americans have soldiers equal to any in the world; and that they can attack and vanquish the Britons in their strongest works. No action during the war, performed by the British military, has equalled this coup de main."[79] In Philadelphia the French minister to the United States, Conrad Alexandre Gerard, was greatly impressed and he suggested that telling the story of

* See Chapter 7, pp. 199–200.

Stony Point overseas would "much elevate the ideas of Europe about the military qualities of the Americans."[80]

The British, distressed "by the aggravating circumstances of the loss of the whole garrison" (General Clinton's words),[81] tried to put the best face on it, and at least one loyalist writer tried to counter American propaganda on the event by noting in the New York *Gazette:*

Can any one be so stupid as to imagine that such a trifling affair could be in any way decisive at present, or influence the conduct of Britain? Or are incidents of this kind unusual in the course of war? I could mention several instances where outposts belonging to the greatest generals that ever led armies into the field, have been attacked and carried; and in wars, too, where those generals have been most successful. People who are so easily elevated, betray their own weakness.[82]

Nevertheless, this first American clear-cut victory in a long time sweetened the patriots' labors for some months to come.

VI

But the year 1779 was to end on a dismal note for the Americans. In October a combined French-American force failed to oust the British from Savannah; and in December General Clinton sailed south from New York with a force of 8,500 men, Lord Cornwallis second-in-command. In February Clinton's army landed thirty miles south of Charleston, South Carolina, and shortly thereafter placed that port town under siege. On May 12, 1780, the siege ended with the surrender of Charleston in "one of the greatest disasters suffered by the Americans during the whole war."[83] The British captured more than 5,400 prisoners and huge amounts of material and weapons.

British broadsides on the event were promptly disseminated into the interior, which propaganda, General Clinton later wrote, "soon had the most happy effects, as numbers with their arms came in every day to headquarters from the remotest parts of the province, many of them bringing in their former oppressors."[84] Now South Carolina as well as Georgia seemed to have submitted.

Meanwhile, in the north, where operations appeared at a standstill, the British renewed their desertion appeals to the American army at Morristown. Said one leaflet addressed *To the Soldiers in the Continental Army, 1780:* "The time is at length arrived when all the artifices and falsehoods of the Congress and of your commanders can no longer conceal from you the misery of your situation; you are neither Clothed, Fed, nor Paid; your numbers are wasting away by Sickness, Famine, Nakedness, and rapidly so by the period of your stipulated Services . . . this is then the moment to fly away from slavery and fraud."

Continuing in this vein the leaflet announced that the troubles between Ireland and Great Britain had been settled (a statement aimed at Washington's Irish soldiers) and urged both American-born and foreign-born rebels to "join your real friends." The leaflet concluded: "You are told that you are surrounded by a numerous militia, this is also false—associate then together, make use of your firelocks and join the British army, where you will be permitted to dispose of yourselves as you please."[85]

A copy of this leaflet—the only one found in the Morristown camp, although Washington was certain many copies had been dispersed by infiltrators and picked up by the troops—was sent to Congress. Washington offered the opinion that this propaganda had had "a considerable effect" on the soldiers.[86]

The morale of the main American army, at a low ebb in the spring of 1780, was further depressed by the news of the fall of Charleston. It became apparent, as the bad news of the seemingly complete submission of the southerners reached the north, that only the approach of new American forces could prevent the loss of the entire south. Prior to Charleston's fall, Washington had dispatched a small force of 1,400 men under Baron de Kalb to give aid to the southerners. The crisis in South Carolina now moved Congress to inject itself into the military picture (as it so often did); it ordered the hero of Saratoga, Horatio Gates, to take immediate command of all American operations in the southern department.

Late in July 1780 Gates arrived in North Carolina to take over command from de Kalb. On August 4, in one of his first moves to bolster morale and encourage the southerners, Gates issued a propaganda sheet announcing his approach with "a numerous, well appointed and formidable army" to deal with the "insulting" British.[87] One hundred copies of this broadside were printed,[88] to be disseminated by his advancing columns.

Unfortunately for General Gates, on August 16 in the Battle of Camden, his mixed forces of regulars and militiamen (about 4,100 men) was swept from the field by Cornwallis' regiments. Early in the melee Gates fled precipitously, leaving de Kalb to fight on until he was mortally wounded.

Gates's defeat, which destroyed his reputation, was somewhat offset in October by the important patriot victory at King's Mountain over a loyalist force. This latter battle had the effect of slowing Cornwallis' invasion of North Carolina. Congress, in the meantime, gave up its military role and turned over to Washington the problem of choosing Gates's successor. The commander-in-chief named Major General Nathanael Greene, a happy choice. Greene promptly rode south to take over the southern "army"—2,300 infantrymen on paper, of whom only 1,480 were present and fit for duty.

VII

While these military events evolved in the Carolinas, in the north there occurred the unexpected defection to the British of one of the best fighting generals on the American side, Benedict Arnold. The fiery Arnold's treason was discovered accidentally on September 25, 1780. Before the plot was fully exposed, he fled to the British camp, leaving behind the unfortunate British adjutant general, John André, who was tried as a spy by Washington and hanged.

The Arnold defection gave birth to two propaganda appeals to his former associates, addresses which showed the hand of loyalist ghost writers. The first paper, directed to "the inhabitants of America," was a general statement by Arnold in which he attempted to explain the motives which had led him "to join the King's arms."[89] There was no word of his negotiations with Clinton for the price of his treason. Instead, he lamented that Britain's offers of reconciliation and peace had been ignored by Congress, which had joined with France, "the enemy of the Protestant faith."[90]

These old British arguments were followed several weeks later by Arnold's second address *To the Officers and Soldiers of the Continental Army who have the real Interest of their Country at Heart, and who are determined to be no longer the Tools and Dupes of Congress, or of France.* Dated October 20, this subversive statement invited the Americans to desert and join the British army.

His Excellency, Sir Henry Clinton [said the statement] has authorized me to raise a corps of cavalry and infantry, who are to be cloathed, subsisted and paid as the other corps are in the British service, and those who bring in horses, arms, or accoutrements are to be paid their value, or have liberty to sell them. To every non-commissioned officer and private a bounty of three guineas will be given, and as the Commander-in-Chief is pleased to allow me to nominate the officers, I shall with infinite satisfaction embrace this opportunity of advancing men whose valor I have witnessed, and whose principles are favorable to a union with Britain and true American liberty.

After making this offer, Arnold's pen seemed to dip into a different well, as he continued:

Friends, fellow soldiers, and citizens, arouse and judge for your-selves—reflect on what you have lost—consider to what you are reduced, and by your courage repel the ruin that still threatens you. . . . What is America but a land of widows, beggars, and orphans?—and should the parent nation cease her exertion to deliver you, what security remains to you for the enjoyment of the consolations of that religion for which your fathers braved the ocean, the heathen, and the wilderness . . . ?

But what need of arguments to such as feel infinitely more misery than language can express? I therefore only add my prom-ise of the most affectionate welcome and attention to all who are disposed to join me.[91]

When the first Arnold address appeared, Washington sent a copy to Congress and commented mildly: "I am at a loss which to admire most, the confidence of Arnold in publishing, or the folly of the enemy in supposing that a production signed by so infamous a character will have any weight with the people of these states, or any influence upon our affairs abroad."[92] But when the second appeal appeared, addressed to his soldiers, Washington was far more annoyed at what he called "this unparalleled piece of assurance." It would, he said sharply, only "add to the detestation" the soldiers felt for Arnold."[93]

The British attempt to use Arnold to subvert the rebel army continued unabated for many weeks. On October 25 the New York *Royal Gazette* reprinted Arnold's address to the American army, and continued to reprint it in every issue, twice a week, through December 6.[94] But the Arnold defection and these ap-peals had little effect on the American cause. Indeed, the patriots countered with a flow of words which soon blackened Arnold's name beyond redemption. Burned in effigy and reviled as the personification of evil, Arnold soon was held in "utmost abhorrence and detestation" throughout the army and the country.[95]

The excitement in the north had temporarily diverted American attention from the critical military situation in the Carolinas, where Cornwallis' force appeared to be invincible (despite Daniel Morgan's victory at Cowpens on January 17). With the existence of the southern American "army" constantly threatened by Cornwallis, in mid-February 1781 General Greene fled for security into Virginia. This movement, to all intents, left the entire area from Virginia to Florida in British hands.

With the enemy cleared of North Carolina, Cornwallis retired to Greensboro where he issued a new propaganda broadside inviting all "faithful and loyal subjects to repair, without loss of time, with their arms and ten days provisions, to the royal standard. . . ."[96] When Greene bounced back into North Carolina to do battle and again was defeated at Guilford Courthouse, the British general issued a second broadside announcing his "complete victory" over the rebels and calling upon the people to surrender and receive British protection.[97]

But despite his victories the Americans stood aside and Cornwallis reported to Clinton: "Many of the inhabitants rode into camp, shook me by the hand, said they were glad to see us and to hear that we had beat Greene, and then rode home again. I could not get 100 men . . . to stay with us even as militia."[98]

There was good reason for this. Although Cornwallis had won every battle he had fought, his army had paid too great a price. His tents were full of wounded and the entire army looked much bedraggled. To the hard-headed North Carolinians, it did not look much like a winning team. And it was not. Cornwallis had already lost the campaign. He was deep in hostile country, a country through which his march seemed to have had no perceptible effect. The stage was set for his fateful retreat to Yorktown.

Greene, on the other hand, who had not yet won a battle, turned south to liberate the Carolinas. He quickly demonstrated that the British conquest had been a mirage. One English strong point fell after another, until by May 1781 the British commander at Charleston, Lieutenant Colonel Lord Francis Rawdon, found himself trying to explain away why the King's troops had relinquished "for the present" parts of South Carolina. In a paper disseminated in the back country, Lord Rawdon said: "We trust that it is unnecessary for us to exhort the loyal inhabitants of those districts to stand firm in their duty and principles; or to caution them against the insidious artifices of an enemy who must shortly abandon to their fate those unfortunate people whom they have deluded into revolt."[99]

But these words could not conceal the fact that the game was ending for Britain. Four months later at Yorktown, Cornwallis and his army found themselves besieged by a combined French–American army of 16,000 men under the rebel commander, General Washington. On October 18, 1781, they lay down their arms in defeat.

In the two remaining war years after Cornwallis' surrender, while the peace negotiations went on, only minor military actions took place. During the period the British were almost entirely on the military and propaganda defensive, and their army became the target for American offers of "pardon and protection" to any turncoat Americans "who may have been seduced from their allegiance to Congress."[100] Washington easily entered into the game and, in an attempt to break up a British corps of American deserters, issued a pardon "to all our deserters in the service of the enemy, who will return to their colors."[101]

At besieged Savannah the Americans also invoked an ancient propaganda technique by prevailing upon an English deserter, one Henry Pumphrey, to write a "seductive" letter to his former comrades. In this letter Pumphrey advised them "to escape from bondage and tyranny to liberty and happiness." He referred them to an offer of the governor of Georgia, who promised free lands and other rewards to any British soldier who defected.[102]

These little operations were, of course, only backwash of the prolonged struggle, whose outcome had already been settled at Yorktown.

6

★★

Kidnappings, Rumors, and Bribes

In addition to the American and English propaganda campaigns, a number of other subversive operations were undertaken during the Revolution. These included attempts by both sides to kidnap each other's leaders, the planting of false rumors and other deceptions, and British efforts to bribe a number of leading Americans.

I

The kidnapping attempts in particular caused many a sleepless night on both sides. Washington was a party to several American plots to carry off from their beds high-ranking British generals, and it is clear the British authorities encouraged similar attempts against key civilian and military personnel on the American side.

This phase of the war was stimulated by the seizure of Major General Charles Lee, reportedly in his night shirt, in December 1776 by a British scouting party.* The news of Lee's capture was a great shock to the patriots, many of whom considered him to be their best military man. Even Washington, before becoming disillusioned with Lee during the Battle of Mon-

* For other aspects of this affair, see Chapter 4, pp. 113–114.

mouth, accepted this evaluation of his subordinate and considered his captivity a great loss.

On the other hand, in the British camp there was much rejoicing; and the incident gave birth to several plans by loyalist elements to try to carry off Washington and other leaders of the Revolution. In this connection, Thomas Nelson reported to Jefferson on January 2, 1777: "The general was informed a few nights ago that a conspiracy was formed by some people in Bucks county near his camp to kidnap him as poor Lee was, but he has more prudence than to be caught in this manner."[1]

The following summer it was the rebels who were rejoicing over a similar exploit—the successful kidnapping of a British major general, Richard Prescott, the commanding officer of the English garrison at Newport. Late one night in July 1777 forty Rhode Island militiamen, led by Lieutenant Colonel William Barton, slipped past the British sentries and seized Prescott in his quarters along with his aide-de-camp.

With a note of admiration a British officer later commented: "It is certainly a most extraordinary circumstance that a General commanding a body of 4,000 men, encamped on an island surrounded by a squadron of ships of war, should be carried off from his quarters in the night by a small party of the enemy from without, and without a shot being fired."[2] In reporting the incident to London, General Howe described the kidnapping "as distressing as it was unexpected."[3]

In rebel quarters the event was received, James Thacher wrote, "with great joy and exultation, as it puts in our possession an officer of equal rank with General Lee."[4] That this was one of the main aims of the American exploit was openly admitted to the British officers who contacted the Americans under a flag-of-truce to inquire about General Prescott's needs.[5] A Providence newspaper, meanwhile, described the exploit in detail, boasting that, whereas it had taken a British lieutenant colonel and seventy soldiers to seize Lee, "a lieutenant colonel

... with only 38 privates and six officers has taken a Commander in Chief, when almost encircled by an army and navy."[6]

Congress was so pleased by the affair that it directed Barton be promoted to the rank of full colonel, and it recommended to Washington that he be used in such service as best adapted "to his genius."[7] The capture of Prescott indeed gave Washington ideas and several months later, when he learned that there was "a Hessian general quartered at one Fisher's, covered only by a small guard," he informed Brigadier General William Maxwell that this might be "a glorious opportunity for a partisan exploit."[8] However, the attempt seems never to have been made.

On the British side kidnapping operations were repeatedly undertaken by loyalist refugees, with only occasional moves by the British army itself. In the first instance, Joseph Galloway was one of the leading plotters; on one occasion he concocted a plan to seize the governor, assembly, and council of New Jersey, but it was never carried out.[9]

More typical of loyalist kidnapping operations was one which came to light in British-occupied Philadelphia in March 1778. One William Hamet, described by a loyalist gazette as "an intrepid young man who had suffered much by the rebel plunders," learned that two American officers were in nearby Jersey and he organized a party to take them. In the dead of night they crossed the Delaware, approached the house where the officers were asleep, broke in, and seized the men in their beds. The Americans' weapons were confiscated and they were carried off to Philadelphia as prisoners.[10]

The unhappy effects of such operations were reported by Caesar Rodney, who complained to the delegates of Delaware in Congress that: "We are constantly alarmed in this place by the enemy and refugees, and seldom a day passes but some man in this and the neighbouring counties is taken off by these villains, so that many near the bay, who I know to be hearty in the cause, dare neither act or speak lest they should be taken away and their houses plundered."[11] Rodney appealed for American troops to be sent to protect the area.

In February 1778 Congress took official notice of these operations and, in a formal resolution, denounced the loyalists who were banded together "for the purpose of seizing and secretly conveying to places in possession of the British forces, such of the loyal citizens, officers, and soldiers of these states as may fall into their hands." Congress declared that all such persons were to be put to death "as a traitor, assassin and spy," if the offence was committed within seventy miles of the headquarters of any American army.[12]

II

It was another matter, however, if Britons and Americans seized each other; and, in 1778, Washington came up with a plan to lay hands on General Clinton at his New York headquarters. Washington sent the plan to Brigadier General Samuel Parsons, assuring him "that taking of Clinton in this manner" was not only practical but also desirable and "honorable." The commander-in-chief gave detailed instructions on how to carry out the exploit,[13] including the following deception: "Namely to let the officers and soldiers in the enterprise be dressed in red and much in the taste of the British soldiery."[14]

For reasons unknown, the attempt on Clinton did not come off. It may, however, have planted a seed in the British commander's mind because in February 1779 Clinton authorized a secret expedition of 1,000 soldiers to try to seize Governor William Livingston in his home near Elizabeth Town. The soldiers, landing under cover of darkness, took possession of Livingston's house at five o'clock in the morning of February 25, only to discover that the governor had stayed away that night at a friend's house. However, the governor's two young daughters, the only occupants of the house, were roused from their beds and forced to turn over the governor's papers to the raiding party's commander, who then ordered a withdrawal.[15]

Several weeks after this incident, Livingston wrote a letter of complaint to Clinton. It was not the kidnapping attempt, said the governor, which troubled him but the fact he had in his possession "the most authentic proofs of a general officer under your command having offered a large sum of money to an inhabitant of this state to assassinate me, in case he could not take me alive." This was such a repugnant plan, Livingston said, that he was sure the British commander-in-chief would not be a party "to a design so sanguinary and disgraceful." The governor said he was giving General Clinton the opportunity to disavow "such dark proceedings," adding mysteriously that, if the British leader had approved such a plot, he should beware since "your person is more in my power than I have reason to think you imagine."[16]

Clinton answered Livingston's letter with a brief statement published in a New York paper, in which he denied he had "a soul capable of harboring so infamous an idea as assassination." Clinton also said: "Sensible of the power you boast of being able to dispose of my life by means of intimates of yours, ready to murder at your command, I can only congratulate you on your able connections."[17] Livingston responded to this with a second missive on April 15, in which he attacked Clinton's reasoning powers, flatly denying he had ever threatened or said anything about murder.[18]

Throughout the remaining years of the war, other sporadic kidnapping attempts were made. In December 1780 Washington once more directed Lieutenant Colonel David Humphrey to "surprise and bring off Genl. Kynphausen from Morris's house on York island, or Sir Henry Clinton from Kennedy's house in the city."[19] This effort was made the night of December 25 but failed when high winds drove the landing boats below the city." "As such incidents always do," a Hessian officer wrote, "it made us take more precautions."[20]

The wife of General Friedrich Riedesel told in more detail the effects these kidnapping attempts had on her husband, when they lived on Long Island in the spring of 1781. Riedesel, it will be recalled, was the German commander captured with Burgoyne's army at Saratoga, and had been released in a prisoner exchange. Said Mrs. Riedesel of her husband's reaction:

Our house was situated close to the shore and was perfectly isolated, so that if they [the rebels] had overcome the watch they could easily have carried him away. Every one was therefore constantly on the watch. Throughout the entire night, at the slightest noise, he would wake up and place himself in readiness for an attack; and thus he lost considerable sleep. I also became so accustomed to watching, that daylight would often surprise me, when I would lie down and catch a few hours sleep; for it was only when my husband believed that I was wide awake and on guard, that he would allow himself to sleep—so terrible was to him the thought that he might again be taken prisoner.[21]

In this same year, 1781, the British made two attempts to seize Thomas Jefferson. One took place in January when the turncoat General Benedict Arnold led a British raiding party into Virginia, reportedly carrying with him a pair of silver handcuffs to clap on the young governor. Jefferson, however, had been alerted and fled the capital of Richmond. The second effort was made in June, when Cornwallis dispatched a cavalry force under Lieutenant Colonel Tarleton to seize Jefferson and members of the Virginia Assembly. Once again Jefferson received advance notice, and he managed to flee Monticello a few minutes before a column of hard-riding British horsemen reached the premises.[22]

In 1782 the Americans brewed another plan to kidnap King George's son, Prince William Henry, who was visiting New York City with Admiral Robert Digby. Washington approved this operation but, in a letter to Colonel Matthias Ogden, he warned "against offering insult or indignity to the persons of the Prince, or Admiral, should you be so fortunate as to capture them."[23] The operation failed to come off. Years later the United States ambassador to Britain, Louis McLane, is reported to have shown Washington's letter of instructions to the King (formerly Prince William Henry and then William IV of Great Britain), who remarked: "I am obliged to General Washington for his humanity, but I'm damned glad I did not give him an opportunity of exercising it towards me."[24]

From the viewpoint of the overall strategy of the Revolution, these little incidents were not very important. Nevertheless, they forced each side to take measures to prevent losses and thus contributed in a general way to the war of nerves.

III

Another aspect of the psychological war was played out by rumors deliberately planted or otherwise. The American Revolution was no exception to the general rule of wartime that, when there is a lack of hard authoritative news about "what's happening," rumors will sprout profusely. For example, in June 1777 such a rumor arose following the American retreat from Ticonderoga. According to this fantastic story, General Schuyler, the northern commander, and Major General Arthur St. Clair had turned traitors, being paid for their treason "in *silver balls,* shot from Burgoyne's guns into our camp," and collected by St. Clair to divide up with Schuyler.[25] In this situation there was enough American shock and disappointment at the retreats in the north for Congress to launch a special investigation of the two men, who were subsequently cleared.

Another rumor, which Washington could "hardly give credit to," stated that the British in besieged Boston in December 1775 were resorting to "germ warfare"; that is, sending out innoculated persons "with design of spreading smallpox through" the American camp and countryside. Later, on March 13, 1776, as the British army prepared to evacuate Boston,

Washington warned his troops in his general orders against going into the city without permission, "as the enemy with a malicious assiduity, have spread the infection of the smallpox through all parts of the town."[26] However, there was no evidence this was anything but a general outbreak of that pernicious disease.

The origin of the planted rumor sometimes is more easily determined. One of the most successful of this type was the rumor Benedict Arnold disseminated in the enemy camp outside besieged Fort Stanwix in August 1777.* In a different context, a planted rumor was spread by British agents in 1777 in an effort to disrupt American recruiting in the southern states. Concerning this, Richard Henry Lee complained to Jefferson that "some evil disposed persons (no doubt hired for the purpose) have industriously propagated among the N. Carolina troops, and among the recruits of Virginia in the upper parts, *that the plague rages in our Army*. In consequence of which, it is said, the recruiting business stops and desertions are frequent. There never was a more infamous and groundless falsehood. The Army is extremely healthy, and the wisest methods are pursued to keep them so. I mention this, dear sir, that some adequate plan may be adopted to stop the progress of such wicked lies as are now, with industry, circulated through the country."[27]

Another planted rumor (of American origin), disseminated among the British and German soldiers in Charleston in 1782, purported to know that the entire British garrison was to be sent to the West Indies. Despite British efforts to deny the rumor, the story caused a great deal of desertion.

A special type of falsehood spread on numerous occasions dealt with the supposed deaths of prominent leaders of the Revolution. In 1776 John Adams was reportedly poisoned in New York City,[28] while two years later a story was spread— and cause much depression among Americans until it was

* See Chapter 2, p. 69.

proved false—that Franklin had been mortally wounded in France by a knife-wielding assassin.[29] In 1780 the loyalist publisher, James Rivington, also printed a rumor that the French minister, Chevalier de la Luzerne, had died by violence during a visit to Washington's camp.[30]

The setting into motion of tales—true, false, or simply exaggerated—also played a role in military deceptions and was a practice Washington applied himself to on several occasions. In 1777, for example, in getting ready to dispatch Morgan's riflemen to reinforce the northern army, Washington wrote Governor George Clinton: "I should think it would be well, even before their arrival, to begin to circulate . . . ideas [about their ability as Indian fighters] with proper embellishments throughout the country, and in the army, and to take pains to communicate them to the enemy. It would not be amiss, among other things, to magnify numbers."[31]

In November 1777 Washington approved a plan of Major General Philemon Dickinson to try to persuade the British that an attack on New York was imminent. In a letter to Dickinson, Washington also suggested the following devices: "A great show of preparatives on your side, boats collected, troops assembled, your expectation of the approach of Generals Gates and Putnam entrusted as a secret to persons who you are sure will divulge and disseminate it in New York; in a word, such measures taken for effectually striking an alarm in that city."[32]

Similarly, in March 1779 Washington wrote to General Sullivan, as the latter prepared for the punitive expedition against the Iroquois:

Nothing will contribute more to our success in the quarter where we really intend to strike, than alarming the enemy to a contrary one, and drawing their attention that way. To do this you may drop hints of an expedition to Canada. . . . You may also speak of the probability of a French fleet making its appearance in the spring in the river St. Lawrence, to cooperate with us. It will be a great point gained, if we can, by false alarms, keep

By his Excellency *G E O R G E   W A S H I N G T O N*, Efq;
General and Commander in Chief of all the forces of the
United States of America.

P R O C L A M A T I O N.

WHEREAS feveral perfons, inhabitants of the United States of
America, influenced by inimical motives, intimidated by the threats
of the enemy, or deluded by a Proclamation iffued the 30th of November laft, by Lord and General Howe, ftiled the King's Commif-
fioners for granting pardons, &c. (now at open war and invading thefe ftates) have
been fo loft to the intereft and welfare of their country, as to repair to the enemy,
fign a declaration of fidelity, and, in fome inftances, have been compelled to take
oaths of allegiance, and to engage not to take up arms, or encourage others fo to do,
againft the King of Great-Britain. And whereas it has become neceffary to diftin-
guifh between the friends of America and thofe of Great-Britain, inhabitants of thefe
States, and that every man who receives a protection from and is a fubject of any
State (not being confcientioufly fcrupulous againft bearing arms) fhould ftand ready
to defend the fame againft every hoftile invafion, I do therefore, in behalf of the
United States, by virtue of the powers committed to me by Congrefs, hereby ftrictly
command and require every perfon, having fubfcribed fuch declaration, taken fuch
oaths, and accepted protection and certificates from Lord or General Howe, or any perfon acting under their authority, forthwith to repair to Head-Quarters, or to the quarters of the neareft general officer of the Continental Army or Militia (until farther pro-
vifion can be made by the civil authority) and there deliver up fuch protections, certificates, and paffports, and take the oath of allegiance to the United States of America.
Neverthelefs, hereby granting full liberty to all fuch as prefer the intereft and protection of Great-Britain to the freedom and happinefs of their country, forthwith
to withdraw themfelves and families within the enemy's lines. And I do hereby
declare that all and every perfon, who may neglect or refufe to comply with this
order, within thirty days from the date hereof, will be deemed adherents to the King
of Great-Britain, and treated as common enemies of the American States.

Given at Head-Quarters, Morris-Town, January 25, 1777.

GEORGE WASHINGTON,

By his Excellency's command,
ROBERT H. HARRISON, *Secretary.*

●●◆●●◆●◆●◆●◆●◆●◆●◆●◆●╳●╳●╳●◆●◆●◆●◆●◆●◆◆●◆◆

Baltimore: Printed by JOHN DUNLAP.

Washington's proclamation of January 25, 1777, was aimed at
countering earlier British appeals to the American people.

the force already in Canada from affording any timely assistance to the savages, refugees and those people against whom the blow is levelled.[33]

As we noted in Chapter 1, alarms were set off in Canada during this period and defensive measures were taken, which may have played a role in allowing Sullivan's expedition to march largely unopposed against the Indians.

IV

It would be very strange if Britain and her American adherents had not tried to persuade or bribe military and political leaders on the patriot side to defect, and indeed they did so on several occasions, their prime targets including Franklin, Joseph Reed, and generals Washington, Sullivan, and Lee. The British attitude in these situations was best stated by Germain in secret instructions sent to Clinton in 1779. "The gaining over some of the most respectable members of the Congress," wrote Germain, "or officers of influence and reputation among their troops, would, next to the destruction of Washington's army, be the speediest means of subduing the rebellion and restoring the tranquillity of America."[34]

The first such attempt at "gaining over" came in response to an American effort to get the patriot viewpoint across to a British officer—General Burgoyne—and influence his actions. The instigator of this very wordy affair was General Charles Lee, who wrote to Burgoyne at Boston with the approval of several members of Congress.

Lee's letter, dated June 7, 1775, was a long American attack on the ministry and British policies. Addressing Burgoyne as an old friend (with whom he had served in the British army), Lee expressed the fear that "the avenues of truth" would be shut to him with regards to the American position. "I assert, sir," wrote Lee, "that even General Gage will deceive you, as he has deceived himself. I do not say he will do it designedly; I do not think him capable. But his mind is so totally poisoned, and his understanding so totally blinded by the society of fools and knaves, that he no longer is capable of discerning facts as manifest as the noon-day sun."[35]

What was the truth concerning the American Revolution? According to Lee, the truth was that Britain could not possibly succeed in stopping it, in conquering America. All the colonists, he said, "from the first estated gentlemen to the lowest planters and farmers," were animated by the same spirit and no less than 150,000 men in arms were determined "to preserve their liberties or perish."[36]

Lee's letter was dispatched northward to Burgoyne, who did not respond until July 8, 1775—several weeks after the crucial Battle of Bunker's Hill. Burgoyne's answering letter, "painfully polite and even more painfully pompous,"[37] argued the government's side. In particular, he tried to emphasize that the British constitution was the best safeguard of the public liberty, that the vital principle of that constitution was "the supremacy of the King and Parliament," a supremacy which the colonists were rebelling against.

To Burgoyne America's arguments for taking up arms were weak and implausible. "Is it the weight of taxes imposed," he asked, "and the impossibility of relief after a due representation of her burden, that has induced her to take arms? or is it a denial of the rights of British legislation to impose them, and consequently a struggle for total independency? For the idea of power that can tax externally and not internally . . . though it may catch the weakness and the prejudice of the multitude in a speech or pamphlet, it is too preposterous to weigh seriously with a man of your understanding."[38]

After proceeding in this manner, Burgoyne wrote that he had a suggestion to make to Lee, that they meet in order that further explanations might clear the air and lead the way to peace. He added: "I know Great Britain is ready to open her arms upon the first overture of accommodation; I know she is equally resolute to maintain her original rights; and if the war proceeds, your one hundred and fifty thousand men will not be a match for her power."[39]

Lee, who was quite prepared to act the part of peace negotiator as well as military genius, first prudently consulted the Provincial Congress of Massachusetts concerning the proposed interview. He told the congress he was prepared to attend if that body approved and if he was accompanied by one of its members.[40] However, the provincial body was very suspicious of British motives and, while it did not come out flatly against the meeting, it suggested to Lee "whether such an interview might not have a tendency to lessen the influence which the Congress would wish to extend to the utmost of their power to facilitate and succeed the operations of war."[41] Lee took the hint; and, in a short note passed through British lines, he rejected Burgoyne's invitation.[42]

The incident did not end there. Both sides took advantage of the correspondence to have their own arguments published to the world. Lee's was printed in the American press, while the British reprinted Burgoyne's letter in broadsides which were scattered around the Boston area. Of these broadsides, General Gage wrote on July 24: "It's hoped General Burgoyne's letter will open peoples' eyes, who are blinded to an astonishing degree by the leaders of the rebellion."[43]

So a private correspondence—which began with both sides hoping they could quietly persuade a key enemy officer of the correctness of their cause—ended in the realm of open propaganda to the people.

v

The next British effort to win over "an officer of influence" in the American army took place in June 1777. The target was Major General Sullivan, second-in-command of the northern army. The propagandist was Peter Livius, an acquaintance of Sullivan and former chief justice of New Hampshire, who had fled to Canada to become chief justice of the province of Quebec. Livius' attempt on Sullivan was in the form of a "seductive" letter, obviously written with the approval of British authorities in Canada. Their hope seems to have been to cause a major American defection in co-ordination with Burgoyne's invasion of the colonies.

The Livius letter was dated June 2. "I have long desired," he began, "to write my mind to you on a matter of the very greatest importance." But circumstances, he said, had made delivery of a letter uncertain until he had found his present messenger. "You know better than I do the situation of your Congress," Livius continued, "and the confusion there is among you, and the ruin that impends; you have felt how unequal the forces of your own people are to withstand the power of Great Britain; and for foreign assistance, I need not tell you how precarious and deceitful it must be."[44]

Proceeding in this vein, Livius painted a dark and dreadful future for the colonists, with Sullivan being "one of the first sacrifices to the resentment and justice of government. Your family will be ruined and you must die in ignominy." But there was an alternative fate. Said Livius:

Now, Sullivan, I have a method to propose to you, if you have the resolution and courage for it, that will save you and your family and estate from this imminent destruction. It is in plain English to tread back the steps you have already taken, and to do a real essential service to your King and country, in assisting to reestablish public tranquillity and lawful government. You know I will not deceive you. Every one who will exert himself for government will be received, and I do assure you firmly upon my honour I am empowered to engage particularly with you.

He was not being asked, Livius continued, to declare himself immediately, or at all, "until you can dispose matters so as to bring the province [of New Hampshire] with you." To accomplish this end, Livius suggested the general might send from the colony all those who were opposed to British rule, and to keep at home those who were favorable. At the same time, Sullivan should send "all the material intelligence you can collect" to Livius himself, or to General Burgoyne, "using my name." Livius assured Sullivan that if he did these things, he would not only receive a pardon and security for his property, but that he also would be further "amply rewarded."[45]

The Livius letter was dispatched from Canada by a messenger who, unfortunately for Livius, was soon picked up by an American scouting party and revealed he was carrying a secret paper hidden in the false bottom of a canteen. Sullivan was not present when the canteen was opened at Fort Edward on June 16, 1777, by General Schuyler, in the presence of four staff officers.[46]

From this point events became slightly complicated. Schuyler, having read Livius' letter to Sullivan, thought it might be an opportunity to obtain intelligence about Burgoyne's plans. Without waiting for Sullivan to return from the field, Schuyler had a letter composed in which he himself posed as General Sullivan. As Sullivan he announced himself ready to return to allegiance to the King, and he declared to Livius that he no longer was a supporter of independence, which he had from the beginning "abhorred from my soul." He also casually announced himself ready to receive Burgoyne's orders regarding the impending campaign.[47]

The faked Sullivan letter was approved by a council of general officers at Ticonderoga on June 20, and sent north by messenger. General Sullivan himself did not learn of the Livius letter and Schuyler's counterplot until the next day, June 21, and then he expressed an opinion that the plan would fail. He explained that he feared Livius, who knew him very well, would detect the deception. He also wished an opportunity to answer the letter himself but, in the interests of the plot, he remained silent—until August 1777. By that date Burgoyne's invasion of New York was well underway and the entire affair seemed quite useless. Whereupon, Sullivan published Livius' offer and his own rejection to the world.[48]

VI

The effect on public opinion of the attempt on Sullivan was mild compared to the excitement several months later when it was revealed that Washington had been the target for a similar attempt. The propagandist on this occasion was a man who had been a fervent and early supporter of the patriot cause, the Reverend Jacob Duché, a Philadelphia minister. Duché not only had read the opening prayers for both the first and second Continental Congresses, but his words had so inspired the assembly that he was offered (and served for a short time) the post of first chaplain of Congress.[49]

The influence which caused Duché to send his subversive letter to Washington apparently was General Howe's seizure of Philadelphia in late 1777. As a well-known patriot clergyman, rector of Christ Church and St. Peter's, Duché was promptly arrested by the British. His release, however, followed within one day. It remains a mystery what happened to Duché in the days and weeks that followed, what influence or pressure may have been brought to bear upon him. All that is known is that on October 8 Duché sat down and wrote a 3,000-word appeal to Washington, asking him to use his influence to end the resistance to Britain.[50]

Duché began on a cautious note. If his letter should happen to find Washington in a meeting or in the field, he said, "before you read another sentence I beg you to take the first opportunity of retiring and weighing well its important contents." Duché then proceeded to a description of his political views, which were, he said, that he had never really believed in "armed opposition" to Britain, nor had he held any ideas of independence or separation from the mother country. In flattering tones, he suggested that Washington surely must have felt the same way.

What, he asked, have been the consequences of independence? "A degeneracy of representation—confusion of councils—blunders without number. The most respectable characters have withdrawn themselves, and are succeeded by a great majority of illiberal and violent men." These men, said Duché contemptuously, were nothing but bankrupts, attorneys, men of desperate fortune—"the dregs" of Congress—with few gentlemen among them of the caliber of a Washington.

After this view of Congress [he continued] turn to the army. The whole world knows that its very existence depends upon you, that your death or captivity disperse it in a moment, and that there is not a man on that side of the question in America capable of succeeding you. As to the army, itself, what have you to expect from them? Have they not frequently abandoned even yourself in the hour of extremity? Have you, can you have the least confidence in a set of undisciplined men and officers, many of whom have been taken from the lowest of people, without principle, without courage. Take away those that surround your person, how very few are there that you can ask to sit at your table?

Having concluded this snobbish note, Duché proceeded to strike down American arguments and expectations of foreign aid, or hopes for help from the Whig opposition in England. The patriots simply had no chance, he said, in the face of the power of Britain. Under such discouraging circumstances, Duché continued, Washington could play a crucial role in bringing about an accommodation, by recommending to Congress "the indispensable necessity of rescinding the hasty and ill-advised declaration of independency," by recommending "an immediate cessation of hostilities."

Duché assured the American leader: "I write not this under the eye of any British officer, or person connected with the British army or ministry. The sentiments I have expressed are the real sentiments of my own heart, such as I have long held."

Duché said he was sure the weight of Washington's influence would succeed with Congress but: "If it should not, you have one infallible resource still left. Negotiate for America at the head of your army."[51]

To deliver this subversive document, Duché enrolled as messenger (to her future misfortune) Mrs. Elizabeth Graeme Ferguson, a lady of Philadelphia society with a minor reputation for literary attainments, who was married to a loyalist. On October 15, 1777, Mrs. Ferguson appeared at Washington's camp outside Philadelphia and requested an interview. Washington, who knew of her, had her ushered in and she handed over the bulky Duché letter of fourteen folio pages. The general opened the letter and began to read.

Washington must have been greatly surprised by Duché's appeal. The next day, in forwarding the letter to Congress, he reported his reaction: "To this ridiculous, illiberal performance I made a short reply by desiring the bearer of it, if she should hereafter by any accident meet Mr. Duché, to tell him I should have returned it unopened if I had any idea of the contents." Washington added that, despite Duché's assertion that no British official was involved: "I cannot but suspect that the measure did not originate with him, and that he was induced to it by the hope of establishing his interest and peace more effectually with the enemy."[52]

Several weeks later Washington wrote of the incident in a letter to Francis Hopkinson, Duché's brother-in-law. He said he had sent the letter to Congress in order to protect himself, "for had any accident happened to the army entrusted to my command, and it had ever afterwards appeared that such a letter had been written and received by me, might it not have been said that I betrayed my country?"[53]

Congress, which had been assailed in such uncomplimentary terms by Duché, was angered by the letter. The former chaplain of Congress became a "Judas," an "apostate" and "the first of villains." The members of Congress also were convinced "that the letter he wrote to our worthy General must have been dictated by a Howe."[54] From the British viewpoint, the entire affair was badly mismanaged. In the subsequent excitement after the public disclosure, the poor, would-be propagandist sailed for England.

Duché did not return to America and to Philadelphia until many years later, in 1792, when the incident was almost forgotten. At that time there took place "the interesting incident of his visit to President Washington; who had been apprised of and consented to it, and manifested generous sensibility on observing the limbs of Mr. Duché, the effects of a slight stroke of paralysis sustained by him in England."[55] Duché lived on for six more years, and died in America.

VIII

The failure of these "seductive" letters seems not to have discouraged the British and, in the following year, 1778, several new attempts were undertaken to win over influential Americans. The leading planner on this occasion was George Johnstone, a member of the commission sent to America in connection with the "conciliatory bills." A member of Parliament and a former British governor of Florida, Johnstone tried to smooth the path for the commission by making contact in England with friends of several Americans. Two of the patriots Johnstone hoped to reach were Robert Morris and Joseph Reed, both members of Congress.

In searching for letters of introduction, Johnstone approached Reed's brother-in-law in England, Dennis DeBerdt, who in the spring of 1776 had also written a letter on behalf of Lord Howe's abortive peace mission.[56] DeBerdt, still hopeful of a reconciliation between the two countries, agreed in 1778 to write a letter of recommendation for Governor Johnstone, whom he described to Reed as "a steady proved friend of

America and its just rights." But along with these kind words for Johnstone, DeBerdt voiced the general English dismay and disbelief that the Americans were allying themselves with the French, "the sworn enemies of British liberty and the Protestant religion."[57] To accompany DeBerdt's cover-letter, Johnstone prepared his own letter to Joseph Reed, in which he assured the latter of his friendship and explained that the commission was authorized to resolve all the differences between England and America "short of a total separation of interests."[58]

After the commissioners reached British-held Philadelphia early in June 1778, Johnstone dispatched the letters to Valley Forge, where Reed was serving on Washington's staff. Reed received his brother-in-law's letter with displeasure, unhappy that DeBerdt had allowed himself to be "used" for a second time by the British government. As for Johnstone's letter, Reed decided to reveal it to Congress. His view of the entire plan of the new commissioners was similar to Washington's: that it was another "insidious" maneuver to distract and divide the patriots. After consulting with Washington on the matter, Reed prepared an answering letter to Johnstone.[59]

However, Johnstone never received Reed's response because of the confusion and excitement attending the British evacuation of Philadelphia. Before leaving the city Johnstone made one last effort to get in touch with Reed. He approached the same lady who carried Duché's letter to Washington, Mrs. Ferguson. In his talk with her Johnstone suggested that Reed, if he would exert his influence to settle the war, might command "ten thousand guineas and the best post in the government, and if you should see him, I could wish you would convey that idea to him."[60] Mrs. Ferguson said later she was "hurt and shocked" at this suggestion, and that she asked Johnstone if he did not think "that Mr. Reed will look upon such a mode of obtaining his influence as a bribe?" To which Johnstone replied: "By no means, madam. This mode of proceeding is customary in all negotiations, and one may very honorably make it a man's interest to step forth in a cause."[61]

When Reed returned to Philadelphia with the American army on June 18, he found a message from Mrs. Ferguson asking for an interview. Their meeting took place three days later, at which time Mrs. Ferguson repeated Johnstone's offer, to which Reed made his famous reply to the effect that he was not worth purchasing, but such as he was, the King of England was not rich enough to buy him.[62]

For several weeks after this incident, Reed was silent about it, presumably to protect Mrs. Ferguson.* Not until Morris and Francis Dana publicly revealed approaches to them by Johnstone, and Congress ordered all letters received by its members be placed before the body, did Reed speak up. His news in July 1778 caused the greatest sensation, and Congress ordered all the Johnstone letters published. On August 11 it further adopted a resolution which cited portions of the letters and Reed's meetings with an unidentified lady, and declared such activities were nothing less than "direct attempts to corrupt and bribe the Congress of the United States of America."[63]

So once again Britain's efforts to win over "some of the most respectable members of Congress" had ended in exposure and failure. At British headquarters in New York, Johnstone became an obvious handicap to the work of the commission and a decision was made that he return to England. He sailed a few months before the other commissioners also gave up the struggle. A year later, in September 1779, the full story of Johnstone's enterprise and Mrs. Ferguson's role was revealed when Reed published a pamphlet which contained most of the letters dealing with the affair.

* The state of Pennsylvania later condemned her loyalist husband as a traitor and seized his property. Although Mrs. Ferguson separated from him, the notoriety for her "thoughtless act" (carrying Duché's letter to Washington) continued to darken her later years.

VIII

There was one more such attempt made by Britain, aimed at persuading one of the most famous men of the Revolution, Benjamin Franklin, to use his influence to bring about an accommodation. This strange episode took the form of the bizarre "Weissenstein" letter, flung into the grate at Franklin's home outside Paris. Marked "secret and confidential," the letter was similar to Duché's letter to Washington, in that the following warning to Franklin was on the outside cover: "Read this in private, before you look at the other papers—but don't be imprudent enough to let any one see it before you have considered it thoroughly."[64]

Signed with an obvious pseudonym, "Charles de Weissenstein," the document was dated June 16, 1778, Brussels. It contained two enclosures: (1) "Project for allaying the present ferments in North America" and (2) "Great outline of the future government in North America." Who was its mysterious author? "It is an Englishman," the writer began, "who addresses you, but an Englishman neither a partisan of mere obstructive faction tending to confound all order of government, nor yet one who is an idolatrous worshipper of passive obedience to the *divine right of Kings*."

Continuing in this manner, with an attack on the past actions of both the Parliament and the ministry, the author patently strove to establish himself in Franklin's eyes as a friend of America. But, at the same time, he did not let the opportunity pass to assail France, America's new ally.

The progress of the new alliance [he assured Franklin] is easily foreseen, and to be traced out——For the present, and for a year or two to come, you will obtain the most ample promises, and ready acquiescence [from France]. Then will come evasions to your applications, contemptuous delays, and of a sudden declaration that you must shift for yourselves. England has been just served thus in the hopes of her present inability to resent the treatment—in that there may probably be a great mistake—but with respect to America there can be no such error, for when will she be able to combat France and compel her to adhere to treaties.

From this argument Weissenstein proceeded to the question of whether America had the power or resources to stand alone "as an independent empire." No, he answered his own question, America could not since the costs of a standing army and the creation of a regular navy were not within the ability of the country. "Yet without these, your rising state will neither be in a capacity to secure itself from hostile ravages, acquire new alliances, or preserve any beneficial purpose. . . . Your sea port towns at the mercy of an enemy, will be too insecure a deposit for the constituent stores of your commerce and the navigation so precarious as to sink almost all the profit."

In view of these unhappy circumstances (but recognizing American suspicions of the British administration and its representatives), the writer then posed the following question to Franklin: "Why not offer some conditions directly to the King himself?" The writer said he was assuming that America "is willing to treat" and he was prepared to transmit "into the King's own hands any proposals on your part, which are not couched in offensive terms."[65]

To facilitate the handling of Franklin's proposals, Weissenstein recommended a secret rendezvous. He suggested that Franklin deposit his reply at a certain spot in the Cathedral of Notre Dame, there to be picked up by a British agent who would have a paper in his hand "as if drawing or taking notes." For more positive identification, the agent also would wear a rose in his hat or in the lapel of his coat.

With what must have been raised eyebrows, Franklin turned from this remarkable letter to the enclosures. There he found further enlightenment in a paragraph which dealt with the British "Indemnity to the principal American leaders." Named to receive "offices or pensions for life at their option, according to the sums opposite their names," were Adams, Hancock, Washington, Franklin, etc. The sums were not listed, but the blank spaces next to the names invited filling in by the recipients. It was further stated that if the King should ever create American peerages, the persons named and their descendants would be among the first to receive them and, in addition: "Mr. Washington to have immediately brevet of Lieutenant General" in the British army.[66]

Franklin's first reactions to these amazing proposals are not known. John Adams, who was living with the Pennsylvania philosopher at the time, later reported that Franklin consulted with him, that it was agreed they would do nothing without informing the French, and that Franklin would prepare an answer. Adams said Franklin seemed convinced that the proposals had come directly from the King.[67]

In his reply to Weissenstein, Franklin began calmly enough, first disputing the point that France would cheat the United States, or fail to support her. He also took exception to the statement that America could not defend itself without Britain's help. "Our militia," he said dryly, "you find by experience are sufficient to defend our lands from invasion; and the commerce with us will be defended by all the nations who find an advantage in it. We, therefore, have not the occasion you imagine of fleets or standing armies, but may leave those expensive machines to be maintained for the pomp of princes, and the wealth of ancient states. We propose, if possible, to live in peace with all mankind."[68]

The main drift of Weissenstein's letter, continued Franklin, seemed to be "to impress me with an idea of your impartiality, by just censures of your ministers and measures, and to draw from me propositions of peace. . . . You yourself, sir, are quite unknown to me. You have not trusted me with your true name. . . . I may be indiscreet enough in many things, but certainly, if I were disposed to make propositions (which I cannot do, having none committed to me to make) I should never think of delivering them to the Lord knows who, to be carried to the Lord knows where, to serve no one knows what purposes."

Warming to his reply, Franklin said that he found the present approach to him "as insidious as that of your conciliatory bills. Your true way to obtain peace, if your ministers desire it, is to propose openly to the Congress fair and equal terms." Further, the offer of places, peerages, and pensions was enough to stamp the author. "This offer to corrupt us, sir, is with me your credentials, and convinces me that you are not a private volunteer in your application. It bears the stamp of British court character. It is even the signature of your King."[69]

According to Adams, the original Weissenstein documents and Franklin's reply were sent to the French foreign minister, Vergennes, who turned the matter over to the Paris police. The police surveillance report was later sent to Franklin. It said that a gentleman had appeared, at the day, hour, and place appointed. The man had wandered around the cathedral, gazing at the statues and pictures, but always keeping an eye out for the spot where Franklin was to deposit his reply. After some time the gentleman left and was followed to his hotel. The name he had assumed, said Adams, "was Colonel Fitz-something—an Irish name that I have forgotten."[70] His real name, according to the French police, was M. Jennings, a former captain of the King's guard in England.[71]

In any event, this attempt to persuade or bribe an important leader of the Revolution to desert his cause ended in failure, as had those in America. The irony of all these efforts was that the one major defection from the rebel side during the war—Benedict Arnold's—resulted not from any direct approach to him, but was initiated by the "base traitor" himself.

7

★★★

Overseas Propaganda

The propaganda war of the Revolution was not confined to the territory of the United States and Canada. Very early in the struggle the Americans realized that they would need outside help if they were to succeed in their war with Britain, and that such aid, economic and military, could come only from Europe. Whereupon, they invoked the instrument of propaganda in the effort to win friends among the European powers.

The American overseas propaganda campaign did not officially begin until July 4, 1776, the date of adoption of the *Declaration of Independence*. In the very first sentence of that famous document, Jefferson said it was "a decent respect to the opinions of mankind" which had called forth the *Declaration*. In reality, however, he was appealing to the one country which had shown more than passing interest in the North American convulsions—to France, which six months earlier had sent a secret emissary to Philadelphia to hint to the colonists that they must first declare their independence of Britain before aid would be forthcoming. The American leaders came to realize that until the thirteen colonies announced a formal state of belligerency, no European power would risk interfering in England's "internal affairs."

The issuance of the *Declaration* was the real beginning of

America's campaign to woo the friendly and unfriendly nations of Europe. In charge of the overseas propaganda program (in the informal sense) was Doctor Franklin, working in co-ordination with the French. Congress had dispatched the seventy-year-old philosopher to Paris late in 1776 as one of three commissioners charged with the mission of obtaining formal recognition of the United States, and economic assistance. The other Americans, who were already in Europe, were Silas Deane and Arthur Lee.

Although Franklin was well known in Europe for his scientific, literary, and philosophical achievements, his arrival in France in December 1776 made an unexpected and tremendous impression on the French public. "No one," wrote Carl Van Doren, "could have foreseen the outburst of enthusiasm which made Franklin overnight the most famous man in the world in French opinion."[1] The reasons for this were various, but undoubtedly most important was the fact that France had been dreaming of revenge against Britain ever since her humiliation in the Seven Years' War. When, to their pleasure, the famed Benjamin Franklin stood on their soil, the French acclaimed him as being not only "a rational sage" like Voltaire, and "a child of nature" like Rousseau,[2] but also as the man who (rumor said) had single-handedly created the American Revolution.

The adulation Franklin received was to be of great use to him, not only in his diplomatic efforts but also in the propaganda campaign he immediately embarked upon. In time, in fact, his own image was to become an American propaganda symbol, reproduced by the enthusiastic French in dozens of portraits, in miniatures, medallions, statuettes, drawings, and prints; and on rings, handkerchiefs, and snuffboxes.[3]

Prior to Franklin's arrival the French themselves had given publicity to two important American propaganda documents— Paine's *Common Sense* and Jefferson's *Declaration of Independence.* Both were published by government order in *Affaires de l'Angleterre et de l'Amérique,* a periodical printed covertly by the French Foreign Office under a faked Antwerp date line. Because its sponsorship was hidden, *Affaires* was considered a safe publication in which the still neutral French could counter British propaganda on the continent. (The British had a number of propaganda outlets in Europe, one of which was a paper called the *Courrier de l'Europe*, published in Holland but with a wide circulation in France.)[4]

Writing from Paris about *Common Sense* in August 1776, Silas Deane informed Congress that the French version had had "a greater run, if possible, here than in America," and had stirred the enthusiasm of France for the American cause.[5] In December Deane also reported that the *Declaration* had become "an old story in every part of Europe" and was "well received."[6] However, in both instances the French had edited each document in an effort to tone down some of the anti-monarchial sentiments expressed in them, and they also added certain "explanatory" notes. Some months later copies of the original *Declaration* reached Europe, and these unexpurgated versions were scattered throughout the continent by the American agents.

Franklin's first significant propaganda activity came shortly after his arrival in Paris, when he obtained the translation and publication of an early draft of the *Articles of Confederation*, and also publication of the thirteen constitutions of the American states. In January 1777, while dining with the young Duc de la Rochefoucauld d'Enville, Franklin either persuaded Rochefoucauld or the latter volunteered to make the translations of the constitutions.[7] They appeared separately in *Affaires,* and were later published together in a compilation edited by Rochefoucauld.

I

That the Pennsylvania philosopher clearly understood the role of political propaganda was revealed in a letter he wrote to Richard Price towards the end of the war. Speaking of the limitations of the ancient Greek and Roman orators, who could reach but a limited audience assembled within hearing of their voices, Franklin remarked: "Now by the press we can speak to nations; and good books and well written pamphlets have great and general influence. The facility with which the same truths may be repeatedly enforced by placing them daily in different lights in *newspapers*, which are everywhere read, gives a great chance of establishing them. And we now find, that it is not only right to strike while the iron is hot, but that it may be very practicable to heat it by continually striking."[8]

In Paris Franklin was able to strike repeatedly in the ready-made platforms offered him by the French papers, covert or otherwise. *Affaires*, in particular, served as a vehicle for numerous Franklinian articles. Very early Franklin made contact with the editor, Edmund Charles Genet (who also was translator for the French Foreign Office), and began sending in propaganda items. During the four years of *Affaires'* existence (it stopped publication in December 1779), the paper reprinted a number of famous Franklin essays, including his *Edict of the King of Prussia*, a parody of the English King's claim to arbitrary rule over America, and his *Rules by Which a Great Empire May Be Reduced to a Small One*.[9]

In addition to these original contributions, Franklin sent Genet many extracts taken from American newspapers, relating to the war in America, and pro-American propaganda writings by his English friend, Richard Price. Letters from colleagues in America concerning political-military events also provided items for the French gazettes.[10] In these ways an American hearing was easily obtained in France.

It was much more difficult, however, to get rebel propaganda into other European newspapers. Yet even here the distinguished American's reputation served him; certain liberal European publishers wrote to Franklin and asked for American news to counterbalance the flood of British propaganda. For example, one such writer, Reinier Arrenberg, introduced himself in a letter to Franklin on March 31, 1777, as second secretary of the Physical Society of Rotterdam as well as publisher of the *Gazetteer Française de Leide*. Arrenberg announced his willingness to pay for any news Franklin could send.[11]

Franklin took advantage of this opportunity and started a flow of American propaganda to Arrenberg which continued for several years. For assistance in operating this "news service," Franklin called upon the American agent in Holland, Charles William Frederick Dumas (see below). Among the stories Arrenberg published was one dealing with the cruel treatment meted out against American prisoners by the English—a theme which was well exploited by the American propagandists during the war.

Besides Arrenberg, a number of other volunteer publishers offered their services. In December 1777 one C. S. Peuch of Utrecht wrote to Franklin requesting prompt and authentic news of America for his *Gazette*.[12] From Germany a Baron de Hupsch, publisher of the *Universal Gazette* in Cologne, begged Franklin in June 1778 to make contributions from time to time to counter, he said, the pro-English propaganda being disseminated by paid journals of the various German states.[13]

All these European volunteers helped Franklin in his job of spreading American views and doctrines throughout the Continent. His most important assistance, however, came from Charles Dumas, his friend at The Hague. A native of Switzerland and an active pro-American, Dumas had been recommended to Congress by Franklin as a man who might gather intelligence in Europe and serve in related capacities. An offer to serve as an American agent was made to Dumas in December 1775, which offer he accepted.

A writer and man of deep learning, Dumas was acquainted with many of the professors and other western European intelligentsia who were active in publishing various Dutch and French-language newspapers. He soon became involved in feeding rebel news items to such liberal papers as the *Gazette de Leide* and the *Courrier du Bas-Rhin,* as well as supplying information to Franklin and Congress' Committee of Secret Correspondence.

In the early years Dumas' letters to the committee often contained appeals "for news." For example, in a letter on June 14, 1777, Dumas reported that Europeans "complain everywhere of knowing nothing of your affairs but what the English wish Europe should know." On this subject, he said, "we have often to wait some months before the truth is unfolded from a heap of impostures, which do not fail sometimes to answer the malice of your enemies in leaving false impressions on minds."[14]

The committee attempted to send American newspapers and letters regularly to Europe, but the British navy was very active and many a packet of rebel papers ended up in London instead of Paris or Amsterdam, or in a watery grave. In this connection, Franklin wrote to Congress suggesting they investigate the possibility of dispatching once a month "little light vessels" to keep up a more regular correspondence. "Even the receiving letters of a certain date," Franklin said, "though otherwise of no importance, might serve to refute the false news of our adversaries on both sides of the water."[15] However, little seems to have been done by Congress; and communications across the Atlantic continued in haphazard fashion.

Operating as best he could under these limitations, Dumas spread the American message in the Dutch provinces and performed numerous outstanding services to the United States. A French historian has written that without his activities, "insurgent propaganda" in the Netherlands would have been insignificant or snuffed out at an early date by the wide-ranging activities of the British ambassador.[16] For five years Dumas filled the breach, until John Adams arrived in Amsterdam and took over personal direction of America's propaganda campaign in that country (see below).

II

In the year 1777 a striking propaganda document—a form of black propaganda*—began circulating in France. It was called *The Sale of the Hessians,* was written originally in French, and is attributed to Franklin.[17] The text centered on the treaties between Great Britain and the German princes for the hire of the mercenaries. Most of these treaties contained a "blood money" provision—that is, the prince would receive levy money for each man killed amounting to about seven pounds per man, with three wounded men reckoned as one killed. Franklin, of course, was well acquainted with these treaties, having served on one of the congressional propaganda committees which prepared an appeal to the German soldiers. The American philosopher was particularly appalled at and contemptuous of the German rulers who, he charged, had "sold the blood of their people."[18]

The Sale probably came from Franklin's pen shortly after news reached Europe (in March 1777) of Washington's victory over the Hessians at Trenton. The document was in the form of a letter, dated February 18, 1777, from Count de Schaumbergh to Baron Hohendorf, Commanding the Hessian Troops in America (both names being fakes). In the letter the Count spoke of his great joy at learning that, "of the 1,950 Hessians engaged in the fight, but 345 escaped. There were just 1,605 men killed, and I cannot sufficiently commend your prudence in sending an exact list of the dead to my minister in London. This precaution was the more necessary, as the report sent to the English ministery does not give but 1,455 dead. This would make 483,450 florins instead of the 643,500 florins which I am entitled to demand under our convention."[19]

The supposed Count de Schaumbergh continued his letter,

* Black propaganda purports to emanate from a source other than the true one.

attributing the differences between British and German casualty lists to a dispute over the listing of wounded men. Regarding the wounded, the count expressed confidence that Baron Hohendorf would not try "by human succor to recall the life of the unfortunates whose days could not be lengthened but by the loss of a leg or an arm. That would be making them a pernicious present, and I am sure they would rather die than live in a condition no longer fit for my service. I do not mean by this that you should assassinate them. We should be humane, my dear Baron, but you may insinuate to the surgeons with entire propriety that a crippled man is a reproach to their profession, and that there is no wiser course than to let every one of them die when he ceases to be fit to fight."[20]

The Sale of the Hessians was first circulated in manuscript form in France, and later reprinted in support of the growing European protests against the sale of German manpower to England. To the British and German leaders the furor was, at least, embarrassing.

III

"All Europe is on our side of the question, as far as applause and good wishes can carry them," Franklin wrote in May 1777 to Samuel Cooper.[21] The British government, finding European opinion favoring the underdog rebels, and noting a growing anti-English attitude, was disturbed, especially so after the Americans gained new prestige with their success at Trenton. In an attempt to halt and reverse this trend, British propagandists appear to have resorted to numerous false reports and rumors. One such report, for example, claimed Franklin was only a deserter who had had a terrible quarrel with Congress and really wished to submit to England. Another claimed the Americans, in talks with the Howe brothers, had already agreed to reconciliation with England.

Until this latter report in particular could be refuted, doubts were created in European minds as to the American cause. In late 1777, when Congress received word from Paris of this story, it quickly adopted a resolution denouncing "the insidious enemies of the United States of America" who had "endeavoured to propagate in Europe false and groundless reports" of a treaty between Congress and the King's commissioners. Congress directed Franklin and the other Americans overseas to inform the European powers "that no treaty whatever has been held between the king of Great Britain or any of his Commissioners and the said United States since their declaration of independence."[22]

A month prior to this resolution's adoption, the momentous news of Burgoyne's surrender at Saratoga was sent speeding to Europe via several fast ships, including the *Ranger* under John Paul Jones. Jones reached Nantes on December 2, 1777 and hurried to Paris, only to learn he had been beaten by twelve hours by Jonathan Loring Austin of Boston, who had sailed aboard a French vessel.

No news received in Europe during the revolutionary war had such tremendous impact on public opinion there, as did the British surrender at Saratoga. It was an event so completely unexpected, that it was, for that very reason, a huge American propaganda success. Franklin, his French allies, and Dumas saw to it that the story of Burgoyne and Saratoga was spread throughout the Continent. Dumas later wrote in a letter of congratulations to the Americans: "This news has made the greatest possible sensation in this country; a deep consternation among those who have all their interest in England, a marked joy among those who hate your enemies."[23]

The three American commissioners, Franklin, Deane, and Lee, reported to Congress the news of Saratoga had "occasioned as much general joy in France as if it had been a victory of their own troops over their own enemies."[24] The commissioners added they had taken the opportunity to press the French ministry for conclusion of the long-sought-for recognition of American independence. Not long thereafter the treaty was finally concluded (on February 5, 1778).

The one event during this period which Britain could point to with pride, although it was spoiled by Burgoyne's surrender, was the capture of Philadelphia. But the Americans disparaged the significance of that event. Richard Henry Lee, in a letter to his brother, Arthur Lee, offered suggestions on what to tell the French ministry about Howe's seizure of Philadelphia. The latter (Arthur Lee) sent an edited version of his brother's letter to Count de Vergennes on December 6, 1777:

> Suffer me here to observe a little [Richard Henry Lee had written] upon the enemy's possession of Philadelphia. In Europe where our affairs are not so well understood perhaps it may make some noise. When first entered into this war we not only considered but openly declared, that we regarded our great towns as indefensible . . . that the possession of them would avail little toward the accomplishment of the views of our enemies. With us, therefore, the enemy's possession of Philadelphia is really of little importance. In truth our towns are only as spots upon the great map of our strength. But it is far from certain that Gen. Howe will retain Philadelphia two months. . . . Boston was once theirs. They have no reason to triumph on that.[25]

IV

The fourth year of the war saw Franklin's attention turn to what appeared to be a fertile field for American propaganda— across the Irish sea. As early as July 1775 Congress had addressed itself to the people of Ireland, seeking support against England, and had suggested that the Irish themselves were not "without grievances."[26] The Irish indeed had many complaints against Great Britain: English laws had nearly ruined their industry; Irish farmers felt exploited by landlords; and the Irish Parliament worked in England's interest by means of corruption.

In addition to their common grievances, America and Ireland were tied together by the fact that the latter country had played an important role sending immigrants to America, many of whom were fighting in Washington's army. These circumstances created a natural bond of sympathy between the Irish and Americans. Thus by 1778, when Ireland's disaffection reached a crisis stage, Franklin's interest was stimulated; and, on October 4, 1778, he printed an address *To the Good People of Ireland*.[27]

In the most sympathetic tones Franklin spoke of the "misery and distress which your ill-fated country has been so frequently exposed to." The British ministry, the Parliament, the King—all came in for Franklin's censure as he reviewed the events which had led the Americans to take up arms. "I have it in my commission," Franklin also said, "to repeat to you, my good friends, the cordial concern that Congress takes in everything that relates to the happiness of Ireland; they are sensibly affected by the load of oppressive pensions on your establishments; the arbitrary and illegal exactions of public money by King's letters; the profuse dissipation by sinecure appointments with large salaries, and the very arbitrary and impolitic restrictions of your trade and manufactures, which are beyond example in the history of the world."

Despite these circumstances, which might call for an Irish rebellion, Franklin urged Ireland to remain "peaceable and quiet" for the time being. But he added, subversively, should the British government, "whom you at this time acknowledge," not remove the restraints on Irish trade, commerce, and manufacturing, "I am charged to assure you that means will be found to establish your freedom."[28]

This appeal was printed on Franklin's press at Passy and turned over to a "Dutch smuggler" at Brest to carry to Ireland. The vessel unfortunately was intercepted by an English privateer and the papers confiscated (and forwarded to the Admiralty). However, Franklin apparently had not put all his broadsides in one basket because other copies made their way into Irish hands. On November 4, 1778—a month after it came off Franklin's press—the *Hibernian Journal,* an Irish Whig newspaper, reprinted the address.[29]

The encouragement of Irish disaffection at this time also was helped by news of the activities of John Paul Jones. Sailing unmolested in the Irish seas, in April and May 1778 Jones raided the English and Scottish coasts, partly in retaliation for the burning of American towns. The news of these raids, and the toll he took of British commerce, not only caused panic in the seaport towns of England but also sent insurance rates soaring on British shipping. Franklin in addition had commissioned several Irish-manned privateers, which also were extremely active against English shipping, seizing dozens of vessels.[30]

Irish domestic agitation, John Paul Jones's successes, and American propaganda began to worry the British authorities. To the ministry it must have seemed that a rebellion in their backyard, in imitation of the American insurrection, was in the making; and that an Irish Washington and an Irish Congress would soon emerge. By late 1779 the Irish crisis reached a climax. When it appeared almost too late to halt Ireland's drift to rebellion, the British moved quickly to stem the tide. In December the government announced an important program of concessions to the Irish—commercial and religious—which had the effect of turning Irish public opinion temporarily away from insurrection.

During the months preceding the height of Irish agitation, the psychological war against Britain threatened to turn into a real invasion by French and Spanish forces. A large portion of the French propaganda paper, *Affaires,* had been devoted to elaborate descriptions of plans for the invasion of England. *Affaires* reminded the British of the many past landings by invaders, and warned that the Channel did not constitute an insuperable barrier.[31]

In the summer of 1779, following Spain's entrance into the

war against England (in May), some 50,000 French troops were mustered along the coast of France while a French–Spanish armada moved towards England with the mission of clearing the seas of the British navy. The invasion threat produced much excitement in London; and a royal proclamation, dated July 9, directed that all horses, oxen, and cattle which might be used by the invading forces be driven away from the coasts, or other steps taken so they would not fall into enemy hands.[32]

The King's proclamation awakened the British people to their danger; and with the awakening came much recriminations against the King's ministers, who were attacked for "obstinately persisting in affirming that the kingdom was in perfect safety" and for their "total want of preparation."[33] The landings, however, failed to come off, apparently because of indecision by the French commander, who tarried in the Channel until a typhoid epidemic among the crews and a storm so disrupted his fleet that he was forced back to Brest.

John Paul Jones, in the meantime, had sailed off looking for prizes; and, in September, he came across the English vessels, *Serapis* and the *Countess of Scarborough*. In the famous battle in which his own ship, the *Bonhomme Richard*, went down, Jones boarded and took the fifty-gun *Serapis*. This remarkable victory—the capture of a larger warship by a smaller one—was the talk of Europe for many months and enhanced the American cause. In a letter of congratulations to Jones, Franklin told the spectacular commander that "scarce any thing was talked of at Paris and Versailles but your cool conduct and persevering bravery during that terrible conflict. You may believe that the impression on my mind was not less strong than on that of others."[34]

Jones took his prizes into the Dutch port of Texel, and his presence there gave Dumas and the French propagandists in Holland an opportunity to organize noisy demonstrations for the new American hero, who was warmly received by the public.[35] Speaking of Jones's activities in a letter to a friend, who had reported the British punitive raids in Connecticut,* Franklin later wrote: "We have given them a little taste of this disturbance upon their own coasts this summer; and, though we have burnt none of their towns, we have occasioned a good deal of terror and bustle in many of them, as they imagined our Commodore Jones had four thousand troops with him for descents."[36]

v

In the sixth year of the war the American propagandists in Europe suffered a setback which was a consequence of British victories in the southern states, in particular the capture of Charleston. Unaware that events were going against them in the south, the Americans set in motion a propaganda letter that boomeranged almost as soon as it appeared. The incident occurred in May 1780, when an American at Lorient forwarded to Franklin a copy of a letter that had been printed in a Philadelphia newspaper on April 8. The letter was supposedly written by the British commander in America, General Clinton, to Lord Germain. In it Clinton voiced doubts about his chances of success in the expedition against Charleston. The letter contained such premonitions of disaster that it seemed Clinton was putting his reservations on record in order to be able to defend himself in case of failure.

Although Franklin said he had doubts "whether some parts" of the letter had really been written by Clinton, in forwarding it to Dumas, he commented: "I have no doubt of the facts stated, and think the piece valuable, as giving a true account of British and American affairs in that quarter."[37] Franklin requested Dumas to publish the letter; and he also dispatched a copy to England, where he hoped his British friends would manage to reprint it there.

* See Chapter 5, p. 153.

Dumas had misgivings about the letter's authenticity; but he delivered it to the editor of the *Courrier du Bas-Rhin,* who published it in June. Whereupon, the British ambassador to the Netherlands, Sir Joseph Yorke, promptly denounced the document as a forgery. Within a few days Yorke's position was fully vindicated by the arrival of news from America of the capitulation of Charleston to the British. The *Courrier's* chagrined editor, who had welcomed American news, felt he had been duped; and in another article he promptly attacked the letter and its American instigators.

In this incident serious damage was done to the American reputation for disseminating "the truth." William Lee, who was in Brussels when the affair was exposed, wrote to John Adams to express concern over it. "You must be sensible," he said, "of the injury it will bring to America and the cause of liberty, if the world is permitted to be impressed with the idea that Congress and its agents are base enough to be guilty of such a mean and pitiful conduct as to forge and publish the greatest falsehoods as solid truths."[38]

This faux pas led Franklin and Adams to begin an investigation into the origins of the letter and, on July 20, Adams reported to Lee: "Within a few days past I have seen a gentleman from America who says it was a mere *jeu d'esprit,* written by an officer in the army. . . . I have been all along afraid that our countrymen would at length imitate their enemies in this kind of imposition. . . . We have no need for such aids as political lies. Our character for truth, sincerity and candor is more real strength than ever can be derived from such impostures, however artfully performed."[39] Adams thus took a stand for a "campaign of truth," in which black propaganda would have little place. Such a policy, however, would have been very constricting indeed on that master of the hoax and faked letter, Benjamin Franklin.

The incident had been clumsily handled only because communications with America were so poor, and the Americans in Europe had no way of knowing how military events were progressing. Thus, in the summer of 1780, as British hopes revived with the great victory at Charleston, American supporters in Europe grew silent. On July 22 Dumas wrote plaintively to Congress: "It is to be wished that we may soon receive news from America which will raise again the courage of friends of the United States, to whom the misfortune of Charleston has caused much pain, in proportion as it has reanimated those who favor your enemies. The latter, in the meantime, forge and utter every day rumors injurious to the United States, such as that they are about to submit."[40]

Although no news of a decisive nature was received from America, by September Dumas was able to report that Dutch public opinion was slowly recovering from "the false notions" caused by the capture of Charleston.[41] Meanwhile, Dumas was busy briefing his American guest, John Adams, who had arrived in Amsterdam the previous month.

VI

Adams' role as an American propagandist in Europe is not as well known as that of Franklin, although he made a number of important contributions in both Holland and in France. The New Englander had first arrived in France in 1778 to replace Silas Deane; and, prior to his return to America in August 1779, he became acquainted with Genet and was asked to contribute articles to *Affaires*.[42]

It was not, however, until Adams' second trip to Europe in 1780 as Congress' "peace commissioner" that he became a full-fledged publicist for the American cause. By this time *Affaires* had been dropped as a publication by the French Foreign Office. But, as Adams reported to Congress on February 23, "those political intelligences and speculations which were formerly published" in *Affaires* were finding outlets in the *Mercure de France* and the *Gazette de France,* both published overtly by the French government under Genet's direction.[43]

Soon after his second arrival in France Adams wrote to Genet, offering himself as a regular contributor to his papers. The English news dispatches from New York, Adams complained, were entirely fabricated. "I see thousands of these things every day that might easily be counteracted," he wrote. "I do not wish you to publish anything against your rules; and if ever I propose anything of that sort, it will be from ignorance or inattention; and I rely upon your knowledge and prudence to check it. But as I am likely to have a little more leisure than I have had for a long time, if you will give me leave, I will assist you a little in your labors for the public good."[44]

Genet accepted Adams' offer; and on May 17 he sat down to his first effort, a lengthy counter-argument to a speech made several weeks earlier in the House of Commons by General Henry Conway. In his speech Conway had said, among other things, that the alliance between France and America was unnatural. Adams, of course, took the opposite view in his letter to Genet, insisting that the two countries were "natural allies" because their interests were the same. Customs, languages, and religion were much less important than other essential interests in deciding the friendship and enmity of nations. In fact, Adams continued, the people of America were "universally of the opinion that, from the time they declared themselves independent, England became their natural enemy" and, since the latter had been for centuries the natural enemy of France, consequently America was "the natural friend of France."[45]

Adams' initial contribution was translated into French and published in the *Mercure de France* on June 3, 1780. A copy of it also was dispatched to London, where friends of the United States managed to get it reprinted in the *General Advertiser*.

On May 28 Adams completed another counter-argument, which also was published in the two newspapers above. This essay was a point-by-point refutation of a speech made by Lord

Germain, which also had attacked the French–American alliance. Adams argued that:

> . . . every step of Congress, every proceeding of every assembly upon the continent, every prayer that is made in the pulpit, and every speculation in the newspapers demonstrates the high sense they have of the importance of this alliance. It is said that this alliance has been of little utility. Has it not employed the British army? has it not cut out work enough for the British navy? has it not wasted for England her annual twenty millions? has it not prevented these from being employed against America? has it not given scope to American privateers? has it not protected the American trade? has it not hurt that of Great Britain?[46]

These arguments were irrefutable and, when published in the London press, must have made sad reading in ministerial circles.

VII

When Adams reached Amsterdam in the summer of 1780, in pursuit of a Dutch loan and recognition of the United States, the Netherlands was in a state of political transition. An important maritime nation, the Netherlands had come into conflict with England for conducting a clandestine trade with the Americans, and for trading in naval supplies with the French. To protect their commerce from British seizure, the Dutch began to explore the idea of joining the newly formed Armed Neutrality, an agreement of the small naval powers of Europe (led by Russia) which aimed at protecting their shipping against all belligerents.

This was the political situation when Adams arrived in Amsterdam. He soon contacted the "indefatigable" Dumas, who became his aide, translator, and contact man; and within a few weeks he learned some of the problems facing an American propagandist in that conservative country. Writing of this to Franklin in October, Adams exclaimed:

It is necessary for America to have agents in different parts of Europe, to give some information concerning our affairs, and to refute the abominable lies that the hired emissaries of Great Britain circulate in every corner of Europe, by which they keep up their own credit and ruin ours. I have been more convinced of this, since my peregrinations in this country, than ever. The universal and profound ignorance of America here has astonished me. It will require time and a great deal of prudence and delicacy to undeceive them.[47]

To enlighten the Dutch, Adams turned to his writing table; and his productions soon were going out to such editors as John Luzac of the *Leyden Gazette* and A. M. Cerisier, of the *Lettres Hollandois,* the latter being a paper originating in the French legation at The Hague. These publications, Adams later wrote to Robert Livingston, "have a vast influence in forming . . . public opinion."[48]

One of the most interesting of Adams' propaganda feats during this period followed a conversation with one Hendrik Calkoen, whom he later described as "the first gentleman of the bar at Amsterdam; a man of letters, well read in law and history, and an elegant writer." Calkoen asked for information on American affairs and, Adams recalled: "I gave him a collection of our constitutions, and a number of pamphlets and papers, and desired him to commit to writing his questions."[49]

Calkoen had many questions, twenty-six in all; and during the month of October 1780 Adams applied himself to answering them. The Dutch lawyer's questions covered military, political, and economic topics and were in the form of challenges to Adams to prove certain points. For example, Calkoen asked Adams to "show that America, notwithstanding the war, daily increases in strength and force."

To this Adams replied (excerpts):

It has been found by calculations that America has doubled her numbers, even by natural generation alone, upon an average about once in eighteen years. This war has now lasted six years; in the course of it we commonly compute in America that we have lost by sickness and the sword and captivity about five-and-thirty thousand men. But the numbers of people have not increased less than seven hundred and fifty thousand souls, which gives at least a hundred thousand fighting men. We have not less, probably, than seventy thousand fighting men in America more than we had on the day that hostilities were first commenced on the 19th of April 1775. There are near twenty thousand fighting men added to the numbers in America every year. Is this the case of our enemy, Great Britain? Which then can maintain the war the longest?[50]

Calkoen also challenged Adams to prove that no single person in America had so much power and influence "that his death, or corruption by English money" could have any significant effect on the American struggle. Here Adams insisted with much fervor that the Revolution's success was not dependent upon any man. "If there ever was a war that could be called *the people's war,** Adams wrote, "it is this of America against Great Britain; it having been determined on by the people, and pursued by the people in every step of its progress."[51]

The British government, Adams continued, had repeatedly deluded itself by hopefully seeking and seeing in such individuals as Hancock, Dickinson, Franklin, Samuel Adams, and himself, "the soul" of the Revolution. But, said Adams, all these men had been absent from the central fulcrum of the Revolution, the Congress, for years, "yet Congress has been as active and as capable as before. . . . In short, sir, all these pretences are the most ridiculous imaginable. The American cause stands upon the essential, unalterable character of the whole body of the people."[52] Not even the defection of such a famous man as General Washington, "which I know to be impossible," declared Adams, could subvert the American cause.

Throughout his discussions Adams sought to demonstrate to Calkoen that Britain could not conquer America, and to bolster

* Adams' emphasis.

his argument he called upon the words of two "unwilling witnesses and cruel enemies"—Generals Burgoyne and Howe. Both these retired British generals had published in 1780 separate statements in defense of their conduct in America, one being *The Narrative of Lieut. General Sir William Howe*, presented to a committee of the House of Commons on April 29, 1779, and the other, Burgoyne's *A State of the Expedition from Canada*.

Adams, citing the words of the two British commanders, demolished any doubts that might have remained about the fighting abilities of the colonists or America's chances of victory. Burgoyne had declared several times in his testimony that "the Americans possess the *quality* and *faculty* of fighting" and that it was absurd for English critics to continue to insist that the Americans were a rabble who could not fight.[53] General Howe also had enlightened a House of Commons committee on the many difficulties facing British military operations in North America. Almost every movement in the colonies, Howe had said, "was an act of enterprise, clogged with innumerable difficulties. A knowledge of the country, intersected as it everywhere is, by woods, mountains, waters or morasses, cannot be obtained with any degree of precision necessary to foresee and guard against, the obstruction that may occur."[54]

Adams' performance was unquestionably effective. He answered Calkoen's twenty-six questions in ten letters, written between October 4 and 27, 1780. Burgoyne's and Howe's pamphlets were translated into French (one into Dutch) for wider distribution. Calkoen not only became an adherent to the American cause (he later helped Adams draw up petitions to the merchants of Amsterdam favoring American independence), but he also undertook to spread American ideas among "a society of gentlemen of letters" which met regularly in Amsterdam.

During his continuing sojourn in Holland Adams also became acquainted with Baron Jan Derck van der Capellen, one of the former regents of Amsterdam, who had been ousted for his liberal and anti-English views. Van der Capellen had begun a correspondence with several American patriots, including Livingston and Franklin, and was one of a number of Dutchmen who had quietly agitated against English influence in the Netherlands.

Adams later wrote of van der Capellen that he had had "frequent and intimate conversations" with him and that "he has been of the utmost service to our cause . . . I dare not say in what a multitude of ways he has served us. Posterity will, perhaps, know them all."[55] One of these services was van der Capellen's secret publication in September 1781 of an appeal *To the People of the Netherlands,* in which he attacked the conservative Dutch authorities who had deferred to Britain. The baron had ended his appeal with the following cry: "Let all be ready, every man with his musket, bayonet and side arms, let them follow the example of the people of America where not a drop of blood was shed till the English struck the first blow, and Jehovah will support our righteous cause."[56]

This inflammatory Dutch pamphlet had an effect reportedly like "an electric shock." Spread clandestinely through the principal cities of Holland, it led the Dutch authorities to offer a $2,500 reward for the arrest of the unknown author or printer. It also was banned from being reprinted, published, or circulated. However, the secret of van der Capellen's authorship was kept well hidden and was revealed only many years after the Revolution by a friend.[57]

What did all this agitation and propaganda mean on the political and diplomatic level? Together with British reprisals against Dutch commerce, American propaganda certainly played a role in the shift of public opinion in Holland away from Britain and towards the French–American alliance. By December 1780, when the Dutch began to seriously consider joining the Armed Neutrality, the worried London government concluded that it would be more convenient for the British navy to have the Netherlands as a belligerent and she declared war on The Hague. Thus by January 1781 the conflict, which had begun with the American insurrection, had spread into a war encompassing France, Spain, Holland, and the Americans on one side, and Britain on the other.

It was under these circumstances that Adams succeeded in winning formal recognition of American independence from the Netherlands in April 1782, and shortly thereafter a substantial loan. Finally, in October of the same year, he concluded a treaty of amity and commerce—the second such treaty for the new American nation.

Adams was not bashful about claiming credit for the American success in Holland. In a letter to Livingston in September 1782 he quoted the Spanish minister at The Hague as telling him: "Sir, you have struck the greatest blow of all Europe. It is the greatest blow that has been struck in the American cause, and the most decisive. It is you who have filled this nation with enthusiasm; it is you who have turned all their heads."[58] Adams was delighted to record "things which were certainly said with deliberation," although he recognized that the charge of vanity might be flung afterwards at him, as it was.

VIII

In the spring of 1782, with the peace negotiations underway in Paris between Franklin and a British representative, another item of black propaganda began to circulate in the salons of Europe. It was a brain-child of Franklin and was in the form of the extraordinary *Supplement to the Boston Independent Chronicle*. Franklin's purpose in publishing this document was to stir public opinion against Britain during the peace talks, in hopes of gaining concessions.

Printed on his press at Passy, the *Supplement* had every appearance of an actual newspaper supplement, complete with advertisements. The main feature of the paper was a letter purportedly from a New England militia captain, who wrote that he had intercepted eight large packages containing the scalps of American frontiersmen, their women and children, and scalps of soldiers. Included with the packages was an address from the Seneca Indians to Governor Haldimand in Canada, asking that the scalps be forwarded to King George "that he may regard them and be refreshed; and that he may see our faithfulness in destroying his enemies."[59]

Each package was further broken down into a complicated inventory, which listed in detail how the various scalps had been obtained. Package number one, for example, contained "43 scalps of Congress soldiers killed in different skirmishes; these are stretched on black hoops, 4 inches diameter; the inside of the skin painted red, with a small black spot to note their being killed by bullets. Also 62 of farmers killed in their houses; the hoops red; the skin painted brown, and marked with a hoe; and a black hatchet in the middle, signifying their being killed with that weapon." Other packages contained the scalps of women, some with no mark except "the short club," to show "they were knocked dead, or had their brains beat out."[60]

Franklin forwarded a copy of this gruesome "masterpiece"[61] to John Adams on April 22, and suggested: "If it were republished in England, it might make them a little ashamed of themselves." As was proper procedure when issuing black propaganda, Franklin was silent about the authorship (as was the case with *The Sale of the Hessians*). To Adams he professed "some doubt" as to the truth of the form of the *Supplement* but none, he said, "as to the substance, for I believe the number of people actually scalped in this murdering war by the Indians to exceed what is mentioned in [the] invoice."[62] The paper was subsequently reprinted in France and reached England, where Horace Walpole read it in an English gazette and immediately pronounced it as too good not to be by Franklin.[63]

The fact that a great deal of propaganda favorable to the American cause was published in England during the war was partly the accomplishment of certain pro-American, anti-government individuals in that country. These persons included the radical friends and correspondents of Franklin and other Americans, who by any strict interpretation of the law were "traitors" to King George's England.

They were not simply unorganized and scattered individuals who happened to disagree with the foreign policy of the British government. There was a certain informal subversive "apparatus," centering on a number of English clubs which Franklin had organized or joined just prior to the outbreak of the war, in particular *"The Society of 13"* or *"Deistic Society of 1774."* The members, who had been brought together by common interests, included such English and foreign intellectuals as David Williams, Thomas Bentley, Joshua Wedgewood, R. E. Raspe, John Horne Tooke, and John Paradise. Associated with them but apparently not members of the club were such well-known writers and scientists as Joseph Priestley, Richard Price, Benjamin Vaughn, and J. R. Foster.[64] Some were members of Parliament.

From this handful of Whiggish intellectuals, many lines went out into British society so that their overall influence was far greater than their numbers would warrant. However, in the early years of the war, it was very dangerous for these men to openly preach their views. For a time the Habeas Corpus Act was revoked; and at least one member, John Horne Tooke, was jailed for three years on a charge of libelling the King in a newspaper article. Yet even under these trying circumstances, such men as Priestley and Price—too well known to be intimidated —continued their pro-American writings and agitation.

Shortly after Franklin's arrival in Paris in 1777, members of the society renewed their contacts with him; and a steady flow of mail—some in ciphers and code—went back and forth across the Channel, often carried by smugglers or European travellers sympathetic to the American cause. These operations sometimes became so conspiratorial that on one occasion, in September 1777, Franklin arranged to meet Benjamin Vaughn *au naturel* in a Paris steam bathhouse![65]

One of the devices for getting intelligence from England was revealed by Franklin in a letter to James Lovell in August 1780. "I have had several volunteer correspondents in England," Franklin explained, "who have in their letters for years together communicated to me secrets of state, extracted from the newspapers."[66] It was with the help of these unpaid English volunteers that news and propaganda materials flowed both ways across the Channel. Towards the end of the war, these men, utilizing their various contacts, managed to slip many a pro-American story into the British press, providing an outlet in England for the voices of Franklin and Adams and the "voice of America."

8

★★

Washington, Congress, and the
Declaration of Independence: Epilogue

It may have been true, as John Adams asserted, that the American Revolution was effected in the hearts and minds of the people "before the war commenced."[1] However, the war was the real test and proof of the people's commitment. Although throughout the struggle the British government resorted to many devices to shake the rebelling colonists from their separatist notions, the stubborn Americans, as we have seen, clung to their *Declaration*. They clung also to one of the most important characters on the colonial scene, a man who became as much a propaganda symbol to the Americans as the words "liberty" and "independence." He was, of course, the enigmatic Virginian who became commander-in-chief of the American army, George Washington.

Washington was one of the indispensable figures of the Revolution, even as Congress was the movement's essential director. For eight long years Washington commanded the American army. During the same period the British government changed commanders four times. For eight years, even during the period of the so-called Conway cabal, when Washington's reputation had fallen, there was only one center of American resistance—*Washington's* army. As the years passed the name of Washington became a propaganda asset of first magnitude.

The reader who dips even briefly into the correspondence of the Revolution is struck by the eminent position Washington attained in the minds of his contemporaries. His physical presence alone seems to have stirred as much awe as his real achievements. Of this, Douglas Southall Freeman once wrote: "Men caught their breath in admiration when they saw him on a spirited horse. Everything about him suggested the commander—height, bearing, flawless proportions, dignity of person, composure, and ability to create confidence by calmness and by unfailing, courteous dignity."[2]

In the eyes of Abigail Adams, who met Washington for the first time in 1775, "the gentleman and soldier" were blended in him, and modesty seemed to mark "every line and feature of his face."[3] To a Frenchman, Washington was "one of those masterpieces of nature," a born leader who inspired respect and confidence at first sight. "He was," wrote the Frenchman, "tall, his face was commanding, his eyes were kind, his language gracious, his gestures and words simple and above all a calm and firm behaviour harmonized all these qualities."[4]

A British officer who spent much of the war in American captivity was impressed by the unique reputation Washington had among his countrymen. Everywhere, wrote Thomas Anburey, Washington's name was spoken with great respect.[5] Patriot propagandists, it is true, cited the exploits of Washington with such great flights of language that another English observer could only record in amazement the American claims after Trenton: "Alexander, Pompey and Hannibal were but pigmy Generals, in comparison with the magnanimous Washington."[6] But Trenton *was* an important stroke, and tall stories are an American tradition.

Washington, of course, was more than a man who looked like a general, or a general whose deeds had been magnified.

Baltimore, *Dec.* 31, 1776.

This Morning Congress received the following Letter from General WASHINGTON.

Head-Quarters, Newtown, 27th Dec. 1776.

SIR,

I HAVE the Pleasure of congratulating you upon the Success of an Enterprize, which I had formed against a Detachment of the Enemy lying in Trenton, and which was executed Yesterday Morning.

The Evening of the 25th, I ordered the Troops intended for this Service, to parade back of M'Kenky's Ferry, that they might begin to pass as soon as it grew dark, imagining we should be able to throw them all over, with the necessary Artillery, by 12 o'Clock, and that we might easily arrive at Trenton by five in the Morning, the Distance being about nine Miles. But the Quantity of Ice, made that Night, impeded the Passage of the Boats so much, that it was three o'Clock before the Artillery could all be got over, and near four before the Troops took up their Line of March.

I formed my Detachment into two Divisions, one to march up the lower or River Road, the other by the upper or Pennington Road. As the Divisions had nearly the same Distance to march, I ordered each of them immediately upon forcing the out Guards, to push directly into the Town, that they might charge the Enemy before they had Time to form. The upper Division arrived at the Enemy's advanced Post exactly at 8 o'Clock, and in three Minutes after, I found, from the Fire on the lower Road, that that Division had also got up. The out Guards made but a small Opposition, though, for their Numbers, they behaved very well, keeping up a constant retreating Fire from behind Houses.

We presently saw their main Body formed, but, from their Motions, they seemed undetermined how to act. Being hard pressed by our Troops, who had already got Possession of Part of their Artillery, they attempted to file off by a Road, on their Right, leading to Princeton; but perceiving their Intention, I threw a Body of Troops in their Way, which immediately checked them. Finding, from our Disposition, that they were surrounded, and they must inevitably be cut to Pieces, if they made any further Resistance, they agreed to lay down their Arms. The Number that submitted, in this Manner, was 23 Officers, and 886 Men. Col. Rohl, the commanding Officer, and seven others, were found wounded in the Town. I do not exactly know how many they had killed; but I fancy not above twenty or thirty, as they never made any regular Stand. Our Loss is very trifling indeed; only two Officers and one or two Privates wounded.

I find that the Detachment of the Enemy consisted of the three Hessian Regiments of Landspatch, Kniphausen, and Rohl, amounting to about 1500 Men, and a Troop of Light Horse; but immediately ⟨upon the be⟩g⟨inning⟩ of the Attack, all those ⟨who were not killed or taken, pu⟩shed di⟨rectly down the⟩ Tow⟨n⟩

and taken Possession of the Bridge leading out of Town; but the Quantity of Ice was so great, that though he did every Thing in his Power to effect it, he could not get over. This Difficulty also hindered Gen. Cadwallader from crossing, with the Pennsylvania Militia, from Bristol; he got Part of his Foot over, but finding it impossible to embark his Artillery, he was obliged to desist. I am fully confident, that could the Troops under Generals Ewing and Cadwallader have passed the River, I should have been able, with their Assistance, to have driven the Enemy from all their Posts below Trenton; but the Numbers I had with me being inferior to theirs below me, and a strong Battalion of Light Infantry being at Princeton, above me, I thought it most prudent to return the same Evening with the Prisoners, and the Artillery we had taken. We found no Stores of any Consequence in the Town.

In Justice to the Officers and Men I must add, that their Behaviour upon this Occasion reflects the highest Honour upon them. The Difficulty of passing the River, in a very severe Night, and their March through a violent Storm of Snow and Hail, did not in the least abate their Ardour; but when they came to the Charge, each seemed to vie with the other in pressing forward, and were I to give a Preference to any particular Corps, I should do great Injustice to the others.

Colonel Baylor, my First Aid de Camp, will have the Honour of delivering this to you, and from him you may be made acquainted with many other Particulars; his spirited Behaviour, upon every Occasion, requires me to recommend him to your particular Notice.

I have the Honour to be, with great Respect, Sir, your most humble Servant,

G. Washington.

Inclosed I have sent you a particular List of the Prisoners, Artillery, and other Stores. RETURN of Prisoners taken at Trenton, the 26th December, 1776, by the Army under the Command of his Excellency General WASHINGTON.

Regiment of LANDSPATCH.
1 Lieutenant Colonel, 1 Major, 1 Captain, 3 Lieutenants, 4 Ensigns, 38 Serjeants, 6 Drummers, 5 Musicians, 209 Officers Servants, 206 Rank and File.
Regiment of KNIPHAUSEN.
1 Major, 2 Captains, 2 Lieutenants, 3 Ensigns, 25 Serjeants, 9 Drummers, 6 Officers Servants, 258 Rank and File.
Regiment of ROHL.
1 Colonel, 1 Lieut. Colonel, 1 Major, 2 Captain, 4 Lieutenants, 5 Ensigns, 2 Surgeons Mates, 25 Serjeants, 8 Drummers, 4 Musicians, 2 Officers Servants, 244 Rank and File.
Regiment of ARTILLERY.
1 Lieutenant, 4 Serjeants, 1 Officer's Servant, 32 Rank and File.
TOTAL———1 Colonel, 1 Lieutenant Colonels, 3 Majors, 4 Captains, 8 Lieutenants, 12 Ensigns, 2 Surgeons, 93 Serjeants, 10 Drummers, 9 Musicians, 15 Officers Servants, 740 Rank and File. 918 Prisoners.

6 double-fortified Brass Three Pounders, with Carriages ⟨com⟩plete.
⟨9 Ammuni⟩tion Waggons.
⟨1000 Stand of Arm⟩s, Bayonets, Cartouch-Boxes, and ⟨other Stores of the⟩ Prisoners.

A reproduction of Washington's letter to Congress on the important victory at Trenton. The letter gave great encouragement to the rebels.

In dealing with his army he was a master of most of the tricks and techniques that every successful commander must use to steel men against hardship and to stimulate them on the battle-field. We have noted Washington's use of his general orders to pass along news that boosted the army's morale. Through his general orders he praised men and units when they per-formed well,[7] or harangued them when discipline became lax. Understanding the importance of camp rumors, Washington also used them to raise the men's spirits—through seemingly casual conversation.[8] He was, one historian has written, the idol of the army: "A message from him could stir an entire corps to enthusiasm. His appearance in camp would produce general jubilation."[9]

Washington's fame was as great overseas as among his fel-low countrymen. Benjamin Franklin, who was not a man given to flattery, once reported Europe's applause in a letter to the General in 1780.

Should peace arrive after another campaign or two and afford us a little leisure [Franklin said] I should be happy to see your Excellency in Europe, and to accompany you if my age and strength would permit, in visiting some of its ancient and most famous kingdoms. You would on this side of the sea enjoy what posterity will say of Washington. For 1000 leagues have nearly the same effect with 1000 years. . . . At present I enjoy that pleasure for you, and I frequently hear the old generals of this martial country (who study the maps of America and mark upon them all your operations) speak with sincere approbation and great applause of your conduct; and join in giving you the character of one of the great captains of the age.[10]

More could be said about this great captain and his influence, but the point is clear: as a propaganda and political asset Washington from the very beginning greatly enhanced the American cause.

I

The Continental Congress was not the hero that Washington was to the people, it could never be; yet its role was even more crucial and significant than his. Of that organization, historian Claude Van Tyne once wrote: "The audacity of the Continental Congress will ever be a matter of wonder. Without unity in instruction, with no power to form a government, without jurisdiction over an acre of territory, with no authority to administer government in any acre if they had it, with no money, no laws and no means to execute them, they entered upon the task of regulating a society in the state of revolution."[11]

It is Congress' important and fascinating propaganda procedures that draw our attention. Within that enterprising organization of fifty to sixty men, there was, of course, no separate propaganda agency. They themselves, the delegates of the thirteen colonies, created propaganda through the process of debate and agreements on policy. A key aspect of this policy-making procedure was the ad hoc committee, appointed to prepare the necessary supporting documents as well as to consider, investigate, and recommend policies.

It was in the congressional committees that were born many of the American propaganda appeals to the Canadians, the orations to the Indians, the broadsides to the Hessians, etc. A useful and flexible system, this committee arrangement provided an outlet and opportunity for some of the best writers in Congress, such as Jefferson and John Dickinson, to put their skillful pens to work on the important policy papers that issued from that body.

Of all the great papers produced by Congress in this manner, perhaps the greatest from the point of view of propaganda was Jefferson's *Declaration of Independence*. Its issuance was, of course, not an isolated event. Six months before, in January

1776, the long smouldering issue of independence had burst into brilliant print with the appearance of Thomas Paine's pamphlet, *Common Sense,* in which the author levelled an attack on the monarchy and argued the merits of separation. Paine's pamphlet set off a great debate in the American press, a useful and important controversy which served in the months that followed to familiarize the American people with the idea of separation from Great Britain.[12]

Later, the rush to independence had begun in earnest when the various delegations in Congress received instructions from their home states to vote for separation, beginning first with North Carolina on April 12 and Virginia on May 15. The climax to the march to the *Declaration* came on Friday, June 7, when Richard Henry Lee of Virginia arose in Congress and introduced the following historic resolutions:

That these United Colonies are, and of right ought to be, free and independent states, that they are absolved from all allegiance to the British Crown, and that all political connection between them and the State of Great Britain is, and ought to be, totally dissolved.

That it is expedient forthwith to take the most effectual measures for forming foreign alliances.

That a plan of confederation be prepared and transmitted to the respective Colonies for their consideration and approbation.[13]

In the heated congressional debate that followed, a conservative group led by Dickinson won a preliminary victory over the radicals by gaining postponement of a decision on the resolutions until July 1. In the meantime, however, they agreed to the appointment of a committee to prepare a declaration of independence—in the event Congress should arrive at a decision.

On June 11 a Committee of Five was elected to draw up the declaration. Chosen were Jefferson, John Adams, Benjamin Franklin, Robert Livingston, and Roger Sherman. On the twelfth members of the other committees, to prepare the plan of treaties and plan of confederation, were elected. Of the Committee of Five, Jefferson was the only member who was free from duties on the other committees, Adams and Franklin being chosen members of the treaties group, and Livingston and Sherman serving on the confederation body.

Subsequently, when the Committee of Five met to discuss the project, Jefferson was chosen to write the declaration. The true reasons for his selection have been the subject of some dispute, but certainly they included the general inclination on the part of the other delegates "to put Virginia at the head of everything" because of that colony's great influence in the south. Whereupon, the 34-year-old Jefferson retired to write the paper.

In two days' time, as Jefferson later recalled, he completed a first draft, which he showed to Adams and Franklin. Both men made minor changes in wording. Jefferson revised the draft, making additional changes, before submitting it to the full committee, which reported it to Congress on June 28. It was not until July 2, when Congress officially voted for independence, that Jefferson's brain-child was examined paragraph by paragraph by the members. For three days—the second, third and fourth—while the distressed young author sat by, Congress edited and, in Jefferson's eyes, mutilated the composition. Whole sections were shorn away. When the delegates had completed their editing, Jefferson's draft stood reduced almost one-fourth of its original length. Congress sent the final approved *Declaration* to the printer on July 4.

II

Although Jefferson in later years said he had "turned to neither book nor pamphlet" to write the *Declaration*, there was ample precedent for it in his earlier writings, in particular a pamphlet he published in 1774, *Summary Views of the Rights of British America,* and his preamble to the Virginia constitution of a few weeks before, both of which contained a recital of grievances against the King.[14] There also was an important precedent in the Virginia *Declaration of Rights,* penned by George Mason.

In detailing American grievances against the King (they constitute the bulk of the *Declaration*), Jefferson obviously had a persuasive intent. Joseph Barton of Delaware illuminated part of this intent in a letter written on July 9. "I could hardly own the King," Barton wrote to a cousin, "and fight against him at the same time, but now these matters are cleared up. Heart and hand shall move together."[15] Later generations of Americans, less involved in such matters and perhaps uncomfortable at polemics, have sought their inspiration in the famous phrases of Jefferson's second paragraph ("We hold these truths to be self evident, that all men are created equal. . . ."), rather than his list of grievances.

But Jefferson's great achievement in the *Declaration* was, as one of his biographers has stated, that he succeeded in placing "philosophic principles into intimate conjunction with propaganda. . . ."[16] Of Jefferson's propaganda technique, another historian wrote: "With the cleverness of a subtle manipulator of public opinion, he personalized the enemy and exposed him to devastating attack."[17] Below run Jefferson's charges:

The history of the present King of Great Britain is a history of repeated injuries and usurpations, all having in direct object the establishment of an absolute Tyranny over these States. To prove this, let Facts be submitted to a candid world.
He has refused. . . .
He has forbidden. . . .
He has refused. . . .
He has called together. . . .
He has dissolved. . . .

He has refused. . . .
He has endeavoured. . . .
He has made. . . .
He has obstructed. . . .
He has erected. . . .
He has kept among us. . . .
He has affected. . . .
He has combined. . . .
For quartering large bodies of armed troops among us:
For protecting them. . . .
For cutting off our trade. . . .
For imposing Taxes on us. . . .
For depriving us. . . .
For abolishing. . . .
For taking away. . . .
For suspending. . . .
He has abdicated Government here. . . .

He has plundered our seas, ravaged our Coasts, burnt our towns, and destroyed the lives of our people.

He is at this time transporting large Armies of foreign Mercenaries. . . .

He has constrained. . . .

He has excited domestic insurrections. . . .

There is part of the list of accusations against stubborn King George. The list contains facts and truths, but they are not facts and truths of an impartial history. They are facts and truths *exaggerated*, aimed at justifying the historic step towards independence and insuring that American "hearts and hands" would move together. For the other side of the question, a contemporary English view, as Ambrose Serle recorded it, tells another story. "A more impudent, false and atrocious proclamation," said Serle of the *Declaration*, "was never fabricated by the hands of man. Hitherto, they have thrown all the blame and insult upon the Parliament and Ministry; now, they have the audacity to calumniate the King and the people of Great

Britain. 'Tis impossible to read this paper without horror at the daring hypocrisy of these men, who call *God* to witness the uprightness of their proceedings."[18] To most Britons in 1776, truth could not be found in very great quantities in the famous American paper.

But, of course, it was the declaring of independence and not the *Declaration of Independence* that had final meaning in the Revolution.

Once the historic document had been adopted by Congress, a great effort was made to quickly disseminate it throughout the colonies. The entire apparatus of the Revolution sped it on its way.[19] To the state conventions, to the committees of safety, to the military commanders, to ministers of the pulpit, and other private individuals, Congress directed copies of the paper. Newspaper editors played an important role in its dissemination. The very first newspaper to carry it was the *Pennsylvania Evening Post*, on July 6. On the ninth it appeared in Dunlap's *Maryland Gazette* at Baltimore, on the tenth in the *New York Constitutional Gazette*, the thirteenth in the *Providence Gazette*, the seventeenth in the *Massachusetts Spy*, the nineteenth in the *New England Chronicle*. Among the southern newspapers that carried it were the *Virginia Gazette*, on July 20, and the *South Carolina and American Gazette* on August 2.[20]

Many Americans, who did not read the *Declaration* themselves, heard it read from state house balconies, from pulpits, and at army formations. Washington reported to Congress on July 10 that he had "caused the Declaration to be proclaimed before all the Army under my immediate command," and that "the measure seemed to have their most hearty assent; the expressions and behaviour both of officers and men testifying their warmest approbation of it. . . ."[21]

By summer's end, 1776, Congress' and Jefferson's important composition thus became known to most of the American people, to the enemy, and, shortly thereafter, to the world.

CONCLUSION

"From the inception of the controversy," Professor Schlesinger has stated, "the patriots exhibited extraordinary skill in manipulating public opinion, playing upon the emotions of the ignorant as well as the minds of the educated."[22] The reader who has travelled with us thus far will agree. As propagandists, the Americans demonstrated great ability. Understanding the uses to which the printing press could be put, they embarked on devastating attacks on the "sceptered savage of Great-Britain," who was charged, by one writer, with a thirst "for the blood of America. Hessians, Hanoverians, Brunswickers, Canadians, Indians, Negroes, Regulars and Tories are invited to the carnage."[23]

That these people actually became involved in the war was no exaggeration, but their activities did little service to England. The Americans, stirred to greater resistance, countered not only with arms but with the propaganda and subversive operations that we have described.

As to these latter activities, the leaders of the Revolution, even in the midst of their most angry flood of words, never lost sight of the fact that they were no substitute for military power. Speaking of this and the search for peace, John Adams wrote in 1781 that only Washington and Greene "and their colleagues in the army" could truly negotiate for America. The British government, which sent armies and fleets to America to persuade the Americans to forego rebellion and independence, ended up being persuaded to relinquish the colonies—persuaded by the stubborn resistance of Washington, Greene, "their colleagues in the army," and the potent French alliance.

Notes, Bibliography, and Index

Notes

★★★

For the larger collections, the author has used abbreviations after the first citation of each work, as, for example, in: *The Writings of George Washington*, subsequently abbreviated as *GW*.

CHAPTER 1

1. *Journals of the Continental Congress*, W. C. Ford and G. Hunt, eds. (Washington, 1904), I, 105–13. Hereafter abbreviated as: *JCC*.

2. Arthur G. Bradley, *Lord Dorchester* (New York, 1926), p. 9.

3. *Ibid.*, 48.

4. Peter Force, compiler, *American Archives* (Washington, 1837), Fourth Series, I, 853. Hereafter abbreviated as: Force, 4, I, 853.

5. *Ibid.*, 930.

6. *Ibid.*

7. *Ibid.*, 1164.

8. *Ibid.*, 917.

9. *Ibid.*, II, 23.

10. Samuel Adams, *The Writings of Samuel Adams*, H. A. Cushing, ed. (New York, 1907), III, 182–88.

11. Force, 4, II, 243.

12. *Ibid.*, 1838.

13. *Ibid.*, 891.

14. *Ibid.*, 893.

15. *Ibid.*, 904.

16. Justin H. Smith, *Our Struggle for the Fourteenth Colony* (New York, 1907), I, 222.

17. Bradley, *op. cit.*, 90.

18. Force, 4, II, 940.

19. *Ibid.*, 919.

20. Edmund C. Burnett, ed., *Letters of Members of the Continental Congress* (Washington, 1921), I, 113–14.

21. *Ibid.*, 189.

22. Force, 4, II, 1342.

23. *Ibid.*, 962.

24. Smith, *op. cit.*, I, 326.

25. Force, 4, III, 742.

26. George Washington, *The Writings of George Washington*, John C. Fitzpatrick, ed. (Washington, 1931), IV, 65–66 n. Hereafter abbreviated as: *GW*.

27. Force, 4, III, 1596.

28. *Ibid.*, 214.

29. *GW*, III, 491–92.

30. Library of Congress, *Washington Papers*, Vol. 18, No. 117.

31. Force, 4, III, 1609.
32. *GW*, IV, 65.
33. Kenneth Roberts, ed., *March to Quebec: Journals of the Members of Arnold's Expedition* (New York, 1938), pp. 89–90.
34. *Journal of the Most Remarkable Occurrences in Quebec, 1775–1776 by an Officer of the Garrison*, New York Historical Society, *Collections* (1880), pp. 175–76.
35. *Ibid.*, 177.
36. Smith, *op. cit.*, II, 95–96.
37. Force, 4, IV, 290; Bradley, *op. cit.*, 119–20.
38. Force, 4, IV, 289.
39. *Ibid.*, 1653.
40. *Ibid.*, 4, V, 411.
41. R. W. McLachlan, "Fleury Mesplet, The First Printer at Montreal," *Proceedings and Transactions of the Royal Society of Canada*, Second Series, XII (May 1906), 224–25.
42. Force, 4, V, 1237.
43. William R. Riddell, "Benjamin Franklin's Mission to Canada and the Causes of Its Failure," *Pennsylvania Magazine of History and Biography* (1924), 111–58.
44. *GW*, IV, 495 n.
45. Isaac N. Arnold, *The Life of Benedict Arnold* (Chicago, 1880), p. 94.
46. Force, 4, VI, 418.
47. *Ibid.*, 5, I, 1241.
48. Bradley, *op. cit.*, 129 n.
49. Force, 5, II, 1144.
50. *Ibid.*, I, 987.
51. *Ibid.*
52. Francis J. Hudleston, *Gentleman Johnny Burgoyne: Misadventures of an English General*

in the Revolution (New York, 1939), pp. 127–28.
53. *JCC*, IX, 981.
54. *Ibid.*, X, 253–54.
55. Smith, *op. cit.*, II, 529.
56. Frank Moore, *Diary of the American Revolution, From Newspapers and Original Documents* (New York, 1860), II, 102–4.
57. John Almon, ed., *The Remembrancer, or Impartial Repository of Public Events* (London, 1778), VII, 251–53.
58. B. F. Stevens, compiler, *Facsimiles of Manuscripts in European Archives Relating to America, 1773–1783* (London, 1892), XII, 1259. Hereafter abbreviated as: *Stevens Facsimiles.*
59. Jean N. McIlwraith, *Sir Frederick Haldimand* (London, 1926), p. 128.
60. *JCC*, XIII, 1190.
61. Burnett, *op. cit.*, IV, 1–2.
62. McIlwraith, *op. cit.*, 189–90.
63. Great Britain, Historical Manuscripts Commission, *Report on American Manuscripts in the Royal Institution of Great Britain* (London, 1906), II, 1–2. Hereafter abbreviated as: Gr. Brit., *American Manuscripts*, II, 1–2.
64. *GW*, XVIII, 386–88.
65. *Ibid.*
66. *Ibid.*, 476.
67. McIlwraith, *op. cit.*, 352–53.
68. Benjamin Franklin, *The Writings of Benjamin Franklin*, A. H. Smyth, ed. (New York, 1906), VIII, 472. Hereafter abbreviated as: *Franklin Writings.*

CHAPTER 2

1. Force, 4, II, 315.
2. Thomas Gage, *The Correspondence of General Thomas Gage, 1763–1775*, Clarence E. Carter, ed. (New Haven, 1931), I, 404.
3. *Ibid.*, II, 204.
4. *JCC*, II, 174–75.
5. *Ibid.*, 178–83.
6. *Ibid.*
7. *Force*, 4, III, 485.
8. Roberts, *op. cit.*, 220–21.
9. *GW*, III, 526.
10. *Ibid.*, IV, 280.
11. *Ibid.*, 280 n.
12. *Ibid.*, 393–94.
13. Force, 4, V, 525–26.
14. *Ibid.*, 5, I, 867.
15. *JCC*, IV, 269–70.
16. *Ibid.*, 412.
17. Force, 5, I, 1105.
18. Thomas Jefferson, *The Papers of Thomas Jefferson*, J. P. Boyd, ed. (Princeton, 1950), I, 493–94. Hereafter abbreviated as: *Jefferson Papers*.
19. Force, 5, II, 514.
20. John D. Barnhart, ed., *Henry Hamilton and George Rogers Clark* (Crawfordsville, 1951), pp. 27–28.
21. Force, 4, VI, 497.
22. *Ibid.*
23. *Ibid.*, 1230.
24. *GW*, VI, 434–35.
25. National Archives, "Papers of the Continental Congress," No. 71, II, 201.
26. Hudleston, *op. cit.*, 84–85.
27. Moore, *op. cit.*, I, 454–56.
28. Thomas Anbury, *Travels Through the Interior Parts of America by Thomas Anbury . . .* (Boston, 1923), I, 171.
29. Hudleston, *op. cit.*, 163.
30. *GW*, IX, 75–76.
31. Arnold, *op. cit.*, 156–57.
32. *Ibid.*, 162 n.
33. R. G. Thwaites, ed., State Historical Society of Wisconsin, *Collections*, Vol. 11 (1888), pp. 175–76.
34. *Ibid.*
35. Barnhart, *op. cit.*, 30.
36. R. G. Thwaites and L. P. Kellogg, eds., *Frontier Defense on the Upper Ohio, 1777–1778* (Madison, 1912), p. 14.
37. *JCC*, IX, 942–45.
38. Thwaites and Kellogg, *op. cit.*, 86.
39. *JCC*, IX, 994–98.
40. *Ibid.*
41. *Ibid.*, X, 110–11.
42. Burnett, *op. cit.*, III, 129–30.
43. *GW*, XI, 343–44.
44. *JCC*, XI, 587–89.
45. Thwaites and Kellogg, *op. cit.*, 254 n; Barnhart, *op. cit.*, 32.
46. Barnhart, *op. cit.*, 33.
47. James A. James, *The Life of George Rogers Clark* (Chicago, 1928), pp. 120–21.
48. James, *George Rogers Clark Papers, 1771–1781* (Springfield, 1912), pp. 95–97.
49. James, *The Life of George Rogers Clark*, 180–81.
50. Barnhart, *op. cit.*, 180–81.
51. James, *George Rogers Clark Papers*, 149–50.
52. *GW*, XVI, 492–93.
53. Louis Gottschalk, *Lafayette Joins the American Army* (Chicago, 1937), p. 315.
54. Thwaites, *Wisconsin Collections*, Vol. 11, p. 181.

55. Gr. Brit., *American Manuscripts*, II, 1–2.

56. *JCC*, XVI, 334.

57. *Ibid.*, XIII, 411; and XIV, 693, 733.

58. *GW*, VI, 192–93.

59. James Thacher, *Military Journal During the American Revolutionary War* (Hartford, 1854), p. 163.

60. *Jefferson Papers*, III, 276–77.

CHAPTER 3

1. Joseph Galloway made the 600,000 estimate in June 1778; *Stevens Facsimiles*, XXIV, 2098.

2. Force, 4, VI, 21.

3. *Ibid.*, I, 1431.

4. William L. Saunders, ed., *The Colonial Records of North Carolina* (Raleigh, 1870), X, 20–24.

5. John Adams, *Life and Works* (Boston, 1850), II, 428. Hereafter cited as: *Adams Works*.

6. Saunders, *op. cit.*, X, 25, 63, 87.

7. *Ibid.*, 43.

8. *Ibid.*, 46.

9. *Ibid.*, 94–95.

10. *Ibid.*

11. *Ibid.*, 138.

12. *Ibid.*, 139.

13. David J. Mays, *Edmund Pendleton, A Biography* (Cambridge, 1952), II, 14.

14. Gage, *op. cit.*, I, 399.

15. *Pennsylvania Magazine of History and Biography*, 34, p. 46.

16. Saunders, *op. cit.*, X, 138a.

17. Mays, *op. cit.*, II, 52.

18. Moore, *op. cit.*, II, 160–61.

19. Mays, *op. cit.*, II, 56.

20. Richard Henry Lee, *The Letters of Richard Henry Lee*, J. C. Ballagh, ed. (New York, 1912), I, 162. Hereafter cited as *Lee Papers*.

21. *GW*, IV, 186.

22. Moore, *op. cit.*, I, 165.

23. *Jefferson Papers*, I, 266.

24. Hezekiah Niles, *Principles and Acts of the Revolution in America* (Baltimore, 1822), p. 141.

25. Mays, *op. cit.*, II, 160.

26. *Ibid.*

27. Force, 5, II, 160.

28. *Ibid.*, 4, VI, 811.

29. *Ibid.*, 5, II, 162.

30. *Jefferson Papers*, I, 290.

31. *Ibid.*, 317–18.

32. Herbert Aptheker, *American Negro Slave Revolts* (New York, 1943), p. 21.

33. Christopher Ward, *The War of the Revolution* (New York, 1952), II, 592.

34. W. B. Hartgrove, "The Negro Soldier in the American Revolution," *Journal of Negro History*, I (Jan. 1916), p. 126.

35. *GW*, IV, 8 n.

36. *Ibid.*, 195.

37. *JCC*, IV, 60

38. Hartgrove, *op. cit.*, 128.

39. *Stevens Facsimiles*, XXIV, 2079.

40. *JCC*, XIII, 385.

41. Burnett, *op. cit.*, IV, 107.

42. *GW*, IV, 267.

43. Richard B. Morris, ed., *Alexander Hamilton and the Founding of the Nation* (New York, 1957), pp. 454–55.

44. Walter Clark, ed., *The State Records of North Carolina*

(Goldsboro, 1901), XIX, 911–14.

45. *Ibid.*
46. *JCC,* XIII, 388.
47. Almon, *op. cit.,* VIII, 367.
48. Moore, *op. cit.,* II, 176–77.

49. Hartgrove, *op. cit.,* 117.
50. Benson J. Lossing, *The Pictorial Field-Book of the Revolution* (New York, 1852), II, 573 n.
51. *Jefferson Papers,* XIII, 363–64.

CHAPTER 4

1. Gage, *op. cit.,* 380.
2. Sir Henry Clinton, *The American Rebellion: Sir Henry Clinton's Narrative.* . . , William B. Willcox, ed. (New Haven, 1954), xvi.
3. Force, 4, VI, 283.
4. Ambrose Serle, *The American Journal of Ambrose Serle, Secretary to Lord Howe, 1776–1778,* Edward H. Tatum, Jr., ed. (San Marino, 1940), p. 77.
5. Force, 4, V, 525–26.
6. *Franklin Writings,* VI, 448.
7. *JCC,* IV, 269–70.
8. Lyman H. Butterfield, "Psychological Warfare in 1776: The Jefferson-Franklin Plan to Cause Hessian Desertions," *Proceedings of the American Philosophical Society,* 194 (June 1950), p. 234.
9. *JCC,* V, 640.
10. *Ibid.,* 653–55.
11. *GW,* V, 450–51.
12. *Ibid.,* 463.
13. Butterfield, *op. cit.,* 237; John C. Fitzpatrick, *The Spirit of the Revolution* (Boston, 1924), pp. 142–43.
14. *GW,* V, 491.
15. Carl Leopold Baurmeister, *Revolution in America: Confidential Letters and Journals . . . of Adjutant General Major Baur-*

meister. . . , B. A. Uhlendorf, trans. (New Brunswick, 1957), p. 41.
16. Force, 5, I, 1110.
17. *JCC,* V, 707–8.
18. Burnett, *op. cit.,* II, 62.
19. Force, 5, I, 799.
20. *Ibid.,* II, 203–4.
21. Edward J. Lowell, *The Hessians and the Other German Auxiliaries of Great Britain in the Revolutionary War* (New York, 1884), pp. 38–39.
22. Force, 5, II, 1264.
23. *GW,* V, 36.
24. Burnett, *op. cit.,* II, 152.
25. *GW,* VI, 284.
26. Frederick Mackenzie, *Diary of Frederick Mackenzie . . .* (Cambridge, 1930), I, 102–3.
27. Baurmeister, *op. cit.,* 62–63.
28. *JCC,* IV, 984–85.
29. Force, 5, III, 1459.
30. *GW,* VI, 453.
31. *Archives of the State of Pennsylvania* (Philadelphia, 1853), V, 146–47.
32. Force, 5, III, 1511.
33. Burnett, *op. cit.,* II, 209.
34. *GW,* VII, 224–25.
35. *Ibid.,* 314.
36. *Ibid.,* 1–3.
37. Baurmeister, *op. cit.,* 128.
38. *GW,* X, 316 n.

39. *JCC*, X, 406–9.
40. *Ibid.*
41. Burnett, *op. cit.*, III, 216.
42. Baurmeister, *op. cit.*, 185.
43. *GW*, XII, 149–50.
44. *Ibid.*, 304–5.
45. *Ibid.*
46. *Ibid.*, 353 n.
47. *Journal of Lt. John Charles Philip Von Krafft, 1776–1784,* New York Historical Society, *Collections* (1882), p. 59.
48. *JCC*, XII, 866–67.
49. *Ibid.*
50. Baurmeister, *op. cit.*, 228.
51. *JCC*, XII, 868.
52. Baurmeister, *op. cit.* 227–28.
53. *JCC*, XII, 1192–93.
54. Baurmeister, *op. cit.*, 380.
55. *Von Krafft Journal,* 151.
56. Max von Eelking, *Memoirs and Letters and Journals of Major General Riedesel,* William L. Stone, trans. (Albany, 1868), pp. 266–68.
57. *Ibid.*, 15–16.
58. *Ibid.*, 22.
59. *Ibid.*, 25.
60. Lowell, *op. cit.*, 287.
61. *GW*, XV, 493–94.
62. Francis Wharton, ed., *Revolutionary Diplomatic Correspondence of the United States* (Washington, 1889), IV, 11.
63. *GW*, XIX, 384.
64. *Ibid.*, XXIV, 175–76.
65. Gr. Brit., *American Manuscripts,* III, 314–15.
66. *Ibid.*
67. *Ibid.*
68. *Jefferson Papers,* IV, 505–6.
69. Gr. Brit., *American Manuscripts,* II, 401.
70. Baurmeister, *op. cit.*, 541.
71. *Ibid.*, 569, 579.
72. Lowell, *op. cit.*, 291.

CHAPTER 5

1. Moses Coit Tyler, *The Literary History of the American Revolution* (New York, 1951), I, 399.
2. *Ibid.*
3. *Warren-Adams Letters, Being Chiefly a Correspondence among John Adams, Samuel Adams, and James Warren,* Massachusetts Historical Society, *Collections* (Boston, 1917), I, 58.
4. Moore, *op. cit.*, I, 21–23.
5. Thacher, *op. cit.*, 31.
6. *GW*, XI, 490.
7. Mays, *op. cit.*, I, 53.
8. Force, 5, I, 99.
9. *Ibid.*
10. *GW*, V, 336.
11. John W. Wright, "The Rifle in the American Revolution," *American Historical Review,* XXIX (Jan. 1924), 293–95.
12. Mackenzie, *op. cit.*, I, 44–45.
13. Charles Stillé, *Major General Anthony Wayne* (Philadelphia, 1893), p. 118.
14. *Ibid.*, 401.
15. *GW*, XXIII, 147–48.
16. *Jefferson Papers,* II, 197.
17. Library of Congress, "Broadside Collection," Portfolio 108, No. 16.
18. E. B. O'Callaghan, compiler, *Documents Relative to the Colonial History of the State of New York* (Albany, 1857), VIII, 582–83.

19. Worthington C. Ford, ed., *Broadsides, Ballads, &c. Printed in Massachusetts, 1639–1800*, Massachusetts Historical Society, *Collections* (1922), p. 266.

20. Sgt. Bedinger's Journal in Danske Dandridge, *Historic Shepherdstown* (Charlottesville, 1910), p. 107.

21. Force, 4, II, 968.

22. *Ibid.*

23. Gage, *op. cit.*, II, 192–93.

24. Force, 4, VI, 242.

25. *Ibid.* 5, I, 437.

26. Burnett, *op. cit.*, II, 17–18.

27. *Ibid.*

28. Ward, *op. cit.*, I, 209.

29. John and Abigail Adams, *Familiar Letters of John Adams and His Wife*, C. F. Adams, ed. (New York, 1876), p. 224.

30. Burnett, *op. cit.*, II, 66–67.

31. Bellamy Partridge, *Sir Billy Howe* (London, 1932), p. 66.

32. Force, 5, II, 398.

33. *Ibid.*

34. *Ibid.* 5, III, 927.

35. Partridge, *op. cit.*, 111.

36. Baurmeister, *op. cit.*, 75.

37. *Jefferson Papers*, I, 659.

38. New Jersey *Archives*, Second Series, I, 245–46.

39. Moore, *op. cit.*, II, 197.

40. Thomas Paine, *Selected Writings of Thomas Paine*, Richard E. Roberts, ed. (New York, 1945), p. 51.

41. George Creel, "Propaganda and Morale," *American Journal of Sociology* (November 1941), 340–41.

42. Partridge, *op. cit.*, 131–32.

43. Moore, *op. cit.*, I, 383–84.

44. Burnett, *op. cit.*, II, 243.

45. *JCC*, VII, 165–66.

46. Almon, *op. cit.*, VI, 99.

47. *Ibid.*, 137–38.

48. *GW*, VIII, 8–9.

49. *JCC*, VIII, 397–404.

50. *Ibid.*

51. Partridge, *op. cit.*, 178.

52. Almon, *op. cit.*, VI, 388.

53. *GW*, IX, 152.

54. *Ibid.*, 174.

55. *Ibid.*, 205–6.

56. *Stevens Facsimiles*, XXIV, 2094.

57. *GW*, XI, 299–300.

58. *Ibid.*

59. *Ibid.*, 277–78.

60. *JCC*, X, 374–83.

61. *Ibid.*

62. Almon, *op. cit.*, VII, 127–31.

63. *Ibid.*

64. *Ibid.*

65. *GW*, XIII, 132–33.

66. *Ibid.*

67. Almon, *op. cit.*, VII, 132.

68. *Ibid.*

69. *GW*, XIII, 210.

70. Baurmeister, *op. cit.*, 146.

71. Almon, *op. cit.*, VIII, 241–42.

72. *Ibid.*, 243.

73. *Ibid.*, 239.

74. *Stevens Facsimiles*, XII, 1274.

75. National Archives, "Papers of the Continental Congress," No. 152, VII, 545.

76. Almon, *op. cit.*, VIII, 363–64.

77. Burnett, *op. cit.*, IV, 33.

78. *JCC*, XIV, 915–16.

79. Moore, *op. cit.*, II, 195.

80. Stillé, *op. cit.*, 201.

81. Thomas J. Wertenbaker, *Father Knickerbocher Rebels:*

New York City During the Revolution (New York, 1948), p. 180.
82. Moore, *op. cit.*, II, 197.
83. Ward, *op. cit.*, II, 703.
84. Clinton, *op. cit.*, 174–75.
85. National Archives, "Papers of the Continental Congress," No. 152, VIII, 579.
86. *GW*, XVIII, 432.
87. Library of Congress, "Broadside Collection," Portfolio 172, No. 7
88. *Jefferson Papers*, III, 525, 550.
89. Arnold, *op. cit.*, 330–32.
90. *Ibid.*
91. *Ibid.*

92. *GW*, XX, 189.
93. *Ibid.*, 264.
94. Carl Van Doren, *Secret History of the American Revolution* (New York, 1941), p. 337.
95. Thacher, *op. cit.*, 231.
96. B. F. Stevens, ed., *Clinton-Cornwallis Controversy* (London, 1888), I, 327.
97. *Ibid.*, 371.
98. Clinton, *op. cit.*, 268.
99. Moore, *op. cit.*, II, 432–33.
100. Gr. Brit., *American Manuscripts*, II, 401.
101. *GW*, XXIII, 469.
102. Gr. Brit., *American Manuscripts*, II, 448.

CHAPTER 6

1. *Jefferson Papers*, II, 4.
2. Mackenzie, *op. cit.*, I, 150.
3. Almon, *op. cit.*, VI, 261.
4. Thacher, *op. cit.*, 86–87.
5. Mackenzie, *op. cit.*, I, 153–54.
6. *Ibid.*
7. *JCC*, IX, 1051.
8. *GW*, IX, 183.
9. Oliver C. Kuntzleman, *Joseph Galloway, Loyalist* (Philadelphia, 1941), pp. 138–39.
10. New Jersey *Archives*, Second Series, II, 126–27.
11. George H. Ryden, ed., *Letters to and from Caesar Rodney, 1756–1784* (Philadelphia, 1933), pp. 267–68.
12. *JCC*, X, 204–5.
13. *GW*, XI, 29–30.
14. *Ibid.*, 51.
15. New Jersey *Archives*, Second Series, III, 160–61.
16. *Ibid.*, 252–53.
17. *Ibid.*
18. *Ibid.*, 266–69.

19. *GW*, XXI, 6–7.
20. Baurmeister, *op. cit.*, 406–7.
21. Friedrike Riedesel, *Letters and Journals Relating to the War of the American Revolution. . . ,* W. L. Stone, trans. (Albany, 1867), pp. 183–84.
22. Nathan Schachner, *Thomas Jefferson, A Biography* (New York, 1951), I, 201, 215–16.
23. *GW*, XXIV, 91.
24. *Ibid.*, 91 n.
25. Thacher, *op. cit.*, 86.
26. *GW*, IV, 389.
27. *Lee Papers*, I, 292.
28. Adams, *Familiar Letters*, 225.
29. Wertenbaker, *op. cit.*, 144.
30. Burnett, *op. cit.*, V, 173.
31. *GW*, IX, 78.
32. *Ibid.*, X, 4–5.
33. *Ibid.*, 201–2.
34. "The Treason of Benedict Arnold, as Presented in Letters of Sir Henry Clinton to Lord George

Germain," *Pennsylvania Magazine of History and Biography* (1898), 410–22.

35. Force, 4, II, 925.
36. *Ibid.*
37. Hudleston, *op. cit.*, 78.
38. Force, 4, II, 1610.
39. *Ibid.*
40. *Ibid.*, 1503.
41. *Ibid.*, 1504.
42. *Ibid.*, 1638.
43. Gage, *op. cit.*, I, 410.
44. John Sullivan, *Letters and Papers of Major-General Sullivan*, Otis G. Hammond, ed. (Concord, 1930), I, 355–60.
45. *Ibid.*
46. *Ibid.*, 360.
47. Van Doren, *op. cit.*, 46; New York Historical Society, *Collections* (1879), 21.
48. Van Doren, *op. cit.*, 48.
49. Edward Duffield Neill, "Rev. Jacob Duché, The First Chaplain of Congress," *Pennsylvania Magazine of History and Biography* (1878), 58–73.
50. W. C. Ford, ed., *The Washington-Duché Letters* (Brooklyn, 1890), pp. 9–25.
51. *Ibid.*

52. *Ibid.*, 8–9.
53. *Ibid.*, 28–29.
54. Burnett, *op. cit.*, II, 527.
55. Neill, *op. cit.*, 73.
56. William B. Reed, *Life and Correspondence of Joseph Reed* (Philadelphia, 1847), I, 197–98.
57. *Ibid.*, 372–75.
58. *Ibid.*, 377.
59. John F. Roche, *Joseph Reed, A Moderate in the American Revolution* (New York, 1951), p. 135.
60. Reed, *op. cit.*, 384.
61. *Ibid.*
62. *Ibid.*, 388; Roche, *op. cit.*, 138.
63. Reed, *op. cit.*, 387–88.
64. *Stevens Facsimiles*, VIII, 835.
65. *Ibid.*
66. *Ibid.*, 836.
67. *Adams Works*, III, 179.
68. Jared Sparks, *The Diplomatic Correspondence of the American Revolution* (Washington, 1857), II, 34–39.
69. *Ibid.*
70. *Adams Works*, III, 179–80.
71. Van Doren, *op. cit.*, 82.

CHAPTER 7

1. Carl Van Doren, *Benjamin Franklin* (New York, 1938), p. 570.
2. Bernard Fay, *Franklin, The Apostle of Modern Times* (Boston, 1929), p. 412.
3. Van Doren, *Benjamin Franklin*, 632.
4. Gilbert Chinard, "Adventures in a Library," *The Newberry Library Bulletin*, Second Series, No. 8 (March 1952), 227; see

also Paul Leicester Ford, "Affaires de l'Angleterre et de l'Amérique," *Pennsylvania Magazine of History and Biography* (1889), 222–26.
5. Silas Deane, *The Deane Papers*, New York Historical Society, *Collections* (1887), I, 213.
6. *Ibid.*, 397.
7. Van Doren, *Benjamin Franklin*, 572.
8. *Franklin Writings*, VIII, 457.

9. Van Doren, *Benjamin Franklin,* 574.

10. Fay, *op. cit.,* 419, 447–48.

11. Hays I. Minis, ed., *Calendar of the Papers of Benjamin Franklin in the Library of the American Philosophical Society* (Philadelphia, 1908), I, 231, 248.

12. *Ibid.,* 319.

13. *Ibid.,* 437.

14. Wharton, *op. cit.,* II, 340–41.

15. *Franklin Writings,* VII, 336.

16. Francis P. Renaut, *La Politique de Propagande des Américains durant la Guerre d'Indépendance* (Paris, 1925), II, 210.

17. Durand Echeverra, " 'The Sale of the Hessians.' Was Benjamin Franklin the Author?" *American Philosophical Society Library Bulletin* (1954), 427–31.

18. *Franklin Writings,* VII, 57–58.

19. *Ibid.,* 27–29.

20. *Ibid.*

21. *Ibid.,* 56.

22. *JCC,* IX, 951–52.

23. Wharton, *op. cit.,* II, 451.

24. *Ibid.,* 452.

25. *Lee Papers,* I, 328–30.

26. *JCC,* II, 212–18.

27. P. L. Ford, ed., *An Address to the Good People of Ireland on Behalf of America, October 4th, 1778,* by Benjamin Franklin (Brooklyn, 1891).

28. *Ibid.*

29. R. B. McDowell, *Irish Public Opinion, 1750–1800* (London, 1944), p. 42.

30. William Bell Clark, *Ben Franklin's Privateers: A Naval Epic of the American Revolution* (Baton Rouge, 1956), p. 168.

31. Chinard, "Adventures in a Library," 234–35.

32. Almon, *op. cit.,* VIII, 152–53.

33. *Ibid.,* 162–63.

34. *Franklin Writings,* VII, 406.

35. Renaut, *op. cit.,* II, 160–61.

36. *Franklin Writings,* VII, 398.

37. *Ibid.,* VIII, 82–83.

38. *Adams Works,* VII, 215–16.

39. *Ibid.,* 231.

40. Wharton, *op. cit.,* III, 876.

41. Minis, *Franklin Calendar,* II, 292.

42. *Adams Works,* VII, 59–60.

43. Sparks, *op. cit.,* II, 629–40.

44. *Adams Works,* VII, 170–71.

45. *Ibid.,* 172–76.

46. *Ibid.,* 180–86.

47. *Ibid.,* 316–17.

48. Wharton, *op. cit.,* V, 689–91.

49. *Ibid.*

50. *Adams Works,* VII, 272–73.

51. *Ibid.,* 279–80.

52. *Ibid.*

53. John Burgoyne, *A State of the Expedition from Canada As Laid Before the House of Commons by Lieutenant General Burgoyne* (London, 1780), pp. 26, 167.

54. William Howe, *The Narrative of Lieut. Gen. Sir William Howe in a Committee of the House of Commons, on the 29th*

of April 1779 (London, 1780), pp. 6, 26.

55. Wharton, *op. cit.*, V, 689.

56. Francis Adrian Van der Kemp, *An Autobiography, together With Extracts from His Correspondence*, Helen Fairchild, ed. (New York, 1903), pp. 55–56. See also Friedrich Edler, *The Dutch Republic and the American Revolution* (Baltimore, 1911).

57. Van der Kemp, *op. cit.*, 55–56.

58. Wharton, *op. cit.*, V, 692–93.

59. *Franklin Writings*, VIII, 437–47.

60. *Ibid.*

61. Fay, *op. cit.*, 477.

62. *Franklin Writings*, VIII, 433.

63. Van Doren, *Benjamin Franklin*, 673.

64. Nicholas Hans, "Franklin, Jefferson, and the English Radicals at the End of the Eighteenth Century," *American Philosophical Society Library Bulletin* (1954), 406–26.

65. *Ibid.*

66. *Franklin Writings*, VIII, 131.

CHAPTER 8

1. *Adams Works*, X, 282–83.

2. Douglas S. Freeman, *George Washington, A Biography* (New York, 1951), III, 334.

3. Adams, *Familiar Letters*, 79.

4. Gilbert Chinard, ed., *George Washington as the French Knew Him, a Collection of Texts* (Princeton, 1940), p. 28.

5. Anburey, *op. cit.*, II, 232.

6. Nicholas Cresswell, *The Journal of Nicholas Cresswell 1774–1777* (New York, 1924), p. 181.

7. *GW*, XIX, 220; XXII, 215.

8. *Ibid.*, XXIV, 325.

9. Allen Bowman, *The Morale of the American Revolutionary Army* (Washington, 1943), p. 101.

10. *Franklin Writings*, VIII, 28.

11. Claude H. Van Tyne, *The Loyalists in the American Revolution* (New York, 1929), pp. 89–90.

12. Arthur M. Schlesinger, *Prelude to Independence: The Newspaper War on Britain* (New York, 1958), pp. 256–80; Philip Davidson, *Propaganda and the American Revolution* (Chapel Hill, 1941), pp. 131–38.

13. *JCC*, V, 425.

14. Edward Dumbauld, *The Declaration of Independence and What It Means Today* (Norman, 1950), p. 21.

15. John B. Hazelton, *The Declaration of Independence: Its History* (New York, 1906), p. 221.

16. Schachner, *op. cit.*, I, 129.

17. Saul K. Padover, *Jefferson* (New York, 1942), pp. 61–62.

18. Serle, *op. cit.*, 30–31.

19. See Hazelton, *op. cit.*, pp. 240–81.

20. Schlesinger, *op. cit.*, pp. 282–83.

21. *GW*, V, 245.

22. Adams, *Familiar Letters*, 397–98.

23. Schlesinger, *op. cit.*, 266.

Bibliography

★★★

This selected bibliography includes only works used or consulted. The author has relied almost entirely on printed works in the possession of the Library of Congress. Those which proved to be very fruitful included *The Writings of George Washington,* edited by John C. Fitzpatrick, 39 volumes (Washington, 1931–44); the century-old but still highly useful compilation by Peter Force, *American Archives,* Fourth Series, 6 volumes (Washington, 1837–46), and Fifth Series, 3 volumes (1848–53); and the various published works of John and Samuel Adams, Franklin, Jefferson, and others who played active roles in the Revolution. Documentary material was consulted in the case of B. F. Stevens' *Facsimiles of Manuscripts in European Archives Relating to America, 1773–1783,* 25 volumes (London, 1889–98); the "Broadside Collection" of the Library of Congress; and the "Papers of the Continental Congress" at National Archives.

For the sake of clarity the author has modernized spelling, capitalization, and punctuation wherever necessary, considering clearness of thought to be far more important than a rigid adherence to eighteenth-century styles of manuscript and type. Readers interested in typography, punctuation, and style are referred to the several illustrations in this volume.

PRIMARY SOURCES

Letters, Journals—

Adams, John. *The Works of John Adams, with a Life of the Author, Notes and Illustrations.* C. F. Adams, ed. 10 vols. Boston, 1850–56.

Adams, John and Adams, Abigail. *Familiar Letters of John Adams and His wife.* C. F. Adams, ed. New York, 1876.

Adams, Samuel. *The Writings of Samuel Adams.* Harry A. Cushing, ed. 4 vols. New York, 1904–8.

Almon, John, ed. *The Remembrancer, or Impartial Repository of Public Events.* 17 vols. London, 1775–84.

Anburey, Thomas. *Travels Through the Interior Parts of America by Thomas Anburey, lieutenant in the army of General Burgoyne.* 2 vols. Boston, 1923.

Archives of the State of Pennsylvania. 12 vols. Philadelphia, 1852–56.

Barnhart, John D., ed. *Henry Hamilton and George Rogers Clark.* Crawfordsville, Ind., 1951.

Baurmeister, Carl Leopold. *Revolution in America: Confidential Letters and Journals 1776–1784 of Adjutant General Major Baurmeister of the Hessian Forces.* B. A. Uhlendorf, trans. New Brunswick, 1957.

Burgoyne, John. *A State of the Expedition from Canada As Laid Before the House of Commons by Lieutenant General Burgoyne.* London, 1780.

Burnett, Edmund C., ed. *Letters of Members of the Continental Congress.* 8 vols. Washington, 1921–36.

Chinard, Gilbert, ed. *George Washington as the French Knew Him, a Collection of Texts.* Princeton, 1940.

Clark, Walter, ed. *The State Records of North Carolina.* XIX. Goldsboro, 1901.

Clinton, Sir Henry. *The American Rebellion: Sir Henry Clinton's Narrative of his campaigns, 1775–1782, with an appendix of original documents.* William B. Willcox, ed. New Haven, 1954.

Cresswell, Nicholas. *The Journal of Nicholas Cresswell, 1774–1777.* New York, 1924.

Curwen, Samuel. *Journals and Letters of . . . Samuel Curwen . . . An American Refugee in England, 1775–1784.* George A. Ward, ed. New York, 1842.

Deane, Silas. *The Deane Papers, 1774–1790.* 5 vols. New York Historical Society, *Collections,* 1887–90.

Dearborn, Henry. *Revolutionary War Journals of Henry Dear-*

born, 1775–1783. L. A. Brown and H. Peckham, eds. Chicago, 1939.

Du Roi. *Journal of Du Roi the Elder.* Charlotte S. J. Epping, trans. New York, 1911.

Eelking, Max von. *Memoirs and Letters and Journals of Major General Riedesel.* William L. Stone, trans. Albany, 1868.

Force, Peter, compiler. *American Archives.* Fourth Series, 6 vols. Washington, 1837–46. Fifth Series, 3 vols. Washington, 1848–53.

Ford, Paul Leicester, ed. *An Address to the Good People of Ireland on behalf of America, October 4th, 1778,* by Benjamin Franklin. Brooklyn, 1891.

Ford, Worthington C. *Broadsides, Ballads, &c. Printed in Massachusetts, 1639–1800.* Massachusetts Historical Society, *Collections.* LXXV. Boston, 1922.

––––––. *The Washington-Duché Letters.* Brooklyn, 1890.

Franklin, Benjamin. *The Writings of Benjamin Franklin.* A. H. Smyth, ed. 10 vols. New York, 1905–7.

Gage, Thomas. *The Correspondence of General Thomas Gage, 1763–1775.* Clarence E. Carter, ed. 2 vols. New Haven, 1931–33.

Great Britain, Historical Manuscripts Commission. *Report on American Manuscripts in the Royal Institution of Great Britain.* 4 vols. London, 1904–9.

Heitman, Francis B. *Historical Register of Officers of the Continental Army.* Washington, 1914.

Howe, William. *The Narrative of Lieut. Gen. Sir William Howe, in a Committee of the House of Commons, on the 29th of April 1779.* London, 1780.

Hughes, Thomas. *A Journal by Thos: Hughes.* E. A. Benians, ed. Cambridge, 1947.

Huth, Hans. "Letters From a Hessian Mercenary," *Pennsylvania Magazine of History and Biography* (1938), 488–501.

James, James Alton, ed. *George Rogers Clark Papers, 1771–1781.* Springfield, 1912.

Jefferson, Thomas. *The Papers of Thomas Jefferson.* J. P. Boyd, ed. 15 vols. Princeton, 1950–58.

Journals of the Continental Congress. W. C. Ford and G. Hunt, eds. 34 vols. Washington, 1904–37.

Journal of Lt. John Charles Philip Von Krafft, 1776–1784. New York Historical Society, *Collections*, 1882.

Journal of the Most Remarkable Occurrences in Quebec, 1775–1776 By An Officer of the Garrison. New York Historical Society, *Collections*, 1880.

Lamb, Roger. *Memoir of His Own Life.* Dublin, 1811.

Lee, Richard Henry. *The Letters of Richard Henry Lee.* J. C. Ballagh, ed. 2 vols. New York, 1912–14.

Library of Congress. *The Washington Papers.* Vol. 18.

Mackenzie, Frederick. *Diary of Frederick Mackenzie, Giving a Narrative of His Military Service . . . during the years 1775–1781 . . .* 2 vols. Cambridge, 1930.

Minis, Hays I., ed. *Calendar of the Papers of Benjamin Franklin in the Library of the American Philosophical Society.* 5 vols. Philadelphia, 1908.

Moore, Frank. *Diary of the American Revolution, From Newspapers and Original Documents.* 2 vols. New York, 1859–60.

Morris, Richard B., ed. *Alexander Hamilton and the Founding of the Nation.* New York, 1957.

New Jersey. *Archives of the State of New Jersey.* Second Series, Extracts from American Newspapers. II (1778) and III (1779).

Niles, Hezekiah. *Principles and Acts of the Revolution in America.* Baltimore, 1822.

O'Callaghan, E. B., compiler. *Documents Relative to the Colonial History of the State of New York.* VIII. Albany, 1857.

Paine, Thomas. *Selected Writings of Thomas Paine.* R. E. Roberts, ed. New York, 1945.

Pomeroy, Seth. *The Journal and Papers of Seth Pomeroy, Sometime General in the Colonial Service.* L. B. de Forest, ed. New Haven, 1926.

Popp, Stephen. *A Hessian Soldier in the American Revolution: Diary of Stephen Popp.* Reinhard J. Pope, trans. 1953.

Reed, William B. *Life and Correspondence of Joseph Reed.* 2 vols. Philadelphia, 1847.

Riedesel, Friedrike, *Letters and Journals Relating to the War of* the American Revolution, and the Capture of the German Troops at Saratoga. William L. Stone, trans. Albany, 1867.

Roberts, Kenneth, ed. *March to Quebec: Journals of the Members of Arnold's Expedition.* New York, 1938.

Rush, Benjamin. *Letters of Benjamin Rush.* L. H. Butterfield, ed. 2 vols. Princeton, 1951.

Ryden, George H., ed. *Letters to and from Caesar Rodney, 1756–1748.* Philadelphia, 1933.

Saffell, William T. R. *Records of the Revolutionary War.* Baltimore, 1894.

Saunders, William L., ed. *The Colonial Records of North Carolina.* X. Raleigh, 1870.

Serle, Ambrose. *The American Journal of Ambrose Serle, Secretary to Lord Howe, 1766–1778.* E. H. Tatum, Jr., ed. San Marino, 1940.

Sparks, Jared, ed. *The Diplomatic Correspondence of the American Revolution.* 6 vols. Washington, 1857.

Stevens, Benjamin F., ed. *Clinton-Cornwallis Controversy.* 2 vols. London, 1888.

Stone, William L., ed. *Letters of Brunswick and Hessian Officers During the American Revolution.* Albany, 1891.

———. *Orderly Book of Sir John Johnson During the Oriskany Campaign, 1776–1777.* Albany, 1784.

Sullivan, John. *Letters and Papers of Major General John Sullivan.* O. G. Hammond, ed. 2 vols. Concord, 1930.

"The Treason of Benedict Arnold, as Presented in Letters of Sir Henry Clinton to Lord George Germain," *Pennsylvania Magazine of History and Biography* (1898), 410–22.

Thacher, James. *Military Journal During the American Revolutionary War.* Hartford, 1854.

Thwaites, R. G., *ed.* State Historical Society of Wisconsin, *Collections.* Vol. 11. Madison, 1888.

———. and L. P. Kellogg, eds. *Frontier Defense on the Upper Ohio, 1777–1778.* Madison, 1912.

Tyler, Moses Coit. *The Literary History of the American Revolution.* I. New York, 1951.

Van der Kemp, Francis Adrian. *An Autobiography, together with*

Extracts from his Correspondence. Helen L. Fairchild, ed. New York, 1903.

Warren-Adams Letters, Being Chiefly a Correspondence among John Adams, Samuel Adams, and James Warren. Massachusetts Historical Society, *Collections.* 2 vols. Boston, 1917–25.

Washington, George. *The Writings of George Washington.* John C. Fitzpatrick, ed. 30 vols. Washington, 1931–44.

Wharton, Francis, ed. *Revolutionary Diplomatic Correspondence of the United States.* 6 vols. Washington, 1889.

Manuscripts—

Library of Congress. "Broadside Collection," 1775–83.

National Archives. "Papers of the Continental Congress," 1774–83.

Stevens, B. F., compiler. *Facsimiles of Manuscripts in European Archives Relating to America, 1773–1783.* 25 vols. London, 1889–98.

SECONDARY SOURCES

Alden, John R. *General Gage in America, Being Principally a History of His Role in the American Revolution.* Baton Rouge, 1948.

Aldridge, Alfred O. *Franklin and His French Contemporaries.* New York, 1957.

Anderson, Troyer S. *The Command of the Howe Brothers During the American Revolution.* London, 1936.

Aptheker, Herbert. *American Negro Slave Revolts.* New York, 1943.

Arnold, Isaac N. *The Life of Benedict Arnold.* Chicago, 1880.

Bemis, Samuel Flagg. *The Diplomacy of the American Revolution.* New York, 1935.

Berkeley, Francis. *Dunmore's Proclamation of Emancipation.* Charlottesville, 1941.

Bradley, Arthur G. *Lord Dorchester.* New York, 1926.

Bolton, Charles K. *The Private Soldier Under Washington*. New York, 1902.

Bonsal, Stephen. *When the French Were Here*. New York, 1945.

Bowman, Allen. *The Morale of the American Revolutionary Army*. Washington, 1943.

Brooks, Noah. *Henry Knox: A Soldier of the Revolution*. New York, 1900.

Burnett, Edmund C. *The Continental Congress*. New York, 1941.

Butterfield, H. *George III, Lord North and the People, 1779–80*. London, 1949.

Butterfield, Lyman H. "Psychological Warfare in 1776: The Jefferson-Franklin Plan to Cause Hessian Desertions," *Proceedings of the American Philosophical Society*, 194 (June 1950), 233–41.

Chinard, Gilbert. *Honest John Adams*. Boston, 1933.

———. "Adventures in a Library," *The Newberry Library Bulletin*, Second Series, No. 8 (March 1952), 223–38.

Clark, Dora M. *British Opinion and the American Revolution*. New Haven, 1930.

Clark, William B. *Ben Franklin's Privateers: A Naval Epic of the American Revolution*. Baton Rouge, 1956.

Clarke, T. Wood. *The Bloody Mohawk*. New York, 1940.

Dabney, W. M. *After Saratoga:* The Story of the Convention Army. Albuquerque, 1954.

Danbridge, Danske. *Historic Shepherdstown*. Charlottesville, 1910.

Davidson, Philip. *Propaganda and the American Revolution*. Chapel Hill, 1941.

Dumbauld, Edward. *The Declaration of Independence and What It Means Today*. Norman, 1950.

Echeverra, Durand. " 'The Sale of the Hessians,' Was Benjamin Franklin the Author?" *American Philosophical Society Library Bulletin* (1954), 427–31.

Edler, Friedrich. *The Dutch Republic and the American Revolution*. Baltimore, 1911.

Eelking, Max von. *The German Allied Troops in the North American War of Independence*. J. G. Rosengarten, trans. Albany, 1893.

Fay, Bernard. *Franklin, The Apostle of Modern Times*. Boston, 1929.

Fitzpatrick, John C. *The Spirit of the Revolution*. Boston, 1924.

Ford, Paul Leicester. "Affaires de l'Angleterre et de l'Amérique," *Pennsylvania Magazine of History and Biography* (1889), 222–26.

Freeman, Douglas S. *George Washington, A Biography*. 7 vols. New York, 1948–57.

French, Allen. *The First Year of the American Revolution*. Boston, 1934.

Frothingham, Richard. *History of the Siege of Boston*. Boston, 1873.

Gottschalk, Louis. *Lafayette Comes to America*. Chicago, 1935.

———. *Lafayette Joins the American Army*. Chicago, 1937.

———. *Lafayette and the Close of the American Revolution*. Chicago, 1942.

Hans, Nichols. "Franklin, Jefferson, and the English Radicals at the End of the Eighteenth Century," *American Philosophical Society Library Bulletin* (1954), 406–26.

Hartgrove, W. B. "The Negro Soldier in the American Revolution," *Journal of Negro History*, I (Jan. 1916).

Hazelton, John B. *The Declaration of Independence: Its History*. New York, 1906.

Hudleston, Francis J. *Gentleman Johnny Burgoyne: Misadventures of an English General in the Revolution*. New York, 1939.

James, James Alton. *The Life of George Rogers Clark*. Chicago, 1928.

Jameson, J. Franklin. *The American Revolution Considered as a Social Movement*. Princeton, 1940.

Kuntzleman, Oliver C. *Joseph Galloway, Loyalist*. Philadelphia, 1941.

Lossing, Benson J. *The Pictorial Field-Book of the Revolution*. 2 vols. New York, 1850–52.

Lowell, Edward J. *The Hessians and the Other German Auxiliaries of Great Britain in the Revolutionary War*. New York, 1884.

Mays, David J. *Edmund Pendleton, A Biography*. 2 vols. Cambridge, 1952.

McDowell, R. B. *Irish Public Opinion, 1750–1800.* London, 1944.

McIlwraith, Jean N. *Sir Frederick Haldimand.* London, 1926.

McLachlan, R. W. "Fleury Mesplet, The First Printer at Montreal," *Proceedings and Transactions of the Royal Society of Canada,* Second Series, XII (May 1906), 197–309.

Miller, John C. *Sam Adams: Pioneer in Propaganda.* Boston, 1936.

———. *Origins of the American Revolution.* Boston, 1943.

———. *Triumph of Freedom, 1775–1783.* Boston, 1948.

Montross, Lynn. *The Reluctant Rebels: The Story of the Continental Congress, 1774–1789.* New York, 1950.

Neill, Rev. Edward Duffield. "Rev. Jacob Duche, the First Chaplain of Congress," *Pennsylvania Magazine of History and Biography* (1878), 58–73.

Padover, Saul K. *Jefferson.* New York, 1942.

Palmer, John M. *General Von Steuben.* New Haven, 1937.

Partridge, Bellamy, *Sir Billy Howe.* London, 1932.

Peckham, Howard H. *The War for Independence: A Military History.* Chicago, 1958.

Pennypacker, Morton. *General Washington's Spies on Long Island and in New York.* Brooklyn, 1939.

Renaut, Francis P. *La Politique de Propagande des Américains durant la Guerre d'Indépendance.* 2 vols. Paris, 1922–25.

Riddell, William R. "Benjamin Franklin's Mission to Canada and the Causes of Its Failure," *Pennsylvania Magazine of History and Biography* (1924), 111–58.

Roche, John F. *Joseph Reed, A Moderate in the American Revolution.* New York, 1951.

Schachner, Nathan. *Thomas Jefferson, A Biography.* 2 vols. New York, 1951.

Scheer, George F. and Rankin, Hugh F. *Rebels and Redcoats.* New York, 1957.

Schlesinger, Arthur M. *Prelude to Independence: The Newspaper War on Britain.* New York, 1958.

Smith, Justin H. *Our Struggle for the Fourteenth Colony.* 2 vols. New York, 1907.

Stillé, Charles J. *Major-General Anthony Wayne.* Philadelphia, 1893.

Stryker, William S. *The Battle of Monmouth.* Princeton, 1927.

Trevelyan, George Otto. *The American Revolution.* 4 vols. London, 1899–1913.

Van Doren, Carl. *Benjamin Franklin.* New York, 1938.

———. *Secret History of the American Revolution.* New York, 1941.

Van Tyne, Claude H. *The War of Independence.* Boston, 1929.

———. *The Loyalists in the American Revolution.* New York, 1929.

Wade, Mason. *The French Canadians, 1760–1945.* New York, 1955.

Ward, Christopher. *The War of the Revolution.* 2 vols. New York, 1952.

Wallace, Willard M. *Traitorous Hero: The Life and Fortunes of Benedict Arnold.* New York, 1954.

Wertenbaker, Thomas J. *Father Knickerbocher Rebels: New York City During the Revolution.* New York, 1948.

Wright, John W. "The Rifle in the American Revolution," *American Historical Review,* XXIX (Jan. 1924), 293–99.

Wrong, George M. *Canada and the American Revolution.* New York, 1935.

STUDIES IN MODERN PROPAGANDA

Bartlett, F. C. *Political Propaganda.* Cambridge, 1940.

Bruntz, George G. *Allied Propaganda and the Collapse of the German Empire in 1918.* Stanford, 1938.

Creel, George. "Propaganda and Morale," *American Journal of Sociology* (Nov. 1941), 340–51.

Lerner, Daniel. *Sykewar: Psychological Warfare Against Germany, D-Day to VE-Day.* New York, 1949.

Linebarger, Paul M. A. *Psychological Warfare.* Washington, 1954.

Mock, James R. and Larson, Cedric. *Words That Won the War: The Story of the Committee on Public Information, 1917–1919.* Princeton, 1939.

Index

★★★